Learning and Teaching in Higher Education

Learning and Teaching in Higher Education

Perspectives from a Business School

Edited by

Kathy Daniels

Associate Dean, Learning and Teaching, Aston Business School, UK

Caroline Elliott

Deputy Dean, Aston Business School, UK

Simon Finley

Associate Dean, Learning and Teaching, Aston Business School, UK

Colin Chapman

Associate Dean, Learning and Teaching, Aston Business School, UK

Edward Elgar
PUBLISHING

Cheltenham, UK • Northampton, MA, USA

Published by
Edward Elgar Publishing Limited
The Lypiatts
15 Lansdown Road
Cheltenham
Glos GL50 2JA
UK

Edward Elgar Publishing, Inc.
William Pratt House
9 Dewey Court
Northampton
Massachusetts 01060
USA

A catalogue record for this book
is available from the British Library

Library of Congress Control Number: 2019949931

This book is available electronically in the **Elgar**online
Business subject collection
DOI 10.4337/9781788975087

ISBN 978 1 78897 507 0 (cased)
ISBN 978 1 78897 508 7 (eBook)

Typeset by Servis Filmsetting Ltd, Stockport, Cheshire

Printed and bound by CPI Group (UK) Ltd, Croydon, CR0 4YY

Contents

Figures

Tables

Boxes

Contributors

Pavel Albores-Barajas, Professor, Operations Management

Bimal Arora, Lecturer, Work and Organisational Psychology

Ilias Basioudis, Senior Lecturer, Accounting

Ahmad Beltagui, Lecturer, Operations Management

Sudeshna Bhattacharya, Teaching Fellow, Work and Organisational Psychology

Michael Butler, Reader in Work and Organisational Psychology

Daniel Cash, Lecturer in Law

Colin Chapman, Senior Teaching Fellow and Associate Dean: Learning and Teaching

Soumyadeb Chowdhury, Lecturer, Information Communication Technology

Elaine Clarke, Senior Teaching Fellow and Associate Dean: Accreditations

Kathy Daniels, Associate Professorial Teaching Fellow and Associate Dean: Learning and Teaching

Matt Davies, Senior Teaching Fellow, Accounting

Caroline Elliott, Professor of Economics and Deputy Dean

Simon Finley, Senior Teaching Fellow and Associate Dean: Learning and Teaching

Keith Glanfield, Lecturer, Marketing

Jon Guest, Senior Teaching Fellow, Economics

Chris Jones, Professor and Head of Economics, Finance and Entrepreneurship Department

Bahar Ali Kazmi, Lecturer, Work and Organisational Psychology

Clive Kerridge, Teaching Fellow, Marketing

Pieter Koornhof, Lecturer in Law

Maria Kozlovskaya, Lecturer, Economics

Alison Lindon, Teaching Fellow, Accounting

Kris Lines, Senior Teaching Fellow, Law

Muhammad Al Mahameed, Teaching Fellow, Accounting

Alison McPherson, Senior Teaching Fellow, Work and Organisational Psychology

Uche Ogwude, Teaching Fellow, Marketing

Matthew Olczak, Senior Lecturer, Economics

Chris Owen, Senior Teaching Fellow, Operations Management

Gayatri Patel, Lecturer in Law

Geetha Ravishankar, Senior Teaching Fellow, Economics and Finance

Umair Riaz, Lecturer in Accounting

Oscar Rodríguez-Espindola, Lecturer, Operations and Supply Chain Management

Keith Schofield, Teaching Fellow, Work and Organisational Psychology

Adam Shaw-Mellors, Lecturer in Law

Jon Taylor, Teaching Fellow, Learning Innovation

Richard Terry, Networked Learning Director

Nicholas Theodorakopoulos, Professor and Head of Work and Organisational Psychology Department

Foreword

It is a great pleasure to write the foreword to this highly relevant and informative book *Learning and Teaching in Higher Education: Perspectives from a Business School*. It has been written at a time when stakeholders (including students, governments, employers, parents) are seeking greater accountability in the delivery of higher education, quality in the student learning experience, work readiness and employability skills development, and learning outcomes that equip students for successful lifelong learning. This book, expertly collated in targeted learning and teaching sections by the editors Kathy Daniels, Caroline Elliott, Simon Finley and Colin Chapman, captures a range of topics that are key to enhancing the quality of learning and teaching in higher education.

The 32 chapters, written with passionate commitment by teaching staff at the Aston Business School, highlight theoretical foundations of learning and teaching that inform good practice; identify strategies for engaging students in their learning, both within and outside the classroom context; suggest initiatives and innovations to enhance teaching practice; outline practices that facilitate learning in small and large groups, as well as creating communities of learners; and discuss the challenges and rewards of sound assessment measures in teaching and learning. The chapters on technology-enhanced learning are most informative in that they provide insights into the effectiveness of learning through technology, including online learning, blended learning and virtual classrooms, accompanied by tips for implementation of these approaches that we can all learn from!

The inclusion of 'creativity' in the Business curriculum; the building of knowledge and engaging students through storytelling; the focus on interactive teaching methodologies such as experiential learning, role play and simulation; and the use of problem-based learning and case studies, are indicative of approaches to teaching that seek to make student learning an enjoyable experience! The inclusion of teaching tips throughout these and other chapters provide encouragement and support for those teaching staff members who are yet to adopt such approaches or may be new to teaching in the higher education sector.

Of importance, too, are the chapters that focus on the challenges of teaching to the diversity of the student population in today's classrooms – students who come from diverse backgrounds with differing learning styles, a range of prior learning experiences, and varying levels of English language competence. The strategies for inclusive teaching and for supporting the learning experience of these students are clearly defined and demonstrate the benefits. All students will find the chapters with suggestions for developing 'work readiness' and employability skills a useful source of information.

There are many books written on learning and teaching and approaches in education that are deemed to be good practice. This book, however, is unique in that it goes beyond the inclusion of just traditional topics in learning and teaching, with a value-added feature of 'Thoughts' which accompany many of chapters. These comprise additional ideas for consideration, additional critical incidents set in Business contexts, and challenging viewpoints for reflection.

This important book is a collection of topics in learning and teaching in higher education, intended for the Business Education context, but it has wider relevance and appeal to all educators and teachers across the disciplines. Although written and edited by experienced and dedicated teachers in the UK, the book and its rich content have equal relevance to educators across the globe, where the trends and issues in higher education are similar. All will benefit from the excellent ideas, the sound advice, the reflections on learning and teaching in higher education, and the Business School perspectives.

Professor Prem Ramburuth
UNSW Business School
University of New South Wales
Sydney, Australia

Preface

There is no requirement to have a teaching qualification in a university. This means that those teaching in a university often have little guidance on how to teach, and little access to tips relating to best practice. This book is a comprehensive overview of all aspects of teaching in higher education, specifically in a Business School, written solely by Aston Business School academics.

All of the contributors to the book have drawn on their considerable experience of teaching, and have reflected on what works well and what does not. Each chapter contains teaching tips, and guidance on further reading if the reader would like to explore a particular area in more detail.

In addition to the chapters addressing the different aspects of learning and teaching, we have included a number of 'Thoughts' scattered throughout the book. These are short reflections on specific approaches that have been used in our Business School, shared as ideas to help you further enhance your own teaching.

The book is divided into six sections:

PART I INTRODUCTION

The book starts with an overview of learning theory. This underpins all of the remaining sections, and looks at the way that students learn and acquire knowledge.

PART II ENGAGING STUDENTS

Getting students to engage with their learning is a crucial first step to effective learning. How can we encourage students to turn up for scheduled learning events such as lectures and seminars, and how can we encourage them to contribute once they do attend? Undergraduate students are coming to university from the different environment of school or college so there is a requirement to help them as they adjust to a new, more independent, way of learning.

In this section we address these issues, and think about some specific ways of engaging students, such as encouraging debate, introducing creativity and helping students to understand critical thinking. We also look at the way that icebreakers can be used to engage students from the start of a module.

PART III ENHANCING TEACHING PRACTICE

Different teaching situations bring different challenges for the university teacher, and in this section we look at these challenges and how they can be addressed. We suggest some innovative approaches to teaching that can make the learning experience more interesting for students.

We address the specific issues of teaching both large and small groups of students, and the associated challenges. We also look at the skill of giving a confident presentation to students, and share some tips and ideas on how those skills can be further developed. Making sure that learning is relevant, and communicating the relevance to students, is addressed. We look at the specific issues of teaching a diverse group of students and teaching those who do not speak English as their first language.

Innovative approaches such as storytelling, experiential learning and problem-based learning are explained in some detail.

PART IV TECHNOLOGY-ENHANCED LEARNING

Using technology in learning is becoming a standard part of the learning experience in higher education, but it is still a new technique to many teachers. In this section we look at the range of ways that technology can be used to enhance learning, and we also look at the way that we can enhance students' digital literacy.

We look at the way to design and use online classrooms, and how to manage online learning in a way that ensures the ongoing engagement of students.

PART V TEACHING CONTENT

It is not possible to cover every topic area taught within a Business School in just one book. However, there are some areas that commonly cause difficulties amongst teachers, and we concentrate on those in this section.

We look specifically at how to teach mathematics, law and corporate social responsibility to business students. These are areas that are typically in all syllabi, but are areas where it can be difficult to get student engagement.

We also address the use of short in-class games and module sponsorship as two ways to liven up teaching content and to gain student interest.

PART VI ASSESSMENT

Our final section addresses assessment. For many students this is the most important part of their learning experience, because that final grade is what communicates their competence to the wider world. However, assessment is also something that students complain about and can find difficult to understand.

We start this section by addressing assessment criteria and how they can be used to help students understand what is required to be successful. We then look at specific ways of assessment – using posters, writing multiple choice questions and using peer assessment. We end this section by looking at tips for providing feedback on assessment that is useful and beneficial for students.

Kathy Daniels
Caroline Elliott
Simon Finley
Colin Chapman

Acknowledgements

When we first asked colleagues if they would be interested in helping to write a book about teaching in a Business School we were overwhelmed with the response. There was huge enthusiasm to capture in writing some of the excellent teaching practices at Aston Business School.

We are proud to work alongside some of the finest teachers of business and law related topics in the university sector, and we have read the chapters with admiration as they have been produced.

Thank you to all our colleagues who have contributed. Thanks are also due to Angie Daniels – writing a book with so many authors requires a lot of coordination. Angie, we couldn't have done it without you.

Kathy Daniels
Caroline Elliott
Simon Finley
Colin Chapman

PART I

Introduction

1. Theorising about learning and knowing

Keith Schofield

INTRODUCTION

Much of the recent rhetoric in higher education focuses on teaching and learning. As we move into the environment where student experiences and expectations are measured, quantified, and publicised, then the mechanisms for understanding how we engage these individuals in their learning becomes more important.

We can use this understanding of how students learn in order to better inform our programme design, teaching, classroom management, and the development of academic practice. Humans are meaning interpreters, we reify the abstract, we seek, we explore, and we learn. The challenge for educators is that we often do not take the opportunity to disentangle the mechanisms of learning from the practices of teaching. Over the coming chapter we will explore different theoretical perspectives on learning; these positions underpin the work which follows where, in each chapter, academics advocate solutions for some of the key issues facing teaching and learning in higher education today.

This chapter will consider different theoretical positions on learning from a largely psychological perspective with clear applications to education. Importantly, we are considering the theoretical approach to learning that we can apply to students; thoughts will be proposed which can be used to understand what we mean when we discuss knowledge, an issue which will emerge throughout the text. Finally, these issues are contextualised within higher education in a practical sense, including the way this underpins curriculum design.

NATIVIST APPROACHES TO LEARNING

The core principle of a view on learning that emerges from nativism is that the ability to learn is innate. In most walks of life, we find that other people outperform us or that others are naturally gifted in different pursuits; applying this principle to the acquisition and use of knowledge means that some are simply better at learning than others.

This perspective has informed much debate over the years, first championed by Darwin's cousin Sir Francis Galton as the precursor to the development of standardised intelligence tests (Nicolas et al., 2013). The extrapolation of this involved research into the hereditary nature of intelligence and higher-order mental processes. The hangover for this exists within society today; the testing regime of children through to adulthood enables continual measurement of progress so that appropriate educational pathways can be recommended based on ability. The methodological development that this perspective fuelled is evident in the use of psychometric measures for recruitment and selection in employment and into postgraduate programmes (Schmidt and Hunter, 2004; Lang et al., 2010).

A number of issues for higher education emerge from this perspective. Without entering the political debate that follows the view that intelligence is fixed and hereditary, the core issue in accepting this position means that the extent to which students can improve is preset. If biological predisposition is all that matters then educational outcomes are predetermined before a student sets foot into a classroom. This is not to say that the innate abilities that we have do not predispose us to preferences or skillsets; rather that to ignore the notion that external factors can influence our acquisition of skill potentially undermines the transformative power of education.

Through developing a critique of the rigidity of this nativist perspective we identify that the application of this view has both strengths and weaknesses. Briscoe (2000), for example, argues that language acquisition is best explained through a nativist lens. In contrast, the 'higher psychological functions' that are required for more complex and abstract thought are best described through notions of relationship and apprenticeship (Vygotsky, 1978).

Arguably, if the nativist perspective is endorsed in education systems then by the time that students reach higher education then their route and their potential to succeed may have already been ingrained. The institution becomes the conduit and the enabler for predetermined individual success or otherwise.

BEHAVIOURIST LEARNING

In contrast to the hereditary perspectives identified through nativist approaches, a behaviourist would argue that all genetic predispositions are redundant. Rather, individuals are focused on exposure to different experiences and learning happens as a result of this. Pritchard (2009, p. 6) explains:

> Behaviourism is a theory of learning focusing on observable behaviour and discounting any mental activity. Learning is defined simply as the acquisition of new behaviour.

The principles of behaviourism are well documented, classical conditioning is where associations are made between natural stimulus and a conditioned stimulus (think Pavlov and his dogs; see Pavlov, 1927). On the other hand, operant conditioning is where learning about behaviours is done through a series of reinforcements and punishments (Skinner, 1948); undesirable behaviours are punished and desirable behaviours are rewarded. Learning, in this sense, is understood as whether or not one repeats the behaviour.

Examples of this approach to learning are often drawn from Skinner's (1953) work with rats (pushing buttons in the cage for food pellets) but that is not to say that the experience cannot be replicated in humans. The simple functions of punishment and reward are ever present in society, given life through iPhone games and sought after in the form of sales bonuses (Anthony and Griffiths, 2014; Glassman et al., 2010).

Adopting this approach within higher education might be understood through the practices that students must adapt to on arrival. It may be that repeated lateness is chastised, that students are embarrassed when a mobile phone is confiscated mid-lecture, that the 'punishment' of receiving a lower than expected grade will prompt a change in behaviour while the 'reward' of a high grade encourages a repeat (Pritchard, 2009). The formation of habit in this sense is, again, understood through the observable behaviour rather than through the psychological functions which traditional higher education charges itself with developing and assessing.

While there are arguments to be made that following these principles students will 'learn to learn', the limitations of a behaviourist approach lie in the focus on behaviours as the *only* measure of learning (Strauss, 2017). Beyond the rudimentary institutional practices, we propose that for many degree programmes there is a limited demonstration of specific behaviour. Rather, the nature of many courses is increasingly cerebral, requiring complex and abstract thought which, by its nature, a behavioural approach to learning rejects.

CONSTRUCTIVIST LEARNING

Rather than limiting definitions of learning to things which cannot be changed (in the nativist sense), or to what can be observed (in the behaviourist sense), a constructivist approach to learning considers the impact of the broader context within which the learner sits. From a psychological perspective, children are said to be able to think abstractly and hypothetically from age 11 (Piaget, 1954). It follows therefore that in a higher education setting we expect to be presented with students who have a certain level of ability, upon which we build through the different learning and assessment opportunities, some of which are covered in this text. Where constructivism is useful for considering learning is the notion of this 'building' of experience, expertise, and knowledge. Fundamentally, this position rejects the possibility that 'mental capabilities function independently of the material with which they operate' (Vygotsky, 1978). Accordingly, context becomes intertwined with knowledge, skill development and acquisition, and the completion of tasks.

The recognition of the value of context presents issues for educators. Vygotsky argued that where education fails its students is in the use of decontextualised assessment mechanisms; knowledge and knowing are rendered abstract creations. To counter this, he proposed that knowledge be understood as something which is constructed through a continual and social approach to learning. Each individual has a Zone of Proximal Development (ZPD); they exist in the centre of this zone where they are able to complete tasks independently. As you move away from the centre, the individual can undertake more complex, difficult or unfamiliar tasks with the support of a 'more learned other'. This shift, from person-centred to context-centred learning, means that what an individual can do alone is not as important as what they can do with the support of somebody with the support of colleagues, teachers, and friends. The role that these 'more learned others' play is to scaffold, to facilitate, to guide, and to support (Wood et al., 1976; Rogoff, 1990).

It follows, therefore, that the core feature of the learning process from this perspective is that of relationship (Bryson, 2016). In order for knowledge to be understood and for learning to happen, there must be a relationship between the learner and their 'more learned other'. This, of course, strikes hard towards notions of apprenticeship (Rogoff, 1990), where the learner is facilitated through a learning journey with somebody who has more experience and knowledge than they do. In the work setting, Lave and Wenger (1991) articulate the methods for doing this through the incremental acquisition of skill, regular testing, and appraisal and growth of confidence.

Accepting that learning happens through a relationship with a 'more learned other' places knowledge as something which is co-constructed through this mutual endeavour. There is no separation between how one engages in thinking, action, and learning (Billett, 2010, 2014); the social world in which we operate becomes central to what and how we learn. The learning environment is as important for influencing how knowledge is interpreted, how sense is made, how the abstract is reified, as any other factor.

KNOWLEDGE AND KNOWING

We largely assume that the purpose of a journey through higher education is to acquire knowledge, some of which is immediately important for the acquisition of a degree, other of which will be relevant for the all-important graduate job. It is, therefore, incumbent on us to explore what we mean by 'knowledge'; how can one be said to 'know'?

Knowledge is often understood in abstract form, it is a transferable and self-contained entity which can be deployed at will. However, if we recognise that the way we engage in the construction of knowledge is through engagement in a relationship with a 'more learned other' and that the context in which we do this will shape how we understand things and what importance it bears, then what we know is itself situated in context; knowledge and context are inextricably linked (Brown et al., 1989). To make sense of it outside of the environment in which it is developed is not impossible but neither can it be assumed. Our role as practitioners of higher education in a business school context becomes ever more challenging; we must enable this development of understanding and construction of knowledge in such a way that its situatedness does not render it institutionalised for fear that our graduates become irrelevant.

As we further explore the nuances associated with knowledge we ought to consider how one is defined as being 'knowledgeable'; surely to be knowledgeable one must not solely count postnominals. In the same way that learning and knowledge is constructed through our social engagement, to be considered as knowledgeable is to be perceived as demonstrating social expertise. Knowledge is displayed in action, one demonstrates that one knows through behaviours, conversations, ways of being (Wenger, 1998; Dawson, 2013). As an academic one 'acts as if one knows' in order to be perceived as such. Accordingly, the students with whom we engage must be prepared to act as if *they* know when they graduate; to simply hold abstract knowledge and be unable to engage with it will not make them productive or successful employees.

MAKING 'LEARNING' HAPPEN IN HE

As knowledge is established as a movable feast, with learners reifying abstract concepts to co-construct their understandings, we move to consider how learning happens as a situated activity (Brown et al., 1989). Foregrounding context and social experience engenders a collaborative understanding of the learning activity, and accordingly we reject traditional transmission models of education where we may expect unproblematic absorption of knowledge. Instead we favour models of teaching which demand engagement from students as in so doing they will be better placed to co-construct their own understanding of concepts and principles with the support of their peers and their lecturers.

Within higher education there are a number of things that students are required to learn. Putting aside the assumption that they wish to engage with their programme and develop an understanding of a specific academic discipline, students must first engage with the prospect of learning how to be a student. Of course, this is different for each individual; some are keen A-level exam passers, others are dedicated BTEC coursework producers, others are mature with families and a career they want to boost, and yet more are at home working remotely online. Accordingly, the environment that we are faced with as teaching practitioners is anything other than stationary; the demands of learners evolve and we must meet them somewhere in order to facilitate their progression.

Let us first consider how students must learn to learn; the context of higher education is vastly different to anything they are likely to have experienced before. We must not, therefore, assume that students are readily equipped to cope with the transition to their new learning environment. They must be responsible for their own learning, feel comfortable in asking for help, be equipped with the skill to access the tools and resources that the institution has to offer (Turner and Tobbell, 2017). The challenge of a perspective which focuses on how and what we teach lies in recognising individual participation in programme outcomes; each student approaches their work in a very different way; the transition to undergraduate and postgraduate study is fraught with challenges to individual identity and engagement in personal as well as institutional practice to enable learning (Tobbell and O'Donnell, 2013).

This issue of engaging successfully in institutional practice cannot be underestimated (O'Donnell and Tobbell, 2007). For without the ability to navigate the systems and processes which bind the institution together, a student cannot be successful in their endeavour to learn. These practices may be perceived as inconsequential, or perhaps more accurately impenetrable, by students and academics alike. Our challenge, therefore, is to not only understand and embrace these practices ourselves but to ensure that they are easily accessible by students.

DESIGNING THE CURRICULUM

Further dichotomies which exist in programme design are through understanding the needs of home and international students and designing curricula which can satisfy both. As higher education shifts to become ever more commoditised, so the competitiveness of institutions can be measured through the attractiveness of their degree programmes. Attractiveness can be determined in the seemingly trivial award title but also in previous student performance, pedagogic approach, and course content.

A text focused on teaching and learning would not be complete without the acknowledgement of the importance of Bloom's (1956) Taxonomy of learning objectives for the classroom. Through his model, learning in action is broken down into the cognitive, affective, and psychomotor domains with further specificity into the type of learning outcomes and assessment objectives which would follow each type of learning. Each will be considered in turn here.

- The cognitive domain spans most levels of thinking. At the lowest levels, students are engaging with knowledge, in the abstract form, learning specific facts and comprehending differences between basic principles and concepts. As the demand on their cognition increases the focuses shifts to application of understanding, more detailed analysis and the synthesis of existing ideas into something new, followed by the evaluation and justification of ideas and principles. Figure 1.1 illustrates how each of these levels relate to one another and the kind of stimulus words which may be used to ensure learning engagement at the appropriate level.
- In the affective domain the focus shifts towards how students feel, or react emotionally, to learning. At the basic level students are passive receptors of content; as we engage them further their participation in the learning process increases in response to stimulus. At the highest levels they begin to value the knowledge that they are acquiring, to organise it within their existing schemas and then to use the characteristics to develop their own abstractions based on the principles they have now adopted.
- The psychomotor domain focuses on physical, action-based, skills which are being learnt. The priority here is on engagement with

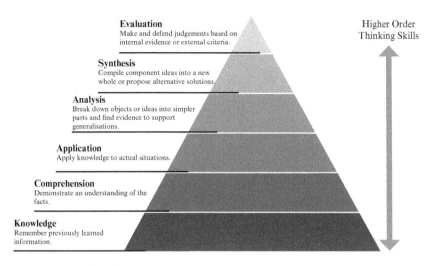

Figure 1.1   Bloom's Taxonomy

sensorimotor skills, increasing familiarity with movements and following guided responses here to develop one's own mechanistic skill. Adaptation of these skills creatively are the most demanding in this domain. Within a business school context it is this domain that is engaged with least.

These principles are valuable to us as educators. Understanding the different levels of challenge and how students respond to these conforms to the accepted notion of institutional programme design. When designing curricula with this in mind we can ensure the appropriateness of different levels of study.

Beyond the principles with which we design a curriculum of study, which Bloom's work largely underpins, the individuation of programmes emerges from the academic skill of the business school. This means that, among other decisions involved in curriculum design (Romiszowski, 2016), curriculum content is often underpinned by the research and consulting interests of the academics who will deliver it. Of course, this can mean that the content which is being created and delivered is cutting edge; students are exposed to the latest thinking and are being taught by well-published experts in their field. The difficulty that this position presents in this new, increasingly externally facing, world of higher education is in the development of programmes and content in collaboration with employers (Bravenboer, 2016). This domain is becoming increasingly focused around the opportunities that degree apprenticeships can offer to both businesses and students alike, so the traditional relationship dynamic of 'student and university' shifts.

We do not advocate here that following Bloom's Taxonomy is the only method for designing curriculum. Critiques of Bloom's work focus on the reductionist nature of each of the stages (Pring, 2014), arguing that it is impossible to simply categorise different learning experiences into a neat flowing structure. Alternative approaches to curriculum design include being collaborative and centring the student voice (Brooman et al., 2015) to not only redesign the structure of programmes but to pay attention to the value placed on institutional practices such as attendance monitoring versus engagement. Further still, and in support of the employability agenda often pursued in higher education institutions, the future may lie in business involvement with curriculum design to support their workforce development agenda (Plewa et al., 2015).

THINKING FORWARD

We have started to scratch the surface here about the different ways that learning can be understood, the complex relationship between learning and knowledge, and how these differences can be used to frame curriculum design. Fundamentally, we argue that a curriculum of study should seek inspiration for delivery from multiple perspectives, and it is for this reason that we champion educators to better understand the learning process as this impacts their choices when teaching and so changes the outcomes for students.

Of course, there is no silver bullet; context, we have argued, is a key factor in understanding the student learning experience and, by extension, the teaching environment. Through the chapters which follow you should be able to identify different elements of learning theory underpinning each example of teaching practice. Some authors will have preferences towards one way of engaging students, others will showcase innovations in teaching practice which make the most of a particular contextual factor such as large group teaching, embedding technology, or recounting experiences of undertaking specific teaching experiences. Throughout, however, it should be possible to gauge how the author views the process of learning, what their position on defining knowledge is, and how these key factors have influenced their curriculum.

SUGGESTED FURTHER READING

Anthony, K. and M. Griffiths (2014). 'Online social gaming – Why should we be worried?', *TILT (Therapeutic Innovations in Light of Technology) Magazine*, 5, 24–31.

Billett, S. (2010). 'Lifelong learning and self: Work, subjectivity and learning', *Studies in Continuing Education*, 32, 1–16.

Billett, S. (2014). 'Mimesis learning through everyday activities and interactions at work', *Human Resource Development Review*, 13, 462–82.

Bloom, B.S. (1956). *Taxonomy of Educational Objectives, The Classification of Educational Goals: Cognitive Domain*, New York: Longmans.

Bravenboer, D. (2016). 'Why co-design and delivery is "a no brainer" for higher and degree apprenticeship policy', *Higher Education, Skills and Work-based Learning*, 6, 384–400.

Briscoe, T. (2000). 'Grammatical acquisition: Inductive bias and coevolution of language and the language acquisition device', *Language*, 76, 246–96.

Brooman, S., S. Darwent and A. Pimor (2015). 'The student voice in higher education curriculum design: Is there value in listening?', *Innovations in Education and Teaching International*, 52, 663–74.

Brown, J.S., A. Collins and P. Duguid (1989). 'Situated cognition and the culture of learning', *Educational Researcher*, 18, 32–42.

Bryson, C. (2016). 'Book review: Engagement through partnership: Students as partners in learning and teaching in higher education', *International Journal for Academic Development*, 21, 84–90.

Dawson, D.C.E. (2013). 'From legitimate peripheral participation to full participation? Investigating the career paths of mature physiotherapy students in a context of changing NHS employment opportunities', Doctoral thesis, Manchester Metropolitan University.

Glassman, M., A. Glassman, P.K. Champagne and M.T. Zugelder (2010). 'Evaluating pay-for-performance systems: Critical issues for implementation', *Compensation and Benefits Review*, 42, 231–8.

Heick, T. (2018). 'What is Bloom's Taxonomy? A definition for teachers' [Online]. Available: https://www.teachthought.com/learning/what-is-blooms-taxonomy-a-definition-for-teachers/ [Accessed 4 November 2018].

Lang, J.W.B., M. Kersting, U.R. Huschleger and J. Lang (2010). 'General mental ability, narrower cognitive abilities, and job performance: The perspective of the nested factors model of cognitive abilities', *Personnel Psychology*, 63, 595–640.

Lave, J. and E. Wenger (1991). *Situated Learning: Legitimate Peripheral Participation*, Cambridge: Cambridge University Press.

Nicolas, S., B. Andrieu, J.-C. Croizet, R.B. Sanitioso and J.T. Burman (2013). 'Sick? Or slow? On the origins of intelligence as a psychological object', *Intelligence*, 41, 699–711.

O'Donnell, V.L. and J. Tobbell (2007). 'The transition of adult students to higher education: Legitimate peripheral participation in a community of practice?', *Adult Education Quarterly*, 57, 312–28.

Pavlov, I.P. (1927). 'Conditioned reflex', *Feldsher Akush*, 11, 6–12.

Piaget, J. (1954). *The Construction of Reality in the Child*, New York: Basic Books.

Plewa, C., V. Galán-Muros and T. Davey (2015). 'Engaging business in curriculum design and delivery: A higher education institution perspective', *Higher Education*, 70, 35–53.

Pring, R. (2014). 'Bloom's Taxonomy: A philosophical critique (2)', in N. Norris (ed.), *Curriculum and the Teacher*, New York: Routledge.

Pritchard, A. (2009). *Ways of Learning: Learning Theories and Learning Styles in the Classroom*, Abingdon: Routledge.

Rogoff, B. (1990). *Apprenticeship in Thinking*, Oxford: Open University Press.

Romiszowski, A.J. (2016). *Designing Instructional Systems: Decision Making in Course Planning and Curriculum Design*, London: Routledge.

Schmidt, F. and J.E. Hunter (2004). 'General mental ability in the world of work: Occupational attainment and job performance', *Journal of Personality and Social Psychology*, 86, 162–73.

Skinner, B.F. (1948). 'Superstition in the pigeon', *Journal of Experimental Psychology*, 38, 168.

Skinner, B.F. (1953). *Science and Human Behavior*, Simon and Schuster.

Strauss, A.L. (2017). *Psychological Modeling: Conflicting Theories*, Abingdon and New York: Routledge.

Tobbell, J. and V.L. O'Donnell (2013). 'Transition to postgraduate study: Postgraduate ecological systems and identity', *Cambridge Journal of Education*, 43, 123–38.

Turner, L. and J. Tobbell (2017). 'Learner identity and transition: An ethnographic exploration of undergraduate trajectories', *Journal of Further and Higher Education*, 1–13.

Vygotsky, L.S. (1978). *Minds in Society: The Development of Higher Psychological Processes*, Cambridge, MA: Harvard University Press.

Wenger, E. (1998). *Communities of Practice: Learning, Meaning and Identity*, Cambridge: Cambridge University Press.

Wood, D., J.S. Bruner and G. Ross (1976). 'The role of tutoring in problem solving', *Journal of Child Psychology and Psychiatry, and Allied Disciplines*, 17, 89–100.

PART II

Engaging Students

2. How to engage students

Alison Lindon and Michael Butler

INTRODUCTION

We envisage our lecture or seminar full of alert students, making notes, asking pertinent questions and enthusiastically joining in with debates. In reality, teachers compete with mobile phones and student conversations. In this chapter, we share two case studies, which provide examples of effective methods in maximising student engagement.

WHAT IS STUDENT ENGAGEMENT AND WHY IS IT IMPORTANT?

Teaching quality is a key criterion of the Teaching Excellence Framework (TEF) and a sub-component is student engagement; providing effective stimulation and encouraging students' *engagement* and effort (Department for Education, 2017).

One definition of student engagement relevant to us is:

> In education, student engagement refers to the degree of attention, curiosity, interest, optimism, and passion that students show when they are learning or being taught, which extends to the level of motivation they have to learn and progress in their education. (The Glossary of Education Reform, 2016)

This definition summarises what we are trying to achieve; retaining student attention during a lecture, sparking their interest, getting active participation, making teaching enjoyable and learning effective. This in turn will provide us, the teacher, with satisfaction and a sense of fulfilment.

CASE STUDIES

This chapter will take you through the following case studies:

1. Retaining student engagement whilst giving a presentation
2. How to encourage active discussion.

We structure each case study by stating the origins of our teaching practice, explaining what we do to encourage student engagement and highlighting the positive reception by students.

CASE STUDY 1: RETAINING STUDENT ENGAGEMENT WHILST GIVING A PRESENTATION

My Learning Experience (Alison Lindon)

My journey as a student has largely driven how I teach today. Lecturers were traditional in their approach; talking through a set of PowerPoint slides. Their ability to explain and mine to listen, process and take notes varied with differing degrees of success. There were some standout lecturers, who captivated their audience simply through talking. One lecturer did make notes on acetate sheets and shared them using an overhead projector, which could have helped my note taking ability. However, the image was always blurred and not big enough for a large lecture theatre which held 400 students.

After graduation, I started to study for a professional qualification. The tutors used a digital pen to highlight and annotate learning material and projected it onto a suitably sized screen at the front of the class. The learning material had areas of explanation, space for making notes on a discussion or attempting calculations. This learning experience was a lightbulb moment, matching my learning style.

Teaching Tip
Many students like to take notes, it keeps their brain more active and the tutor highlighting and annotating notes as they progress helps the student to keep up with the flow of the lesson.

In my teaching I use a laptop that has the digital pen/write onscreen capability and link this to the overhead projectors in the lecture and seminar rooms. My lecture material is a workbook, including explanatory notes and calculation illustrations (if relevant), in which I can highlight key points and it has questions where I can write up answers and questions for students to practise during the lesson. Sometimes I do teach from PowerPoint slides but I still like to highlight and annotate these using the digital pen.

Whether the lecture is qualitative or numbers based, the method is similar: highlight key words and annotate with key words (see Figures

W4- Consolidated retained earnings

	£
→ Parent company retained earnings at consolidation	27SO
+ parent share of post-acquisition profit of subsidiary: (100% × 150 (w1))	150
	2900

Vc. SOFP

<u>Non-controlling interest</u>

In illustration 2 we saw P acquire 100% of S, but what happens if P acquires
control but not 100%? Example:

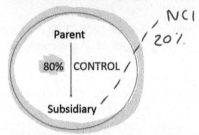

In this case P has acquired 80% of S and therefore has control (> 50%) but
another party has the remaining 20%. This other party is known as the non-
controlling interest (or minority interest) and is the subsidiary's shareholders
external to the group.

Figure 2.1   An example of notes for a numbers based topic

2.1 and 2.2). It took me a while to develop my ability to write concisely
onscreen, rather than writing long sentences which took too long and I ran
out of space for!

Teaching Tip
*I find it useful to have a colour coding system for my teaching notes: any-
thing written in blue is to say and anything in red is to write onscreen for the
students' benefit.*

During my presentation I like to ask questions as we go; in larger groups
this can be trickier because students are wary of venturing an answer in
front of others in case it is wrong. However, regardless of the class size I
always regularly pause to ask if anybody has any questions. Even in large
groups you tend to get a couple of questions.

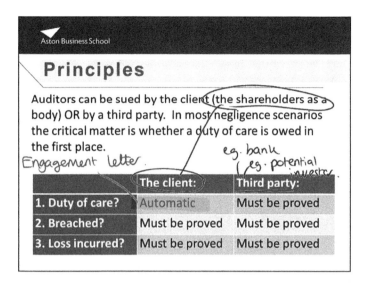

Figure 2.2   An example of notes for a qualitative topic

It is important to break up a long lecture and give students the opportunity to practise a couple of short questions, attempted on their own or as a group during the main body of my presentation. In the second half of the lecture, when fatigue is setting in, I set a longer question to have a go independently for about 20 minutes. Whilst students are working on this question I go around and speak to them to find out how they are getting on. This is possible even with the really large groups, quick questions can be answered there and then. If a student is struggling, I suggest an office appointment.

Teaching Tip
Walking around provides an opportunity to gauge how students are coping with the material and how much detail to go into when debriefing the question. In other words, 'As in any live event, the presenter picks up on feedback from the audience – and adjusts their performance accordingly.' (Merrifield, 2018)

I know what suits my learning style but I was interested to find out whether my students preferred the '*traditional*' talk through slides presentation style or the '*digital pen*' style of highlighting and annotating the screen in addition to talking. On a second year financial reporting module, I employed both styles of teaching. Following this, I conducted a short student survey.

The first two questions (Figure 2.3 and Table 2.1) asked the students

Learning and teaching in higher education

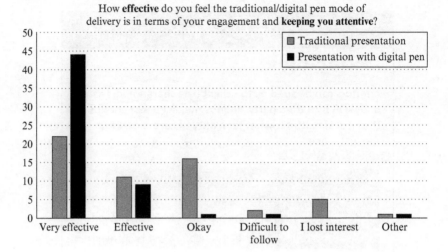

Figure 2.3   Effectiveness of traditional/digital pen mode of delivery

Table 2.1   Traditional v digital pen presentation

	Traditional presentation	Presentation with digital pen
Very effective	22	44
Effective	11	9
Okay	16	1
Difficult to follow	2	1
I lost interest	5	0
Other	1	1

how effective the two respective modes of delivery were in terms of their engagement and retaining their attentiveness.

The results show people favoured the presentation with the digital pen style of presentation. No one 'lost interest', whereas five people reported losing interest under the traditional presentation style.

The third question (Figure 2.4) asked whether the digital pen style helped students to make notes.

The response to this question was overwhelming, 52 respondents indicating that the digital pen did help them to make notes during lectures and seminars.

The survey also enabled students to add comments in relation to the digital pen and whether it helped them to stay more engaged with the

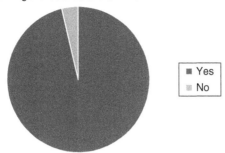

Did my use of the digital pen help you to make notes
during the lectures and seminars?

- Yes
- No

Figure 2.4   Use of digital pen helping to make notes

learning in lectures and seminars. Common themes emerged in terms of advantages from using the digital pen:

Pace of delivery

Students noted that the pace of delivery slowed when I highlighted and annotated the screen, so they could keep up:

> 'Helped me stay more engaged as I could write down what you were saying as you wrote it down. I think when lecturers have just slides they go too fast for us to write things down and keep up which makes us lose interest.'

Interactive/note taking

A number of students mentioned that they found the lectures more interactive and note taking easier:

> 'Very helpful, it made the lecture more practical than just sitting and listening to you talk. Keeps you active and attentive during lectures.'
>
> 'It helps in terms of focusing on what key points to pick up on. To see where the numbers flow and where they come from when you highlight them. It's more beneficial than looking at a stationary or even animated PowerPoint slide.'

Walkthrough examples

Students appreciated me writing up calculations onscreen:

> 'When you write with the pen it feels like you are doing the exercises with us at the same time so we are more engaged.'
>
> 'I think it helped me follow the calculations and to understand how everything is done by seeing you go through them rather than just talking through a solution that was already on the screen.'

'It was definitely effective when going through examples, especially step by step; more so that just having power point slides and reading from them . . . I was more likely to go on my phone or not pay attention when it's not interactive, but using the pen and annotating kept me more focused and interested in the lecture.'

Interestingly, one of the students made reference to a colleague who uses a normal pen to annotate printed-out notes which in turn are projected via a visualizer and said this was equally effective. So I don't think it matters whether the pen is digital or normal, the conclusion is that a large proportion of students value seeing learning material annotated and highlighted.

CASE STUDY 2: HOW TO ENCOURAGE ACTIVE DISCUSSION

The Importance of Participation (Michael Butler)

Like many teachers, role models influenced my teaching practice, especially the encouragement of active discussion during a lecture or other learning session. In my case, it was my first training course, 'Training the Trainer', which reinforced the important role of active discussion. The course participants had left school, were working, but were either early in their careers or changing career direction.

The course leaders led us through a series of exercises in which the core idea was conveyed more traditionally and in which we received key information in a short introduction. There was then plenty of active discussion related to our experiences, and we all had to participate, to confirm our understanding of the core idea. Related experiential activity followed in which participants divided into pairs or small groups, and then we would come back together in a whole group to share key learning and difficulties with putting into practice the core idea.

I later understood that the course leaders adopted Kolb's experiential learning cycle (see Figure 2.5). They started in the abstract conceptualisation quadrant, and then moved in a clockwise direction.

Perhaps the most important ingredient was the atmosphere in the room generated by the course leaders. It was trusting and participants were open, with the course leaders getting to know participants individually, so they could link their material to personal needs. They used appropriate humour to increase enjoyment and learning. There was high energy sustained over two days. We became 'friends' – I use quotation marks because I mean we wanted to help each other, be the best we could, knowing that when we all

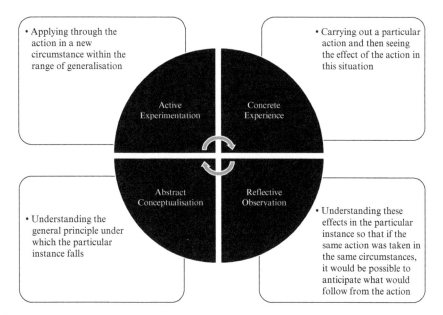

• Applying through the action in a new circumstance within the range of generalisation

• Carrying out a particular action and then seeing the effect of the action in this situation

Active Experimentation

Concrete Experience

Abstract Conceptualisation

Reflective Observation

• Understanding the general principle under which the particular instance falls

• Understanding these effects in the particular instance so that if the same action was taken in the same circumstances, it would be possible to anticipate what would follow from the action

Source: Adapted from Zhang and Kyriakidou (2012, pp. 114–15).

Figure 2.5 Kolb's experiential learning cycle

went back to our different UK workplaces contact would be less frequent as we went back to our daily routines.

My future training style, then teaching practice, had to replicate what the course leaders were achieving. My early attempts were very patchy, mostly failing. Participation would end quickly because I had naively assumed that when you ask a question, active discussion will follow – it does not. This puzzled me and I used Kolb's later work, experiential learning theory (Kolb and Kolb, 2005; see Butler and Gheorghiu, 2010, for further explanation and application), to reflect on how to *encourage active discussion during a lecture*.

ACTIVE DISCUSSION – FIVE-STAGE PROCESS

A five-stage process for active discussion is summarised in Figure 2.6 and described in more detail below. The process works in all group sizes, though I have used it most recently with an undergraduate class of 140, and an MBA class of 35.

First, I build the expectation that active discussion will take place. At the

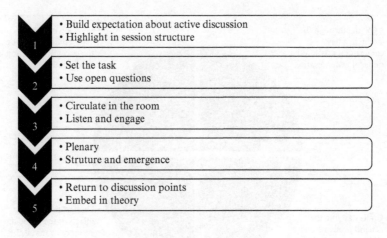

Figure 2.6   Five-stage process for active discussion

start of the session, when outlining its learning objectives, the structure of the session includes a segment for active discussion. Students get used to this taking place every week.

Second, I set the task that will generate the class discussion. To achieve this, I use PowerPoint to ask an open question(s). PowerPoint is helpful so that everyone in the room can see the question(s) and the details about the task they will do. Students self-form into small groups speaking with the person next to them.

Teaching Tip
When asking students to discuss an issue allow them to talk with whoever they are sitting next to. If students are placed into groups a lot of teaching time is lost with them finding their group members and deciding where to sit.

Third, having paused so that the students can get on with the task and work out their initial responses, I then circulate in the room to hear as many discussions as possible. Sometimes I am asked a question which I will either answer or push back for another group member to answer. I do this to show that they have answers themselves, and can take ownership of the discussion. During this stage, I will start working out how to connect the variety of discussions. I plan a structure for the plenary so there is a coherent sequence to the student responses. I include an international perspective from exchange students, which reveals the variety of perceptions on many topics.

Fourth, when the time allocated to the task is up, the plenary starts.

I invite a nominee from each group to reflect the debate in the group. Everyone uses a microphone so we hear the ideas, and a clear recording is made of the lecture. I thank each participant to encourage future speakers to come forward. It is important to be flexible, as students intervene to support the idea they have heard or offer a different opinion.

Teaching Tip
Students may not be proactive and signal that they want to speak, for example, by putting a hand up. Instead, the teacher needs to look for cues, for instance, facial expressions.

Fifth, I summarise the central points of the discussion. Students transition from listening and discussion to note taking. It is important to remember in the more formal part of the lecture to return to the discussion points. This embeds theory by relating it to the students' ideas (for a wider discussion about how to link theory, practice and student engagement see Butler and Rose, 2011).

CONCLUSION

A common theme to take away from both case studies is trying to get our students to 'do more' in order to improve engagement, whether that be active note taking during a presentation or active discussion. We have put this into a simple hierarchy (Figure 2.7), with a low level of engagement

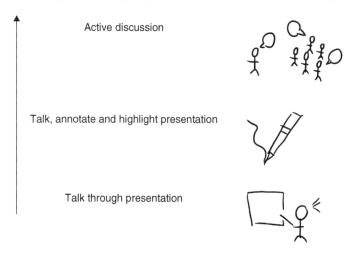

Active discussion

Talk, annotate and highlight presentation

Talk through presentation

Figure 2.7   Hierarchy of student engagement

being listening on its own; a higher level being making notes whilst actively listening; and the highest being participating through discussion.

Several real-world issues emerge which make implementing our ideas more difficult in practice. Some students may not want to engage in active discussion because they are less confident or seemingly disinterested when compared with their peers. We build confidence by verbally stating that having a go is just as important as knowing an answer, and establish from the outset of the module an atmosphere in the room that supports talk.

Key takeaway ideas from this chapter include:

1. Experiment with your presentation style, if a digital pen is not easily available; consider whether you could try annotating lecture material using a visualizer and a manual pen.
2. Experiment with the five-stage process for active discussion. Gradually it becomes easier to implement and can be adapted to individual preferences.
3. Increased student engagement can lead to improved learning and a more enjoyable teaching experience.

SUGGESTED FURTHER READING

Butler, M.J.R. (2010). 'Innovative Management Education through Work-Based Assessment – The Case of "Strategy for Future Leaders"', *Learning and Teaching in Higher Education*, 4 (2), 142–5.

Butler, M.J.R. and L. Gheorghiu (2010). 'Evaluating the Skills Strategy through a Graduate Certificate in Management – An Experiential Learning Theory Approach', *Education and Training*, 52 (6/7), 450–62.

Butler, M.J.R. and P. Reddy (2010). 'Developing Critical Understanding in HRM Students – How You Teach is Important', *Journal of European Industrial Training*, 34 (8/9), 772–89.

Butler, M. and E. Rose (2012). 'Introduction: A New Model of Learning Blending Employability Skills, International Focus and Multimedia Elements', in M. Butler and E. Rose, *Introduction to Organisational Behaviour*, London: CIPD, pp. 1–10.

Department for Education (2017). *Teaching Excellence and Student Outcomes Framework Specification*, [online] Department for Education, p. 25. Available at: https://www.gov.uk/government/publications/teaching-excellence-and-student-outcomes-framework-specification [accessed 2 July 2018].

The Glossary of Education Reform (2016). *Student Engagement*. [online] Available at: https://www.edglossary.org/student-engagement/ [accessed 2 July 2018].

Kolb, A.Y. and D.A. Kolb (2005). 'Learning Styles and Learning Spaces: Enhancing Experiential Learning in Higher Education', *Academy of Management Learning and Education*, 4 (2), 193–212.

Merrifield, M. (2018). *University Lecturers should be Engaging Raconteurs*, [online] Times Higher Education. Available at: https://www.timeshighereducation.com/ blog/university-lecturers-should-be-engaging-raconteurs [accessed 2 July 2018].

Zhang, C. and N. Kyriakidou (2012). 'Learning Theories and Practices', in M. Butler and E. Rose, *Introduction to Organisational Behaviour*, London: CIPD, pp. 108–56.

3. Icebreakers for business school students

Ilias Basioudis

INTRODUCTION

With the beginning of every programme, many educators (or instructors and facilitators)[1] are strategising about how best to start productive and engaging classroom conversations. Students (or participants) who speak even briefly at the first class meeting are more likely to participate in discussions going forward. This normally leads to student ongoing interaction and increased learning, and hence a well-chosen icebreaker can help everyone join in at the first day of class.

WHAT IS AN ICEBREAKER?

Icebreakers can be an effective way of starting a programme, or a training session. An interactive and often fun session that is run at the start of the first class of a programme can help students to get to know each other, get to know the instructors, develop classroom community and learn about the objectives and other important aspects of the programme.

Icebreakers[2] are discussion questions or quick, low-stakes and often fun activities that involve students at the beginning of a session and are used to help students relax and ease people into a group meeting or learning situation. They can be a good way to learn about who is in the classroom, reduce anxiety and tension, and engage all students in thinking together about programme content.

AIMS

The main aims of using icebreakers are:

- to improve the student learning experience

- to actively involve students in their learning process
- to create a positive group atmosphere to help people to relax
- to break down social barriers
- to energise and motivate and encourage student–instructor interaction from the beginning
- to help students to think outside the box
- to help students to get to know one another
- to help the educator understand his/her student population
- to set and communicate expectations
- to give potentially verbal feedback in the first class.

Whether it is a small or a large class size we teach in the business school, we all want to feel that we share some common ground with our fellow students. By creating a warm and friendly personal learning environment, the students will participate and learn more. Be creative and design your own variations on the icebreakers you find here. Try different things and most of all . . . have fun!

ENGAGEMENT INSTEAD OF RESENTMENT (OR, HINTS AND TIPS)

The following steps should ensure that your icebreakers are a success and lead to comfort and engagement (instead of anxiety and resentment) within your students in the class.

Teaching Tip
1. *Identify the ice, in other words figure out what creates the anxiety and tension in your class (or group).*
2. *Focus on melting the ice rather than breaking it. Think about the 'ice' that needs to be broken, and then watch students moving from anxiety and disengagement into comfort and engagement. The amount of 'heat' needed to melt the ice will depend on the needs of your class (or group), but one well-crafted activity or a series of activities will help towards melting the ice eventually (see examples of icebreakers below).*
3. *Know your audience and consider your context. As a general rule, before deciding which activities to use, make an attempt to assess the group for the following: average age, number of students, familiarity with one another, purpose of the group gathering, types of students present and what dynamics will the various personalities create, and potential considerations for physical abilities.[3] Also, very importantly, you should know the time and space you have got available for the icebreaker(s).*

4. *Lead with intention, by presenting the icebreaker with contagious enthusiasm, and staying positive, giving clear instructions, and leading with energy.*

5. *Be flexible and keep it simple. Successful ice melting requires that you have a few activities prepped and ready. Have a collection of activities, then use a particular activity (or more than one activity, if necessary) when appropriate. Complicated activities normally add to the anxiety and tension of participants, so you would need to keep everything as simple as possible.*

6. *Be extremely sensitive and prudent. Consider the needs of each student, their background, their culture and religion, their physical ability, and remember that your goal is to reduce anxiety and not to create it, to break the ice and not to uncover the whole iceberg, to engage instead of resent.*

MY APPROACH

First impressions are always important and this is certainly true in the classroom. Remember, there is only one first day of class. With this in mind, I use the following introductory icebreaker, called 'The Little Known Fact'.

In small-sized classes, and in the first class of the programme, I make sure that I am the first one to arrive in the classroom and then personally greet the students as soon as they arrive. I then introduce myself and instead of calling their names, I ask them to tell me who they are so that I can find them on my class list. Note that I always request the class list to be given to me with student photographs, so I can more easily identify students and remember their names in the future. I also ask them to share one little-known fact about themselves (which can serve as a humanising element in future interactions). This also gives me a chance to ask students their nicknames (or the English equivalent names for students from overseas) as I add them to my class list, conveying that I am not merely taking attendance but am making an effort to learn their first names (or nicknames) and am planning to converse with them. Another important point is that because I teach students from many different cultures and nationalities in the same class, I always ask those with difficult or unusual names to coach me in the pronunciation of their names, which reverses the usual dynamic by making me the student and them the teachers and serves as another way to approach students and start melting the ice. As I work my way through the class, I inevitably end up chatting with students, which helps in melting the ice and putting everyone at ease before the class has even begun!

In addition to adding their nicknames on my class list, I normally ask a volunteer student from the class to also write the first name (or nickname) of each student in the class on the board. At the end of introductions, the board is filled with names and I say something about being a true community of learners who actively learn from one another and I encourage them to mingle with each other and start creating friendships.

In large-sized classes, I still take care to arrive first in the classroom and personally greet every student when they arrive, but I don't ask students to introduce themselves or I don't call their names, as time does not allow this to happen. Instead, I use one of the following icebreakers (called the 'true or false'). I randomly ask a small number of students to introduce themselves and make three or four statements about themselves, one of which must be false. I allow some time for students to think of their three or four statements. Next I get the rest of the class to vote on which fact is false. It brings some fun in the first class and helps to start some interaction within the group.

Another icebreaker I have used in the first meeting of a large size class is the 'word association'. I generate a list of words related to the topic of the programme. For example, in my first year Introductory to Financial Accounting programme, I ask participants what words or phrases come to mind relating to 'financial statements'. They might then suggest: 'assets', 'liabilities', 'capital', 'profits', and so on. I write all suggestions on the board, perhaps clustering by theme. I use this opportunity to introduce essential terms in the programme and discuss the scope (what's in and what's out) of the programme from the outset.

Perhaps, a lead-in activity to the 'word association' icebreaker above is the 'knowing the syllabus' which I basically use in the first meeting of all my classes. I split students into small groups and allow them to introduce themselves. Following introductions, I ask each group to generate a list of questions they have about the content of the programme. I then hand out the printed programme outline and the groups go over it together to answer their questions. Upon completion of this small group activity, the whole class then reconvenes and the groups ask any questions that were not addressed in the syllabus. A comprehensive review of the details in the programme syllabus and a thorough discussion of the syllabus then takes place which sets the expectations and creates a positive climate of learning.

Another activity is the 'programme content knowledge'. This icebreaker which I have used in my first year Introduction to Financial Accounting programme is related to a survey (or quiz) the students complete during the freshers' week. Most of the questions in the survey are based on the programme material and testing students' knowledge of the programme content. Some other questions are about class philosophy and (acceptable or disruptive) student behaviour. And some questions collect basic student background information. I analyse the survey and we discuss the answers in the first class. The content questions make them realise what they don't know and get them curious to find out, and the philosophical questions get us talking about various concepts, such as independent study, ethics, values and critical thinking, my expectations, among others!

I have also used the following icebreaker in the past which I call the 'nutty question'. It is similar to the 'The Little Known Fact' as described above. I arrive early, meet students at the main door of the classroom, and in addition to asking their names I also then typically ask a nutty question – for example, vanilla or chocolate? Hogwarts or Narnia? Pepsi or Coca-Cola? iPhone or Android? Starbucks or other? McDonald's or Burger King? What month were you born? What month do you enjoy most and why? Recommend a movie for my weekend. If a song played when you walked into the classroom what would it be? Your favourite car? Do you have a pet? What would you do with an hour completely to yourself? Stuff like that – students certainly look amused and surprised! I carry on doing the same thing at the start of every class until the first class test in week five of the term. If the question is different every time they start expecting you to ask, but beware; if you stop asking they will complain! At least you will get to know your students.

Another favourite is 'the best experience' icebreaker. This involves placing flipcharts and different colour markers around the classroom. Each chart has a different sentence stem. Here are a few examples:

- 'In order to succeed in the university . . .'
- 'In order to fail in the university . . .'
- 'In order to succeed in business you need . . .'
- 'In order to fail in business you need . . .'
- 'The best class I've ever had . . .' and on adjacent flipchart 'what the instructor did . . .'
- 'The worst class I've ever had . . .' and on adjacent flipchart 'what the instructor did . . .'
- 'Students in programmes help me learn when they . . .'
- 'I am most likely to participate in classes when . . .'
- 'Here's something that makes it hard to learn in a programme . . .'
- 'Here's something that makes it easy to learn in a programme . . .'
- 'What is your goal for the programme?'

Students are invited to walk around the room and write responses in all sentences in the flipcharts, chatting with each other and the instructor as they do so. The answers are always interesting, often humorous, and surprisingly poignant. Also, two very different class portraits may emerge. The instructor walks to each one and talks a bit about one or two of the responses. The instructor may move the flipcharts around the room so that the best and worst class portraits are separated. The instructor can move to the best class section of the room and tell students that this is the class every instructor wants to teach, but it can't be done alone. Together, the instructor and students have the power to make this class one of those 'best class' experiences!

On the last day of class at the end of the term I pull out the flipchart created on the first day (with only the last question above), so that students can see that they have actually met their goals!

Another successful activity I use every year is 'surprise testing' in the class (Basioudis, 2008). This activity is used many times during the term but not on the first day of the class. Multiple-choice question tests take place during certain lectures with no prior announcement, and as such an element of surprise in the class is introduced. These tests add a whole new dimension to the student learning experience. There is always a buzz on the corridors after each test has finished. These tests foster interactions and actively engage students with the subject matter.

OTHER ICEBREAKERS

There are many other icebreakers that you could use. Here I look at a few of the more popular types and how they can be used successfully in many business school classrooms.

Bingo is a fun activity. Make a 5x5 grid to use as a Bingo sheet. In each box, write a 'fun fact', or something that at least one of your students will probably relate to. Some examples might be: have travelled to Europe; play a sport; is left-handed, and others that can also be related to your programme directly. Then have your students walk around and talk to others until they find matches; the first to find all of them and complete the 5x5 grid successfully yells 'bingo' and wins.

The 'yes/no' icebreaker: with this one students answer a series of 'yes/no' questions by moving to the side of the room designated for 'yes' or 'no' answers. For example: Are you under age 20? Are you under age 25? Do you work? Do you work full-time? Do you play sports? Do you go to the gym? Do you live on campus? Try to ask questions that will make students move from the 'yes' to 'no' side of the room and vice versa with every question, so you can give them a chance to speak to each other and socialise each time they move and meet different students after each question. This also gets the students (and the instructor) to visually see who they may have some things in common with and get a quick demographic of the class. The last question is about where the students live. They are to space themselves out in the room according to how close or far they live from campus and in what direction (campus is the centre of the room, and you can hang signs on the walls to help students with cardinal directions). Then students are told to look around and meet with the two other students who live closest to them. Once they are in these small groups, they can exchange names, phone numbers, email (for potential study buddy or travelling together).

Another approach is the 'Common Sense Inventory': assemble a few common sense, true or false, statements directly related to the programme material. Ask students to evaluate each statement as true or false. In a large size class, have students get into groups, introduce themselves and then share their answers in small groups. Allow students to debate their differences. Instruct the groups to reach consensus and have a presenter from each group share their response to at least one question. Either 'debrief' by going over the answers and clarifying misconceptions or take the 'cliffhanger' approach and let the class wait for the correct answers to unfold throughout the term. If you take the 'cliffhanger' approach, you might consider re-administering this inventory at the end of the semester as a method of reviewing and/or reflecting on the programme (see Kharrudin et al., 2019 for an example of this approach).

'Photography': looking at images instantly ignites emotions and associations, and creates connections between people faster. Display a number of photos around the room or lay them on the desks where students can walk around and see them easily. Have them select a photo or two that resonates with them and visualises their thoughts. Once everyone has had time to think and choose a photo, have each student share their photo and have them explain why they chose them. If split into groups, then ask each group to look for common themes, maybe.

CONCLUDING THOUGHTS

The first day of class is the first chance to find out some information (how detailed depends on the size of the class) about your students in the programme. Whatever information you can gather builds rapport with your students and connects you with them as learners.

On that very first class, you have also got the opportunity to get students connected with each other and the programme content. So, a well-crafted icebreaker would help immensely towards that goal in building constructive relationships with students and discovering concrete ways you can link programme content to student realities.

In sum, on that very first class, let students wade around in some intriguing content details, collectively discovering that the ice can be melted and the water is warm and feels good. My hope in every programme I teach is that they'll even be motivated enough to dive in and swim out towards deeper waters by themselves!

NOTES

1. Others include: professor, lecturer, teacher. In this chapter the word used is primarily 'instructor'.
2. The term icebreaker can include energisers (i.e., activities that ignite energy in the group) and learning games (i.e., activities that engage programme content).
3. Other things to find out about your students in the programme may be: current jobs, career objectives, characteristics of programmes in which they've learned a lot, instructor feedback that is and isn't helpful, peer contributions that support learning, assessment that they like and dislike, etc. The goal is to try to connect with them as learners, to build constructive relationships and to discover concrete ways that you can link programme content to student realities.

SUGGESTED FURTHER READING

Basioudis, I.G. (2008). 'The introduction of "surprise tests" in teaching accounting', *Accounting Education: An International Journal*, 17 (2), June, 205–8.
Kharuddin, K.A.M., I.G. Basioudis, B. O'Connell and C. O'Leary (2019). 'Assessing the impact of teaching business ethics on accounting students' ethical decision making', working paper, Aston Business School.

Thought 1

Alison Lindon and Michael Butler

Before you begin teaching there are a couple of vitally important issues to consider: the learning environment and its relationship to the room layout. The best time to consider them is before you first walk into the lecture theatre or classroom, and then confirm that everything is in place when you arrive. Ask yourself the following two questions:

1. Is the learning environment optimal (or are there any distractions)?
    Small things can make a lot of difference. For example, check the white board/flip chart paper. Is there work there from the previous lecture? If so remove it or students could find themselves reading that instead of listening to what you are saying. Also, a quick tidy up makes the learning environment more conducive – remove the litter of coffee cups and chocolate wrappers left by the last group of students!

2. Is the room set up in the best way for your session plan?
    It is worthwhile considering the room layout for what you are trying to achieve in your session. It may be necessary to move tables and chairs into a better arrangement (if possible), and do not be afraid to ask participants to help you and to confirm what layout they prefer.
    If you are planning to deliver a presentation, it is best that participants are all seated facing forwards (for example, in rows), all with an adequate view of the screen. Some rooms have been designed to facilitate group discussion by having tables that students can sit around, supported by a smaller monitor. Ensure that all the screens have been turned on and contain the same information. In this type of room, it may mean that you need to position yourself in the middle, so all students can see and hear you.

If you are planning to write up notes on a white board, consider whether the writing will be large enough for the people at the back of the room. Ask students at the back of the room if they can read your writing.

If you are intending to carry out group work or group discussion and the room has not been designed to facilitate group discussion, then grouping tables works well. Or if you plan to facilitate the discussion of the group as a whole you could even consider arranging the chairs in a circle if the space allows.

4. Trumping truancy: maintaining student attendance and engagement

Gayatri Patel

INTRODUCTION

All stakeholders in Higher Education have a common aim and interest in improving learning and teaching outcomes, and enhancing student experience. One of the key, yet admittedly obvious, ways to meet this challenging aim is through student participation in the learning and teaching of the module, to ensure they achieve their full potential in Higher Education (HE). Whilst independent learning is, justifiably, applauded as one of the cornerstones of HE, student engagement through attendance in classes makes a significant contribution to their progress and achievement at both modular and programme level. For the purposes of this chapter, the focus will be on the attendance in classes on traditional platforms of teaching at HE through lectures, tutorials and seminars. However, the practices discussed here are equally applicable to non-traditional methods such as webinars, online tests or listening to podcasts.

Despite the introduction of innovative practices in the teaching methods at HE, the traditional approach of a lecture, followed by small group teaching, is still a common method of teaching practice. Amongst the growing debates questioning whether the traditional delivery of content through lectures and tutorials should continue as common teaching practice, such platforms continue to be beneficial as they provide a clear direction for students, aid in understanding key and complex concepts through the comfort of asking instant questions for clarification and feedback, and provide a unique forum for discussion.

Lectures and tutorials also facilitate the development of soft skills such as note taking, organisation, discipline and time management. Most importantly, lectures and tutorials create, expose and maintain a commonality amongst the student cohort on any programme, and make a significant contribution to facilitating the creation of a learning community not only between students, but between students and lecturers. Students who choose not to attend put themselves at a significant disadvantage through the break in the lineage of receiving knowledge on key concepts and principles for the module in the delivery of lectures, and miss the opportunity to acquire skills for a deeper understanding with the content of the module, and in developing essential employability skills of engaging in clear and articulate discussions. At a wider and more programme level, the lack of attendance causes a breakdown in essential contact and communication with lecturers and fellow students, the maintenance of which is essential in forming a trusted learning partnership, which can be sought upon in difficult times for support on academic or pastoral grounds.

The significant role that student attendance in classes plays in achieving learning and teaching outcomes, and in enhancing the student experience at HE, has led some institutions and departments to make the attendance compulsory. Aside from the bureaucracy involved in ensuring appropriate repercussions are in place for nonattendance, possibly on the lecturers themselves, compulsion for attendance seems reactionary at best as the student learning experience has to be lost before action is taken, and patronising to the students at worst, which itself may cause troublesome behaviour within the classes. Instead, tackling the nonattendance should be more proactive and progressive in nature.

With the increased access to recorded material on virtual learning environments, physical attendance at lectures and tutorials should be prominently considered at the module design stage. Innovative methods need to be adopted to ensure students are intrinsically motivated and *want* to attend classes, rather than being *required* to do so. What follows is a recollection based on my experience of teaching, where I chose to focus on assessment practices on my module and have designed and implemented a method to encourage students to attend lectures, with very successful outcomes.

THE PROBLEM

The dwindling student attendance, to varying degrees, in lectures and tutorials over the course of the year is not a phenomenon that is unique to any module, programme or institution. Similarly, for my module, there was a noticeable decline in the attendance of lectures and tutorials over the year, and then a rapid increase in attendance towards the assessment period. It was noticeable that even the students that were largely well disciplined and engaged with the module refrained from attending lectures and tutorials, before the sudden increase in attendance towards the end of the module.

The module in question is an optional module on the programme, and students largely select the module based on a genuine interest and passion for the subject. The feedback for my module has always been overwhelmingly positive, with students often commenting on the enjoyable content. In light of this, keen to understand the reasoning behind the attendance, I drew upon the issue of attendance in my last lecture of the year, and asked students to specifically comment on it in the formal and informal feedback. The responses were all aligned to two main points, both of which were related to the method of assessment (which was an exam at the end of the year worth 100 per cent of the total mark for the module).

First, the nature of the exam at the end of the year permitted students to prioritise other more prevailing demands of assessments, from other modules, throughout the year. This also explained the sudden increase of attendance and communications from students as the exam drew closer.

Teaching Tip
Think about what assessment is being used throughout the programme on which you are teaching, to ensure that your approach to assessment fits effectively with the overall demands on the student.

Second, the students explained that the nature of the examination permitted selective study of certain subjects, in depth, to a sufficient level so as to pass the module with high marks. This was further evidenced in the nature of the answers provided in the exam, which demonstrated depth of knowledge in a few selected subject areas, but lacked the breadth of understanding in the module and therefore the ability to understand the wider implications of the content studied.

The lack of physical attendance to lectures and tutorials has a detrimental impact on the learning and teaching outcomes of the module. First, there is a lost opportunity for the incremental development of the knowledge, skills and understanding of the module content that is built upon over the year. The nature of HE education is such that it relies on gradual development of knowledge over the year to facilitate deeper learning and understanding, to acquire unique skills, which fundamentally distinguishes the skills acquired at the level of Further Education. This was reflected in the level of the answers provided in the exam for my module, which were largely a regurgitation of information that indicated knowledge acquired over a short period of time, rather than deep critical thinking, evaluation and synthesis, which is a product of gradual development of subject skills and knowledge over a longer period of time. More broadly, the majority of the students on this module received a grade of a lower second class, with very few students achieving an upper second class or higher.

Second, the selective attendance and reading of the subjects within the module fundamentally deprived the students of the opportunity to understand the breadth of the subject, which is fundamental for students in understanding the interconnections between the modules to meet the programme level learning outcomes. It also limited the understanding of the wider implications of the issues examined beyond the curriculum. At modular level, this is very concerning as students were able to pass the module, demonstrating that they have achieved the learning outcomes of the modules, without having studied the full module content. At programme level, my own analysis showed that very few students managed to draw connections and comparisons of the content studied on my module, to others that were naturally linked on the programme.

The third detrimental impact of the lack of attendance to lectures and tutorials on the module was the breaking down of the active learning community for the module, as students were largely unaware of who else was studying the module. Aside from the lack of peer support for the module, the students also missed the opportunity to develop their soft skills in relation to communication, discussions and being able to articulate, challenge and defend a position through participation in the tutorials. In this way, the learning partnership between the lecturer, students and peers had been ruptured.

Teaching Tip
Create a learning community, where students feel a benefit from discussing issues with their fellow students. This means building discussion time into lectures and tutorials.

THE SOLUTION

In line with my strongly held belief of the importance of assessment for learning (Black and William, 1998), I began to implement changes to the module to address the problem of attendance by focusing on the assessment practices of the module. To address the issue of the delayed priority given to the module, the exam was removed and replaced with 100 per cent coursework, with the assessment questions distributed to the students in the very first lecture.

This immediately provided the students with a way to engage with their learning and they could begin the assessment at their convenience. In addition, the nature of a written piece of coursework facilitated students to engage deeply with the core and critical issues that were assessed, and work on their critical analysis and evaluation skills. The nature of an assessment by coursework discourages large regurgitation of descriptive information, thereby pushing the students to produce enhanced level of answers.

The coursework itself is divided into two sections, which are equally divided in terms of marks. Section A of the assessment requires the students to submit an essay to a single question. The question itself is purposively designed to be very generic in nature, inviting students to research and write on areas within the course that they themselves have selected to focus on and felt passionate about writing.

To ensure breadth of study, the students are required to indicate which subjects they will be including in their study, and are not permitted to choose the same subjects of study for the second section of the assessment.

The second section of assessment is titled the 'tutorial report'. For this section, students are required to write a 500-word piece of writing in a form of an academic blog post, on one key aspect of the topic studied in each tutorial cycle. The writing must be critically evaluative of the key issues, principles, or concepts that were examined. Due to the nature of the module, students are encouraged to form an academically informed position and to clearly articulate an argument within the 500 words. The reading and preparation for each tutorial cycle is directly aligned to this part of the assessment. Students are encouraged to discuss their arguments between each other and to challenge each other's viewpoints as well as reflect upon their own. At the end of each tutorial cycle students are in the position to write up this aspect of the assessment.

THE IMPLICATIONS

Following the changes in assessment, I recorded my own observations, and undertook a mid-term, and full-term written feedback in the written format, both formally and informally, as well as using oral feedback. The attendance and engagement of students had dramatically increased and was sustained throughout the year, in comparison to the previous years. Students, during classes and their feedback, demonstrated a genuine interest in the subject area and felt passionate about their writing. A deeper level of learning was reflected in the quality of the assessments that were submitted, with a significant increase in the marks, with the majority of students under the new method of assessment now acquiring an upper second class or higher.

First, at modular level, Section A of the assessment (that required students to write an essay question) ensured a breadth of understanding of the content of the module. This is primarily because students were required to discuss a certain number of issues in their essay, without any repetition of subject content in Section B.

Teaching Tip
By setting coursework that covers all the content of the module the possibility of selective studying of certain topics can be designed out of the module.

As a result, the attendance levels in lectures and tutorials dramatically increased as every aspect of the module could potentially be included as part of their essay.

Students' feedback showed that they preferred to have an overview of the whole module, and then decide the topics for the assessment in which they were most interested and were able to research and write on them at length. The tutorial reports provided an invaluable opportunity to undertake deeper level of learning and understanding, on a weekly basis, throughout the year.

Students were extremely well prepared for their tutorials, as they were aware that they would receive feedback, from myself and their peers, on their own understanding of the subject area and the position they were advocating in their tutorial report. This made significant strides in developing a proactive learning community, as over the course of the module students felt more comfortable in actively participating in discussions in the tutorials. In this way, the reports provided the invaluable opportunity for students to incrementally develop a deeper and more critically evaluative understanding of the content over the full year, rather than crammed in the last few weeks or days before the assessment.

Second, as students engaged in a deeper level of learning of the module the benefits were clearly evident at programme level. There was an increased number of students drawing comparisons and references of the content covered in other modules, as well as an increased level of interest in undertaking a final-year dissertation based on the subject matters covered.

In addition, having inspected the methods of assessment across the programme, the demands of the tutorial reports are unique to this module, providing students with a unique set of skills. For example, many graduate positions now require the new recruits to contribute to the online presence by writing a blog post on current affairs that have implications for the institution that they have joined. Writing a concise, focused and yet formal piece for the first time for your employer, whilst still on probation, can be daunting. As such, the requirements of the tutorial report fills this gap of skills that students will now be acquainted with on the programme.

CONCLUSION

The replacement of an exam with coursework that requires students to study the breadth of the module, as well as the depth of the subject content aligned to the tutorials or other teaching methods, has increased the student attendance and, more importantly, the engagement with my module. Students were not only passionate about their writing, but were also developing a deeper level of understanding and a whole body of skill sets, *incrementally*, over the year. This gradual acquirement of complex body knowledge, skills and understanding is the core difference between the learning outcomes and experiences from FE to HE.

REFERENCES

Black, P. and D. Williams (1998). 'Assessment and classroom learning', *Assessment in Education: Principles, Policy and Practice*, 5 (1), 7–74.

SUGGESTED FURTHER READING

Moore, S., C. Armstrong and J. Pearson (2008). 'Lecture absenteeism among students in higher education: A valuable route to understanding student motivation', *Journal of Higher Education Policy and Management*, 30 (1), 15–24.

Thought 2

Kathy Daniels

Sometimes discussions with students can be stilted because the students have a very narrow understanding of the topic that is being discussed. This became evident in a discussion about the role of trade unions in today's society.

As the discussion developed it became clear that students were thinking about trade unions in a very narrow way. They were seeing trade unions as the voice of the working class, and something that was for older employees. This does not fit with the statistics relating to trade union membership which show that trade union members are as likely to be male as female, and a high proportion of trade union members have a qualification at degree level or above.

It was decided to address these stereotypes before the next discussion on the same topic, but with a different group of students, took place.

At the start of the session students were asked to get a piece of paper and to draw the image that came into their head when they heard the words 'trade union representative'.

This caused quite a lot of amusement, and some comments about drawing skills, but all students engaged. The lecturer walked round the room looking at the drawings as they developed.

Figure T1   A typical drawing

The majority of students in the room drew a male person who was angry. Those who had the art skills to distinguish further also tended to draw an older person.

This then led to an interesting discussion about the perception of trade unions, and the data relating to trade union membership was presented. Then a debate about the role of trade unions in today's society could proceed with a more open understanding of what a trade union actually does, and who might join a trade union.

5. Helping our students to think critically

Elaine Clarke

INTRODUCTION

There is an abundance of excellent resources on critical thinking. In this short chapter I don't aim to add to the definitions, frameworks and exercises that you could easily find through a Google search and an hour or so of your time. I have two main aims here, the first of which is to argue for the deliberate and overt teaching of critical thinking skills rather than hoping our students already have them, or that they will emerge gradually and unconsciously through subject study. In business and management studies we should be preparing our students to conduct themselves as 'business people' and 'managers', to be able to contribute to the performance of any organisation they join, be it commercial, not-for-profit or social enterprise. The second aim is, therefore, to link critical thinking to what students will encounter in the world of work so that we can design real-life learning experiences, fitting them to enter the workplace with a mindset and skills that will increase their effectiveness.

CRITICAL THINKING

Critical thinking has never been more important than it is now as technology evolves ever more quickly, radically changing the way we live our lives and operate in the workplace, accompanied by an explosion of the information available to us at any minute of the day. The problems we face are different and we must be able to search for, sort, prioritise, analyse, interpret and apply information like never before. A recently published manifesto for the future of management development (Abell et al., 2018, p. 18) characterises management as a 'world of dilemmas and trade-offs' where a 'crucial skill to be developed is "to get to the essential". Often this is more about defining the problem than resolving it. Managers have to learn to stand back to see the "big picture" before focusing back in on the essential. . . . Management requires a constant alertness for secondary and tertiary effects. Asking the right "what if?" questions is a key requirement.' What is this if not an imperative for critical thinking on the part of the future managers we are helping to form?

WHAT IS CRITICAL THINKING, AND HOW IS IT OF VALUE IN THE WORKPLACE?

Some years ago, following the redesign of a suite of undergraduate courses, I had volunteered to write a first-term, first year module on Critical Thinking that was to span all courses. I duly wrote the module handbook, setting out the learning outcomes, weekly topics, and designing seminar exercises for each week. I then had to leave it to a colleague to actually deliver the module. Imagine how disheartening it was to hear after two or three weeks, and throughout the semester, that the students weren't very happy with the module and didn't understand what it was for. The most commonly quoted grumble was that they felt they weren't learning anything.

The following year I was running a second-year work-experience module that was based either on students' part-time or voluntary work, or on a summer internship. As part of the work-in-progress review for this module, students had to do a short presentation, including saying which of their first-year modules, if any, they were finding most relevant in the workplace. Imagine how gratifying it was for me, and not a little surprising, to hear that one year later in *every single presentation* the students commented that their first year Critical Thinking module was proving of value. The students didn't know I had written a good part of it, so I don't think they were telling me what they thought I wanted to hear.

Teaching Tip
Sometimes we tutors have to wait some time before students recognise the value of what we are trying to teach them. Don't give up too soon. Maybe tweak your approach and seek the support of fellow tutors.

Why would we be surprised, however, that students find learning to think critically to be of value in the workplace? It pervades so many activities geared towards fulfilling the missions of organisations. Let us take Halpern's (2002, pp. 6–7) definition of critical thinking:

> Critical thinking is the use of those cognitive skills or strategies that increase the probability of a desirable outcome. It is used to describe thinking that is purposeful, reasoned, and goal directed.

To increase the probability of a desired outcome could be described as what we all want, no matter what we are aspiring to. Here, it is specifically linked with critical thinking – this being the tool to be applied to aid our journey towards the outcome. We need to teach our students critical thinking to increase the likelihood of their success in entering employment and in excelling at it.

Halpern's use of the terms 'purposeful' and 'goal-directed' resonates particularly in organisational contexts where, no matter the type of organisation, our graduates will quickly find that objectives and targets abound, either directly for the individual or indirectly through, say, departmental targets. More and more of our working life is measured and we are judged against achieving those targets: sales growth, production outputs, lowering wastage, click-through rates, average time spent on web pages, conversion rates, and so on. Technology allows performance against targets to be accessed at any time, and staff at all levels can find themselves challenged on their performance at any minute of the day. Critical thinking, applied in the right context for the task, can put us in a better position to achieve our goals in a purposeful (and therefore, more likely, an 'effective') manner.

'Reasoned' is reflected in other definitions of critical thinking which use such terms as 'objective' and 'rational'. The way to provide proof in an argument and/or to ensure maximum objectivity, reason, or rationality is to seek evidence to support a view, and to scrutinise the evidence others have provided. This will involve verifying the evidence and questioning the credibility and interests of the sources. We are inundated with data, for example on budgets, competitors, customers, forecasts, that we need to sort, scrutinise and evaluate in order to use it as evidence to support arguments and guide rational decision-making. Where perfect and complete data isn't available, we need to give our students the confidence and competence, through critical thinking, to support their case when a decision must nevertheless be made.

Individuals practised in critical thinking will be more effective at:

- Looking at issues from various perspectives
- Understanding the connections between ideas
- Identifying inconsistencies in data and arguments
- Evaluating their own work and that of others
- Arguing a case and reinforcing it with evidence
- Calculating various scenarios, implications and potential consequences
- Making decisions
- Solving problems

all of which are predeterminants for success in their studies and in the workplace.

We must not forget that the reflective practice in which we increasingly engage our students is critical thinking too. We use it to heighten their awareness of their own work, and their approaches and responses to situations. A lack of self-awareness will hinder progress within an organisation, so efforts to focus thoughts on greater self-knowledge are well-founded. Individuals who are practised in critical thinking also show an ability to manage their own emotions, again a valuable asset when dealing with the ebb and flow of organisational life.

We need, therefore, to give critical thinking some serious space.

WHY AND WHERE SHOULD WE TEACH CRITICAL THINKING?

There is a considerable body of evidence that shows outcomes for students are improved when they have overtly been taught critical thinking. This contrasts with the view that students will absorb and recognise critical thinking through their subject studies. The evidence does not support this latter view. Although students might engage in critical thinking in fulfilling a subject task, they are less likely to be aware that they are doing it.

Teaching Tip
A conscious approach to critical thinking and the opportunity to practise techniques enable students to take a more purposeful approach and to become more sophisticated in their thinking and communication skills.

Cottrell (2017) lists the benefits of critical thinking for students: improved attention and observation; more focused reasoning; improved ability to identify the key points rather than becoming distracted; improved ability to respond to the important messages; knowledge of how to get one's point across; precision in one's thinking and work; being more accurate and specific; and skills of analysis that can be used in a number of situations. We can use this list of benefits applied to both their studies and the workplace (and we will probably have to do it repeatedly) to convince students of the value of overtly studying critical thinking. Halpern (2002) touches upon *attitudes* that underpin effective thinking: a willingness to plan, to be open-minded, to be persistent, a willingness to admit errors and change one's mind when the evidence changes, not to respond in an automatic or routinised way, and consensus seeking in the light of the evidence. We should likewise make the desirability of such attitudes evident to students in discussions and in written documents, providing concrete opportunities for them to develop them.

Overt teaching of critical thinking will lead to greater learning and success throughout their studies, not just at a given end point. Students will go out from their degrees already having enriched their learning through critical thinking. Their approach will make them more likely to be successful in the multi-faceted recruitment processes our students face these days, even before they move on to demonstrating their prowess in the workplace. I remember the HR Director of a global cosmetics firm stating that what she craved, but rarely saw in graduates she interviewed, was an ability to debate an issue – to get into the cut and thrust of an argument and to be able to defend their point of view. Enter critical thinking.

Teaching Tip
We have to build specific training in critical thinking into the curriculum in such a way that students know they are doing it, why they are doing it, and that builds their competence and confidence the further they move forward in their studies.

Starting from the assumption that there are particular skills we can teach students to train them in critical thinking, we need to consider where this should be happening. In the example given earlier, students had one 15-credit first-year module. It took them some time, however, to recognise the value of what they had been taught. Is this a problem as long as they do recognise it at some point? I would say yes, it is a problem. We should be concerned to ensure that students see the value earlier. Their 'negative' attitude towards the module might have prevented them from learning as much as they could at the time, and from being able to apply it to the way they approached tasks in their other modules. The fact that they didn't recognise the value until late in their second year means a lot of time was wasted when they could have been building on, and refining, their thinking skills.

We need, therefore, to link the teaching in that one module with materials and/or assessment they are covering in the other modules running concurrently. For example, if they are doing an Introduction to Marketing module in their first year, why not also look at a problem from the point of view of customers, competitors, the production team, an external media agency, the internal marketing team, the sales team and so on? Make it clear to the students that they are looking at an issue from a variety of perspectives, and that this is an element of critical thinking.

Teaching Tip
Think about working together with other tutors to plan your approach before
making final design changes to modules before the start of term.

If you are linking with one concurrent module, I suggest you link with all others that are running concurrently too, to show the breadth of critical thinking, and to create an integrated experience for students. Each module could address a different element of critical thinking; for example, taking the list above, one module could run an exercise that looks at the links between ideas (how about Organisational Behaviour for this?), while another could focus on identifying assumptions and inconsistencies in data and arguments (perhaps put something like this in your Introduction to Accounting module). It must always be made clear that this is building upon what students have been taught in their Critical Thinking module (so co-ordination and scheduling by module leaders is important).

It might be possible to use one case study that allows different modules to pick up on all of these elements, with the case study then forming the final assessment in the Critical Thinking module. A separate module also makes it easier to measure assurance of learning in critical thinking, providing clear evidence of whether we have succeeded, at that stage, in making critical thinkers of our students.

It is possible, of course, to use several modules without there being a separate Critical Thinking module too. In this case, you are relying on overtly teaching Critical Thinking in different modules. This again creates a significant task of coordinating, scheduling and communicating. It needs strong leadership to sell the idea, to agree what is being done where, to ensure it is being done, and to ensure students are getting a consistent message and the agreed opportunities to develop and recognise their critical thinking skills.

In either case, we must ensure that the tasks reflect situations the student might encounter in the workplace. We must also look to continuing overt engagement in critical thinking beyond the first year of an undergraduate course, or the first term of postgraduate study. Like any skill, practice will improve performance and conscious practice will improve it even further.

HOW SHOULD WE TEACH CRITICAL THINKING?

'It is not unusual to assume our point of view is well-founded, that we know best, and that we are logical and reasonable. Other people observing us may not share this view' (Cottrell, 2017, p. 4). It is also not unusual for people to share their opinions, but less usual for them to provide us with reasons to support those opinions.

Studies have shown that students tend to think of critical thinking as being the same as 'being critical' of something, that it is about looking for weaknesses and exposing them. The list above on what is involved in critical thinking can serve as the structure for exercises, setting them in a context relevant to the internal workings of an organisation, or to the external environment that affects the performance of the organisation. For example:

Looking at issues from various perspectives: this could involve identifying the positions of people mentioned in a piece of writing, or a video, or imagining what the positions of people not mentioned might be. It could also be about evaluating any evidence from alternative points of view.

Teaching Tip
A widely used introductory exercise is to use two or more newspaper articles or editorials on the same subject – newspapers are notoriously partisan, so alternative points of view should be easy to find. If the subject matter is about something that affects business, so much the better, as this can lead to a wider discussion.

Understanding the connections between ideas: analysing a case study or undertaking a (mini) literature review can be helpful here. Text needs to be broken down into relevant parts to aid in seeing the nature of what is written and the relationships. The manifesto mentioned in the introductory section (Abell et al., 2018) talks about 'pattern recognition' being a key skill for managers, whatever their responsibilities. Understanding the parts and their relationships can then lead to a more sophisticated skill of synthesising the information to form new ideas. Mind maps are particularly helpful for bringing relationships to light.

Identifying inconsistencies in data and arguments: material for such an exercise could come from the same sources as mentioned above, however if you also want to build your students' confidence in their quantitative abilities, use market research data, or production or accounting data.

Teaching Tip
If you can persuade your business contacts to allow you access to non-sensitive genuine data, you will probably find that you can turn it to many uses, and it usually awakens students' interest more than data from a textbook.

The key message to students here is that they shouldn't just accept what they see. The first step is to identify any assumptions so that they can be isolated. This in itself can give rise to rich discussions. It is then a question of considering the evidence that supports any arguments; what were the sources of the evidence, how credible are they, what are their interests, how consistent is the evidence from those different sources? It could be that in the subject you are teaching there are particular standards to take into account, so how does the evidence fit with these standards? Does every step in the argument follow on logically, or support earlier assertions?

Evaluating their own work and that of others: to undertake this exercise with regard to the work of others, students need to have undertaken the steps above. They need now to go two steps further and evaluate the arguments and draw conclusions. Ask students to set out the opposing arguments and make a judgement about whether they are based on and stem from sound evidence. If the arguments did not flow logically, what was needed to make this happen? By the time students have been through the steps above, they should also be in a position to identify hidden messages as well as the obvious ones, to recognise those techniques writers or speakers use to reinforce a particular position they wish to convey. Ask them to draw conclusions about the strength of the case presented and to justify those conclusions.

Teaching Tip
Students will be much more effective at evaluating their own work if they have first evaluated the work of others.

Students will have learned what is meant by objectivity and can be asked to apply this to themselves, maybe in the form of self-assessment or as part of a peer-assessment process, certainly in some formative exercise. Students' reflective practice is also likely to be much more considered after training in critical thinking, and therefore of more value to them in positively influencing their future practice. It is important students understand that reflection is also critical thinking, and that they can apply critical thinking techniques to it.

We can help our students further by providing them with the 'language of reasoning'. Fisher (2011) talks about 'argument indicators' such as 'my opinion is', 'the evidence implies', 'this explains why', 'by contrast', 'the best option is'. Whereas we would normally be reluctant to spoon-feed our students, here is one occasion where I recommend that we draw together a handout for students of phrases that would indicate a critical approach, and refer to it regularly, so that they become familiar with them and practised in using them. Language is a tool for them to express their critical thinking, it is not the critical thinking itself – they will need to provide that. Sensitive and constructive use of language to defend points of view will undoubtedly be called upon in the workplace.

Arguing a case and reinforcing it with evidence: students might well approach an exercise in arguing a case with trepidation, as this is where they could feel exposed and lack confidence. If, however, you have taken them through exercises like those above, you can reassure them that they have already argued a case and reinforced it with evidence. They have argued the strength of the arguments of others, so that *is* arguing a case, and they *have* reinforced it with evidence by evaluating the very evidence that was provided and selecting that which was sound. We should, however, for the sake of their success in their studies and to enhance their employability, ask them to go further.

Now they need to research information to argue a case (whether you give them a stance to argue, or they decide for themselves), they need to assure themselves of the validity of any evidence, organise the information appropriately, structure their reasoning logically, and make clear and justified conclusions stemming from the evidence. Most business and management students will have to produce a significant piece of self-managed work, usually in the form of a dissertation, and this is a prime vehicle for applying their critical thinking skills. I propose, however, that we do not wait until they start their dissertation to ask them to argue a case and reinforce it with evidence. Let us give them plenty of opportunity to practise, so that the quality of the dissertation experience and the outcome reflect the skills that are core to managers of the future.

Calculating various scenarios, implications and potential consequences: case studies are a good basis for imagining different scenarios. They are usually rich in characters, roles, data and quandaries. Students will enjoy exercises generating 'What ifs' and exploring potential implications of these. Anticipating outcomes and preparing contingencies are essential skills for the workplace.

Making decisions and solving problems: the above steps will equip our students to make rational, reasoned decisions to move forward, to solve problems and to communicate their conclusions with a clarity that convinces others. Even in situations where data, evidence or time to think are not available, a practised approach to thinking critically will lead to greater effectiveness in decision-making under duress, or when spontaneity is required.

CONCLUSION

The ability to think critically is more important than ever. Evidence does not support the view that students will absorb it automatically; we therefore need to teach it openly. A conscious approach to critical thinking, where students are aware of its value to their studies and their employability, will lead to a quicker build-up of competence and the confidence to apply it.

It takes strong and consistent leadership at programme and modular level to maximise the benefits of overt teaching of critical thinking, and to ensure it is transferred across subjects and levels. Like any skill, we must consciously provide opportunities at every level of study for students to practise so that their sophistication in thinking and communicating grows along with their subject knowledge.

We must set critical thinking activities within the context of the workplace so that by the time students apply for graduate jobs, they are comfortable with the language of business, they know that there will be 'dilemmas and trade-offs' to face, and they have the confidence of a practised critical thinker to embrace the challenge.

SUGGESTED FURTHER READING

Abell, D.F., D. Purg, A. Bracck Lalic and N. Kleyn (eds) (2018). *MANIFESTO: Changing the Course of Management Development: Combining Excellence with Relevance*, Bled, Slovenia: CEEMAN (International Association for Management Development in Dynamic Societies).

Cottrell, S. (2017). *Critical Thinking Skills: Developing Effective Argument and Analysis, 3rd Edition*, Palgrave Study Skills, London: Palgrave.

Fisher, A. (2011). *Critical Thinking: An Introduction, 2nd Edition*, Cambridge: Cambridge University Press.

Halpern, D. (1999). 'Teaching for critical thinking: Helping college students develop the skills and dispositions of a critical thinker', *New Directions for Teaching and Learning*, Winter, 80.

Halpern, D. (2002). *Thought and Knowledge: An Introduction to Critical Thinking, 4th Edition*, Abingdon: Taylor & Francis.

Thought 3

Daniel Cash

In terms of aspects that have been well received during my teaching practice, perhaps the development of a 'topic of the week' during seminars has been the most productive. When designing the 50-minute seminar, I have instituted that the final 5 minutes be left for a predetermined topic that is concerned with the students' development, rather than their academic understanding.

Topics that have been discussed include: understanding support networks; navigating the first year of university; the importance of preparation; preparing for assessments/examinations; physical wellbeing; mental wellbeing; extra-curricular activities; and career planning.

The sections are not designed to be exhaustive, nor are they designed to be overly directional. Their aim is twofold: the first aim is to highlight something to the students and provide them with knowledge which can be followed up after the session, i.e. alerting them to the presence of the Enabling Team in the university (however, this is done throughout the year in a variety of ways owing to its importance); and the second aim is to allow the students to be exposed to a professional person who has been in their position, and hear that person's viewpoints on these important topics – the topics will never be delivered in a uniformed manner, and that is the point; the aim is to develop a human connection between tutor and student, which has been designed to facilitate the 'opening up' of that relationship so that important aspects of the students' progression may be brought forward by the student.

The topics have been very well received, and have led to a number of instances where students have accessed services, spoken with faculty members about their plans and how best to execute them, and also encouraged feedback in a group setting on important issues (which is impressive given the lack of engagement in such settings when such topics are raised). If the topics are agreed upon in advance by the module team, there is a real opportunity to shape not only the academic progression of the cohort, but their *real* progression which can have an equally demonstrable effect.

6.   How to introduce and integrate creativity

Bimal Arora

INTRODUCTION

Stories of distracted, disinterested and disgruntled students and the disconnect between students and teachers, and more worryingly, disruption
and incivility by students in classrooms, are growing concerns, which we
often hear about in higher education institutions (HEIs). Like many other
business educators, I too have experienced some of these issues first-hand.
I try to work towards addressing these difficult issues through continual
reflection and improvements, peer exchanges, and engaged teaching and
learning practice. Over the years, I have also realised that it is possible, to
some extent, to address these challenges by introducing and integrating
creativity in my teaching and learning practice, and so I have been engaging with the notion of creativity. I always had the gut feeling that I could
leverage creativity to improve my teaching and learning practice, but until
a few years ago I knew little about creativity. I wonder if that's the case
with most business educators, or more broadly with educators in the HEIs?

CREATIVITY IN THE CLASSROOM

An insightful session on creativity in classrooms I attended helped enhance
my awareness and further aroused my interest and curiosity on the topic.
However, I left the session with unanswered questions on how I integrate
creativity in my teaching and learning practice, and particularly in my
classroom. These questions got me thinking and researching on creativity
in HEIs, and since then I availed every opportunity to learn and develop
my own capabilities and skills on integrating creativity in my teaching.
More importantly, I learnt that creativity as a graduate attribute is growing
in demand among employers, particularly business corporations, and that
creativity, besides being an individual trait, should be considered as a social
and public good (I discuss these issues in more detail later in the chapter).

A key differentiator in my journey and engagement with the notion of creativity has been my own motivation. Hence, motivation is an underlying theme in this chapter – both the value and importance of motivation for individual creativity and work, and motivation generated because of being creative – for students, for business educators and for HEIs.

In this chapter my objectives are to offer some insights and guiding principles for business educators – to develop their own motivation to explore and engage with the notion of creativity; to develop interest in building their capacities to support students with improving creative thinking skills and abilities; to support with some ideas for stimulating their thinking for designing of curriculum for the purpose; and to work towards contributing to developing a supportive institutional environment.

I would like to emphasise though that as creativity is a widely misunderstood and complex notion, the purpose with this chapter is largely to raise consciousness, bust some myths, and offer some directions towards achieving these objectives. Research on creativity is abundant and growing, and a lot of guidance material and tools are available and should be referred to if this chapter succeeds in motivating you to view creativity in a fresh light, to improve your teaching, learning and student engagement practices. (I have provided some references and links to useful resources at the end of this chapter.)

CREATIVITY AS SOLUTION FOR BUSINESS, MANAGEMENT AND SOCIETY IN A VUCA WORLD

The managerial acronym VUCA describes environments or situations that produce high levels of:

- Volatility
- Uncertainty
- Complexity
- Ambiguity.

Despite newly emerging transformational technologies, gadgets, standards and processes – meant to make life and work simpler for us – the world is in fact becoming more complex, unpredictable and unsustainable. From the very basic challenge of making our day-to-day life decisions; to managing local and global workforces to achieve the desired levels of productivity and performance; to coping with and resolving distant-sounding grand challenges and wicked problems around climate change, sustainable development and corporate sustainability, we need leaders and managers who are able to think and act creatively – leaders who can find innovative solutions to the problems for both current and future generations, in whatever situations and contexts they arise.

Not surprisingly, creativity features prominently in the projections of future skills by international organisations such as the International Business Machines corporation (IBM), World Economic Forum (WEF) and the McKinsey Global Institute (MGI), and is becoming an established field of academic inquiry and engagement. Creativity is considered as a catalyst for innovation, invention, performance and a signifier for personal fulfilment, motivation and satisfaction for individuals. Scholars describe creativity as the cultural capital and one of the official twenty-first-century skills (Kaufmann, 2016). However, Adobe's State of Create 2016 study highlights the 'creativity gap' between aspiration and reality with only 1 in 4 reporting themselves to be 'living up to their creative potential' around the world. We as educators should bear the responsibility and can help bridge this gap by developing in students the knowledge, skills and aptitude for successfully navigating the VUCA world. We all need to view creativity among students as a social and public good, not just for business, organisational and economic rationales.

BUSINESS SCHOOLS AND STUDENTS' CREATIVITY

People hold divergent opinions and generally view creativity as an individual's ability to be imaginative or develop original ideas, or the cliché – 'think outside the box'. Thus, several intuitive ideas and conceptions are applied to the notion of creativity. Research, however, suggests that all these are just aspects, making creativity a much misunderstood construct. While the wider society holds a view of creativity as an exceptional individual's gift, attribute and talent, the idea of 'second generation' creativity 'supports the proposition that all individuals have the potential for creative ways of learning, thinking and being' (Philip, 2015). Scholars argue that creativity is not a talent or skill possessed only by exceptionally gifted individuals, and can be harnessed and developed among students through learning and development processes and activities. Business schools, therefore, should invest in motivating faculty and staff members to develop curricula, pedagogies and co-curricular activities, as well as aligning the broader institutional policies and environment, to support fostering creativity among students.

Robyn Philip, who defended her PhD thesis on the topic of creativity in contemporary HEIs, argued that creativity is usually implicit in curricula, and 'teaching for creativity and teaching creatively remain problematic', as analytic modes of knowledge delivery and assessments are prioritised (Philip, 2015). Many business educators try to inculcate creativity among students, in their own unique ways. However, we need to make it an *explicit* objective and agenda in all aspects and functions of our teaching, learning and student engagement activities and experience.

According to Norman Jackson, creativity involves 'the capacity to generate and connect ideas and create frameworks to judge the worth of ideas and potential solutions'. Importantly, Jackson et al. (2006) connected creativity with *positive attitudes* and high levels of *motivation and passion*, reflected through perseverance, willingness and ability for hard work – qualities and characteristics much in demand by organisations in general and business corporations in particular. Creativity demands as well as generates motivation to do something. Therefore, integrating creativity in business school curriculum and pedagogy has the potential to generate motivation among students. This develops a motivation to actively engage and participate in learning and to contribute in creating a positive learning environment and learning, which can be valuable for students' own future, their employers and the society more broadly.

INTRODUCING CREATIVITY IN A BUSINESS SCHOOL

Business schools should invest in harnessing and fostering creativity. Usually the challenges faced in nurturing creativity among students in business schools may involve issues such as inflexible management attitudes and practices; the approach towards student engagement; experience; assessments and marking; faculty perception about creativity and their motivation; the wider institutional environment; and the national policies on education, teaching and learning.

The efforts and processes demanded in teaching creativity may challenge, and even destabilise, established norms of teaching, learning and management practices. Therefore, introducing creativity in a business school should be a carefully considered and well-deliberated decision, taken in consultation with faculty members, programme and administrative staff, and other relevant stakeholders, including students. Such a process may contribute to addressing and arresting some of the negativity associated with fostering creativity in students, particularly amongst faculty and other management members.

The foremost issue business schools and educators should address is about defining creativity. Beghetto and Kaufman (2013), highly accomplished creativity scholars, have argued that 'without a clear understanding of the nature of creativity itself, such well-meaning advocacy may do more harm than good; educators may experience calls for teaching creativity as just another guilt-inducing addition to an already-overwhelming set of curricular demands'. In fact, the definition of creativity may even vary from one business discipline and function to another, and from one country and culture to another. Attempts at finding and pursuing a single definition suitable for all contexts is not advisable. Of course, scholarly definitions of creativity should be used to arrive at and adopt the most suitable definition of creativity for your own institution.

A useful step to define creativity relevant to your institution could be to form a working group or a special interest group (SIG), comprising interested faculty and management team members, within the Business School.

Teaching Tip
Besides developing the definition of creativity, SIG could be tasked with developing and supporting school, departments, course, programme and module wide tools and faculty-level engagement strategies and activities – to develop interest, motivation, capacities, confidence and skills on integrating creativity in curricula, pedagogy, programme/module design, delivery and assessments.

School-wide student surveys on creativity at the beginning and end of terms/academic year may be introduced and institutionalised to measure progress on fostering students' creativity. Results of such surveys can be used to create a positive competition among departments and faculty members, and awards can be instituted to celebrate the achievement of faculty members, departments and students that demonstrate exceptional performance and creativity.

INTEGRATING CREATIVITY IN CLASSROOMS

Of course, not all business educators may be confident in their abilities to design and deliver creative learning processes, methods and outcomes. The digital learning technologies may be seen as adding to the complexities. Also, I may not be overstating in suggesting that prescriptive and heavily lectures-driven teaching methods and styles, and traditional forms of summative assessments, mostly discourage student creativity. Such practices are less likely to encourage students to make efforts and apply themselves to creative thinking and engagement.

Further, educators are increasingly operating in strong cultural, procedural and standardised environments that have significant impacts and implications on what they can and cannot do to develop their own approach, methods, practice and processes to harness and inculcate students' creativity. Norman Jackson, however, suggested that: 'In spite of, or perhaps because of, these constraints, teachers who care about creativity are able to overcome these barriers to create through their pedagogy curricular spaces and opportunities for learning that encourage and reward students for their creativity.'

SO WHERE AND HOW DO WE START THE JOURNEY?

Following Jackson, I suggest that learning objectives, activities and processes to foster creativity in business schools 'must develop self-efficacy, encourage risk taking in safe environments and help students to engage with messy/complex and unpredictable situations where there are no right and wrong answers'. Researchers have recognised a range of intellectual attributes, attitudes and behaviours associated with creativity, and I outline three characteristics advocated by Jackson: ability to visualise ideas; effective use of memory; and convergent and divergent ways of thinking.

Keeping the above three characteristics in mind, any learning and development programme in a business school can be designed or redesigned to harness and enhance creative abilities of students. To encourage and foster students' creativity, we as teachers need to act and engage as a facilitator, resource person, stimulator, mentor and guide, and offer freedom, space, time and appropriate – and sometimes unusual – challenges to students to think both critically and constructively, and to make decisions about their own learning process, pace, performance, achievements and outcomes. Teaching for creativity, therefore, will require a pedagogic approach that facilitates and enables, is responsive, and open to possibilities and collaborations, and which values the process as much as the performance and outcomes.

Creativity might sound soft and fluffy (Kaufman, 2016). Therefore, to harness and foster creativity among students necessitates substantive integration of aspects and factors of creativity in a classroom, and entails creatively creating certain conditions. Inspired by Jackson et al. (2006), I offer some specific suggestions that may help facilitate harnessing and fostering students' creativity in a classroom:

Teaching Tips
- *Course and curriculum should explicitly refer to and highlight the harnessing and fostering creativity of students by specifically mentioning creativity in the learning objectives, module description and/or learning outcomes:*

- ○ *Explicit reference to creativity, along with an institutionally agreed definition (if developed/available), may introduce and help students think, reflect and generate positive interest in the course/module.*
- ○ *Develop and make available to students a separate guideline on creativity, specifying the meaning, need and importance of creativity for students, as well as the linkages with the course, programme, module and assessment approach encouraging and reflecting application of creativity.*
- *Course and curriculum design should reflect the aspects for harnessing and fostering creativity of students:*
  - ○ *By making context specific provision and opportunities for dialogues, time, space and contestations – to allow students to immerse and engage in critical thinking and reflections for developing their own creativity. Make provisions for both individual and group engagements, and extensive use of case studies, real-life examples of policy, practices, with historical and contemporary relevance to issues and challenges.*
  - ○ *By thinking of varied and diverse working situations, possibilities, collaborations – to be inclusive and enable all students to be creative. Carefully planning and allowing sufficient time, motivation and gentle nudges for students who take longer to feel confident in participating in dialogues and class/module activities.*
  - ○ *Encouraging and allowing students the freedom to work in new and context appropriate ways.*
  - ○ *Challenging students – with realistic, demanding and exciting work and assignments – that encourage and allow students to relate classroom and course activities to their own experiences and situations.*
  - ○ *Encouraging students to link course-specific theories with real-life situations and their own experiences and perceptions.*
- *Assignment and assessments approach and design to allow for outcomes that offer opportunities and reflection among students.*
- *In terms of removing barriers, we could address:*
  - ○ *Regulatory inhibitors: review and address common assessment regulation difficulties that lead to standardisation of outputs or elevation of risk (mistakes being costly).*
  - ○ *For instance, a learning outcome such as 'Demonstrate the capacity to learn from failure'; 'Deal with incomplete information'; 'Respond effectively to unexpected challenge or opportunity' etc.*
  - ○ *Provide all students with the opportunity to retake or resubmit a proportion of summatively assessed work.*
  - ○ *Allow all students to craft a learning outcome to fit a body of work that has been self-driven and/or determine personalised assessment criteria.*

○ *Refocus some assessment to emphasise creative fluency, flexibility, unusual connections etc.*

○ *Integration of impossible challenges – 'Develop creative proposals for how a business could be made out of oranges'; 'Design a premium product that costs nothing to produce' (and related use of relevant creative assessment criteria).*

● *In terms of additional opportunities, we could make much of the HEAR (Higher Education Achievement Record) to incorporate clearer evidence of the development of creative attributes (Student CPD and/or extra-curricular activities, knowledge and skills).*

SUMMARY

Introducing and integrating creativity in business schools and classrooms can help enhance student motivation and learning experience. Besides the course, curriculum, classroom, assignment and assessment, school and department's overall environment should encourage creativity among faculty and staff members. Continuing debates within and across disciplines and dialogues with stakeholders about the subject and the need and role of creativity among students can help take the agenda forward.

I conclude the chapter quoting Jackson (2006), and with my best wishes for your efforts and endeavours to learn and develop the necessary skills for introducing and integrating creativity in your school, curriculum and classroom.

Being creative is a fundamentally human characteristic. People generally feel more fulfilled and motivated if they are able to be creative. If education is about helping people to develop their full potential then helping students to understand and develop their unique creativities is a worthwhile educational goal. Enabling students to be creative should be part of a higher education experience.

REFERENCES

Beghetto, R.A. and J.C. Kaufman (2013). 'Fundamentals of creativity', *Educational Leadership*, 70 (5), 10–15.
Fields, Z. and C.A. Bisschoff (2014). 'Developing and assessing a tool to measure the creativity of university students', *Journal of Social Sciences*, 38 (1), 23–31.
Jackson, N., M. Oliver, M. Shaw and J. Wisdom (2006). *Developing Creativity in Higher Education: An Imaginative Curriculum*. Abingdon: Routledge.
Kaufman, J.C. (2016). *Creativity 101*. Berlin: Springer.

McWilliam, E. and S. Dawson (2008). 'Teaching for creativity: Towards sustainable and replicable pedagogical practice', *Higher Education*, 56 (6), 633–43.
Philip, R.L. (2015). 'Caught in the headlights: Designing for creative learning and teaching in higher education', PhD Thesis, Queensland University of Technology, Australia.
Sheridan-Rabideau, M. (2010). 'Creativity repositioned', *Arts Education Policy Review*, 111 (2), 54–8.

SUGGESTED FURTHER READING

http://www.creativeacademic.uk/resources.html.
http://www.normanjackson.co.uk/creativity.html.
https://www.timeshighereducation.com/news/how-universities-can-cultivate-creativity-their-students.
https://www.creativityatwork.com/2014/02/17/what-is-creativity/.
https://www.ted.com/topics/creativity.
https://theconversation.com/we-need-creative-teaching-to-teach-creativity-34407.
https://theconversation.com/us/topics/creativity-series-13677.

7. How to invigorate group presentations

Matthew Olczak

INTRODUCTION

In the teaching of business subjects, we want our students to apply the concepts and theories studied to analyse real-world scenarios and policy issues. One common way to do this is to ask the students to prepare and then deliver an oral presentation on an assigned case. Often the students will work in a small group preparing and then presenting this to the tutor and other students taking the programme.

GROUP PRESENTATIONS

I have used this approach extensively when teaching competition (antitrust) policy to final year economics undergraduates. Here, we apply economic theory in order to evaluate policy interventions adopted by governments internationally. One example would be the case brought by the European Commission alleging that Microsoft had abused its dominant position. In other cases, we consider the decision by competition authorities over whether to allow two businesses to merge. In general, cases are selected on the basis of how well they illustrate the application of the economic theories studied and, as I also highlight to the students, as examples of the more controversial cases that have been brought.

Outside of competition policy there is an extremely wide range of other topics that would also fit well with group work leading to an oral presentation. These include the UK's decision to leave the European Union; the Bank of England considering a change in the interest rate; a business's decision over whether or not to enter an overseas market, and many others.

At the start of the programme, I allow the students to self-select into groups of five. Whilst there are pros and cons of allowing students to choose their own groups, overall I believe this is a worthwhile approach due to the lower likelihood of 'free-rider' issues, i.e. students not participating in the activities but still earning the group mark, when working with familiar peers.

Teaching Tip
If you do decide to allocate students into groups yourself make sure that you have a way of dealing with complaints about group members who do not contribute.

Each group then expresses their preference for which cases they want to study from a prepared list to assist with case allocation. The group's task is to run a one-hour session where they present their case to the rest of the cohort. The session includes time for discussion and then a conclusion regarding whether the group agrees with the real decision that was made. The presentation is marked according to various criteria including use of economic theory, arguments for and against the decision, teamwork and the quality of delivery, and this then results in an overall group mark.

In order to clarify expectations, when the cases are allocated at the start of the programme each group is provided with several supporting documents. First, a template outlining the broad expected content of the presentation (see Annex). Second, a list of key references for their case. These include the official report on the case decision, academic literature and opinion on the decision and briefing notes on the case prepared by consultancies who worked on it. In addition, in preparation for the presentation, each group is encouraged to meet with the tutor at least once to discuss their initial findings and the content of their presentation.

Teaching Tip
Make sure that students know how the presentation is going to be assessed, and how the marks are split between content and presentation technique.

The benefits of setting tasks of this nature are that students apply the concepts and theories studied to real-world problems and formation of policy arguments. Furthermore, the task enables the students to develop a wide range of transferable skills that will be invaluable when they move on into graduate employment. These include the ability to work well with others to gather, synthesise and critically evaluate a wide range of evidence and then to effectively communicate the key arguments orally.

My experience of using this approach in my teaching has been extremely positive. It is very clear that students like the application of the concepts and theories studied to real-world cases. In general, groups worked well together to research the cases in detail and identified and evaluated the key arguments well. Often the groups were able to develop arguments well beyond simply stating those outlined in the references provided. Furthermore, the students put together well-structured presentations and delivered these clearly.

GROUP DEBATES

Although the presentation approach worked well, I felt it could be improved further by recasting the presentations into a debate format. This adjustment transformed the student learning experience. The approach is very similar to the practice of mooting, which is commonly used in the teaching of law, but much less so in other disciplines.

I now ask one group of students to represent the competition authority and another group to defend the firms involved in the case. As an example, in one debate one group represents the European Commission in the case against Microsoft referred to earlier, whilst another group defends Microsoft against the allegations. A tangential benefit is that more students can then work on a given case.

Much of the initial setup of the exercise remains as before. However, I now hold an initial meeting with both groups of students together to set the scene and highlight some key features of the case. Then, about a week before the debate is scheduled, I meet with each group at least once so that they can check their arguments in secret from their opponents and seek any clarification they require from me on specific features of the case. This interaction with the groups in advance of the presentation plays a key role in ensuring that factually incorrect and weak presentations are much less likely.

I also provide guidance to the students on the format for the debate. For a typical case, the competition authority group is given the first 15 minutes to make their arguments. Then the group representing the firm gets 15 minutes to respond. Next, the groups get the opportunity to cross-examine each other (approximately 10 minutes). I then field questions from the other students in the audience and, typically, ask a few questions myself. After this, each group is given one minute to summarise their key arguments. The outcome of the case is put to an audience vote, thus helping to keep them engaged throughout the presentation. At the end I highlight some of the more general insights from the case.

As before a group mark is given for the presentation (see the feedback template at the end of this chapter), now including a sub-component for the group's performance in the cross-examination part of the debate.

A concern that is sometimes raised by students once I have assigned them to a role and they have done some preliminary research on their case is that they don't agree with the standpoint of their side of the debate. My response is that their job is to play devil's advocate. This is a position graduates working as consultants, lawyers and government officials often find themselves in when working on real-world cases. It is, therefore, a skill that will serve the students well in their future careers. I also make clear to the students that they will not be assessed on winning the debate and the final vote. Instead they need to demonstrate good understanding of the arguments and application of relevant theory. In addition, I make clear that I will take into account that in some of the cases one of the groups has a harder position to defend. These reassurances have always been sufficient to alleviate the students' concerns.

REFLECTION AND FEEDBACK

The switch to the debate format has made the material more fun to teach. It is also evident how much more engaged the students have become, both during the preparation and delivery stages. This has led to significant improvements in the quality of the presentations. Presentation sessions often result in heated, but very well-informed, debate between the two groups. Some teams become so engrossed in the topic that a number of them would probably still be debating now had I not brought the class to a close!

Student feedback has also been incredibly positive, as exemplified by the following example:

> I think the assessed presentations really helped us learn a lot more about the module content in an applied way and also reinforced our learning of the module's theories. Working in a group situation and presenting helps us develop our soft skills such as teamwork, presentation and communication skills which are very important for everyone's future career. . . It was a great way to end the year and a great way to end the university experience for me. I think the debate worked out well because the other group were brilliant and although you probably couldn't tell we are quite good friends outside of the debate scenario so it was fun, but I still didn't think it would get quite as heated as that! We're still good friends though.

It is interesting to reflect on why the debate format works so well. Arguably, it taps into the natural competitive instinct of business school students. The desire to outdo their fellow students in the debate is apparent, even more so when the other group are their close friends!

Initially, especially given the fact that a proportion of the programme content examines the possibility of similar behaviour between firms, I wondered whether collusion between groups, i.e. sharing of information on the case and coordinating on particular arguments, would be prevalent. To the best of my knowledge, this does not seem to have materialised. Even if it was to occur, the benefits for student learning appear to be substantial. Interestingly, what does appear to be more common is the planting of questions in the audience amongst peers. However, again the beneficial effects of this on student learning should not be underestimated.

More generally, a knock-on effect of the switch to a debate format has been increased attendance and engagement of students in the audience. It is clear that they benefit from seeing the arguments debated rather than just presented in front of them. Furthermore, they like the opportunity to question the groups and vote on the decision.

The design of the debate presentation task can also be closely aligned with a range of subsequent assessments. The preliminary research undertaken and feedback received can lead on to a requirement that the students write a report that evaluates the decision made in the case they have presented. Here the students should no longer be required to play devil's advocate and instead can form their own opinion on the efficacy of the decision made in the case. Students may also be required to bring in a range of examples from the cases presented in their reports or in a final exam.

CONCLUSION

Overall, debate-based assessments of this nature are a fantastic way to enhance student engagement in applying concepts and theories studied to real-world policy applications. Furthermore, the wider transferable skills developed stand them in good stead as they enter the graduate job market.

SUGGESTED FURTHER READING

Economics Network (2018). Group presentations on a topical economic issue, https://www.economicsnetwork.ac.uk/themes/recruitment/games/presentations (accessed 27 April 2019).

Stead, R. (2004). Stimulating the participation of the audience in student presenta-tions, The Economics Network, https://www.economicsnetwork.ac.uk/showcase/ stead_presentations (accessed 27 April 2019).

Taylor, R. (2002). Linking student presentations to exams, The Economics Network, https://www.economicsnetwork.ac.uk/showcase/taylor_presentations (accessed 27 April 2019).

ANNEX

Group Debate Presentation Assessment Feedback Template
Topic:
Student names:

Comments	Mark
Content	
Introduction to the Case (5%)	
Understanding of the Case (15%)	
Presentation of Arguments (25%)	
Links to Relevant Economic Theory (15%)	
Cross-examination and Response to Questions (15%)	
Summary of Arguments (5%)	
Presentation	
Evidence of Teamwork and Resulting Good Organisation of Presentation (10%)	
Quality of Delivery (10%)	
General comments	
Possible areas to develop in your individual essays	
Final mark:	%

Thought 4

Gayatri Patel

Student engagement with the literature relating to a module has always been a challenge, particularly the core reading. The lack of engagement with the course reading can have fundamental implications to meeting the learning objectives of the material, as it is likely to lead to fundamental gaps in the core knowledge required for the module.

My first attempt to address this issue was to make the core reading list more streamlined and prescriptive, highlighting the relevant pages that were required as the bare minimum for the module. Unfortunately, this seemed to have lowered the expectations even further, as students sought to read even less and, in some cases, asked for further summaries of core reading.

I changed the approach in the following year. I removed the title of core reading from the tutorial preparation sheet, and instead provided a very extensive list of reading. Alongside each reading, I provided a summary of its content, as well as indicating which learning outcomes of the tutorial the literature met. In this way the students were encouraged to take ownership of their own reading and learning, but also to engage in the reading material that they found most interesting and accessible.

At the beginning, the students were apprehensive with the lack of a core reading list for the module. However, as I explained my reasoning behind the practice, which was embedded in exploratory readings and taking ownership of their own learning, students became more acquainted with it. In fact, the beginning of each tutorial cycle began with a discussion on the reading, as students engaged in discussions as to which of the readings were most useful, interesting and engaging. These exchanges of ideas and viewpoints amongst students itself led to the increase of reading and engagement with the literature, as the students explored the reading list.

An additional advantage has been that the students were now comparing, contrasting, evaluating and synthesising the work of academics, which enabled students to achieve the very high marks for this module. This practice of removing a prescriptive or compulsory element of the reading material forced students to take a mature approach to their learning. Students took responsibility for their own reading, and ensured that they engaged with the appropriate literature to meet the learning outcomes of the modules.

8. Bridging the gap: writing in higher education

Daniel Cash

INTRODUCTION

As student numbers within the higher education (HE) system continue to increase in the UK, there is a need to assess how best HE practitioners impart certain skillsets on the ever-growing cohort. Whilst there are many aspects that need to be considered, this chapter focuses upon a central aspect, and that is how a student may most effectively communicate their understanding with the written word. The chapter aims to communicate a considered approach to facilitating an increased understanding of the process of writing at HE level and beyond.

In particular, this chapter is looking at the changing demands on a student as s/he moves from further education (FE) to HE. A student in FE might be used to smaller classes and more structured support. Moving into HE can leave the student feeling adrift.

Before the chapter begins, there is a paradox that needs to be addressed. As already stated, student numbers in the UK are steadily increasing, and as such there is a need to address how the Higher Education sector approaches the challenge of 'bridging the gap' for students coming from FE institutions. However, this is not technically correct, as in 2017 when the Universities and Colleges Admissions Service last recorded application figures, there was a 5 per cent reduction in UK student applications, and a 7 per cent reduction in students applying from countries within the European Union; in 2017, 564 190 people applied for places on HE courses.

Yet, this statistic does not necessarily mean that fewer people will move from FE and into HE, as it has been suggested that the reality is that it means fewer people will have their applications rejected, due to the infiltration of market forces within the HE sector. Therefore, whilst statistical data may not allude to the pressing need to adapt to an ever-growing intake of students, the reality is that student recruitment is still operating at advanced levels, and as such there is a need to examine how these students are taught when they arrive at the HE institution. The reduced likelihood that applications will be rejected might also mean that the skills of the student coming from FE are more varied, adding in additional challenges for the HE teacher.

WRITING IN HE

When one considers how best to communicate through the medium of writing, it is important to acknowledge that one of the inherent wonders of this art is that there is no one prescribed way one should write. Yet, for the transmission of teachable principles, there are *fundamentals* which can be offered, particularly when we consider the cohort HE teachers will be working with. Another point to note is that different HE institutions in the UK (and, in truth, around the world) attract different cohorts, which have different backgrounds.

So, there are a number of elements which can be included to change the nature of this discussion, but for this chapter the aim is to provide for *principles* which can be incorporated, upon which a given HE practitioner can then adapt their approach to their given cohort.

Yet, despite these points, there is one element that will be maintained throughout; whilst different disciplines require different things, learning and adopting efficient writing processes is of crucial importance to a vast number of disciplines. In the current climate, the notion of 'pressure' is perhaps now fundamental to societal processes, with students being under increased pressure to secure employment within volatile economic times, and the HE sector under increasing pressure to improve levels of 'employability'. It is for this reason that the issue of writing is identified in this chapter, because research has suggested that graduates' ability to write effectively and efficiently is the biggest concern for employers in the marketplace, with studies implying that employers are concerned about how students are taught this most crucial skillset within HE.

As a result of this aim, the chapter will operate on a simple basis. After providing the context for this work, the chapter will go on to examine *five key principles* that it is suggested should be considered when working with students who have recently entered HE. How those principles are incorporated would be the decision of the practitioner, and therein lies the advantage of this principled approach; the objective is to provide a considered foundation.

However, in order for the sentiment of the principles approach to be transmitted properly, there is a requirement that practitioners be fully committed to the aim of 'bridging the gap' between FE and HE. It is not suggested that this is not the case within HE institutions, but it needs to be acknowledged that the first year of an HE course is perhaps the most crucial for a student's development, so the concept of dedicated support ought to be fundamental to the teaching of that particular cohort.

APPLICATION

The basis of this approach has been derived through personal experience and research into the process of teaching. I developed and applied this approach within a core module on an LLB course entitled *Legal Skills and System*, which provides for exposure to core skills required for the completion of a Law Degree, and also provides for fundamental knowledge of key components of the legal sector. In this chapter the focus will be on the *skills* element, as there is no uniform approach to how this module is delivered across the country (some schools may have chosen to separate the *skills* and *system* elements).

Within my module, the decision was taken to establish a multi-faceted approach to assessing the cohort's written ability, all based upon the principles that will follow shortly. Technically, the cohort is provided with a difficult essay-style question that requires a student to examine and dissect the question itself; this is done purposefully to encourage the development of a certain skill which will be required throughout the students' development. At the same time, the cohort is exposed to teachings which seek to alter perceptions about the art of writing, all of which are based upon the five key principles. The next stage is for the students to complete their assignment to the best of their ability and submit the assignment, upon which they will receive *detailed* yet *ungraded* feedback. The purpose of this is to develop a 'bridge' upon which the students can make mistakes without the pressure of the mistakes becoming indelible. Upon receiving their feedback, the cohort is provided with increased support to guide them to the next phase of the assessment, which is to submit the revised work alongside a self-reflective piece detailing their own perception of their development within the first year of their time at the HE institution.

Yet, whilst the technical components of the assessment fit neatly into one paragraph, what underpins that assessment is far more extensive. What follows are the *five key principles* upon which this module has been developed, and upon which I suggest the teaching of writing practice in the first year of a Degree should progress:

- Principle I – Support
- Principle II – Simplicity

- Principle III – Deconstruction
- Principle IV – Process
- Principle V – Identity.

Before applying these principles there is the need to think of some specific differences between the typical FE and HE learning experience.

INTERACTION WITH THE TEACHER

In FE the focus is on smaller group sizes, which are exposed to the FE teacher on a more consistent basis; within HE, it is rare that the cohort will be exposed to the HE practitioner more than twice a week, and in that week one of those instances will be via a 'lecture' of sorts (different institutions may differ in how these sessions are delivered) – yet, the effect is the same, in that the cohort is exposed to the practitioner *as a large group*, within which the possibility of detailed support is almost non-existent. Upon that basis, the extra time afforded to students at this stage can have a demonstrable effect in allowing the student to make the transition between FE and HE in a relatively comfortable manner.

Teaching Tip
I have found that an extended open-door policy is a clear advantage to the student, as the transition from FE to HE sees the cohort exposed to very different practices.

A CLEAR SYLLABUS

The requirements at FE are clear; there is a syllabus to follow which students can access on the Internet. Examiners are looking for certain elements to be 'included', which is mapped to a standardised process, i.e. 'box ticking'. Whilst preparing for FE assessments students can access detailed examiners' reports and understand what is required. It is a more prescriptive form of learning.

Whilst HE institutions do all have 'marking criteria', the emphasis is different, and this can be difficult for students to understand. Students need to understand the importance of meticulousness in their learning and being able to support their assessments with referenced information. They also need to be able to contextualise their writing, showing an understanding of how the information that they are reporting can be applied.

Teaching Tip
Discuss in tutorials how the assessments will be marked. It can be useful to
work through previous examples of assessments which received a high or a low
mark, and to discuss the reasons for the marks that were given.

FORMATIVE FEEDBACK

Finally, the act of providing in-depth formative feedback (coupled with extended appointment availability) has been a distinct success. The students have the ability to see clearly where they are up to in their progression, with aspects signposted for further development.

For example, one common issue is that a first-year student's work is not where it needs to be grammatically. To resolve this issue, the ungraded feedback highlights instances where this issue has arisen, and provides feedback for why the issue has arisen and what may be done to resolve it. This, admittedly, is incredibly time-consuming and moves further away from the traditional model of HE teaching, but this expense now will be of direct benefit to the student and the university later on.

This approach is also a fantastic vehicle to inspire, in that providing truly constructive feedback here will be of real benefit, as it is often the first piece of major work the students are undertaking in their degree; discussing the issues but highlighting aspects such as endeavour provide for confidence when the student needs it most.

Teaching Tip
When giving formative feedback, particularly if it is the first piece of work the
student has completed in an HE setting, always emphasise the positive aspects
of the work. Students can be quickly discouraged.

Having explained the context of learning we now return to explore the five principles.

PRINCIPLE I: SUPPORT

It is perhaps safe to say that, traditionally, the HE sector has been founded on the principle of self-directed learning. There are a number of advantages to this approach, ranging from the increased incorporation of skillsets for those who engage with the process and chart their own development, all within a considered framework. However, that approach pre-dates the drastically different dynamic of current cohorts, with cohorts over the last two or three decades representing incredibly different variables than what came before.

In today's HE sector, the rates of applications from a number of groups represent a marked difference from the traditional composition of HE cohorts, with more women, people from different ethnic backgrounds, people from different socioeconomic sectors, and those identifying as disabled (amongst a long list) being far more representative. What this perhaps means is that whilst the traditional approaches to teaching may have benefits, there is a need to understand how the sentiments of those approaches may translate to today's cohorts.

Of course there is no one perfect approach which will cater for all of these diverse groups but, in incorporating fundamental principles, there exists an opportunity to provide a foundation for all groups, upon which they may then independently chart their own course. Whilst ethnicity or gender may or may not influence one's ability, what *will* influence one's ability is the paradigm that exists between the notions of training standards, and the ability to incorporate those training standards.

For instance, one's socioeconomic status, and the intricacies of what may be attached to that status – a crude example may be the requirement to care for a family member whilst studying, or residing in an overcrowded living space – will have an effect upon one's development and, ultimately, one's skillset when one arrives at the HE institution. It is for this reason that the first and most important principle offered here is *support*.

That support is offered in a number of ways, but it should always be offered from within a defined framework. I would be hard-pressed to find an HE practitioner who would not have an opinion on the delicate balance between providing support and removing the responsibility from the student; this is a valid concern and one which must be constantly assessed and planned for. However, this does not mean that support can be ignored.

To ensure support I make it clear to students what I offer – an open-door policy and the opportunity to make a more formal appointment to come and see me. However, I also make it clear that I will not be chasing up students to come to an appointment, and that students have to take responsibility for seeking support if they want it.

The purpose of this is to impress upon the cohort that there is a 'safety net' available, but that the student still has the responsibility to initiate the procedure; it is important to acknowledge that this is done from within the confines of openness and confidentiality – an 'open-door' policy is key to achieving the objectives of this approach.

Teaching Tip
If time allows, have a time for student appointments immediately following a
lecture (in the same room if it is not booked for another lecture). If students
are already present in the room it is less daunting for them to come and see
you, compared to them seeking out your office in a different location.

Whilst this might not seem to be focusing on writing, the reality is that these
are all components of a much larger picture. That picture details instances
which allow for students to feel comfortable to try and fail, and then to seek
support and develop. Once that sentiment is instituted within the cohort,
the technical aspects of the art of writing can then be developed.

Support for developing the skill of writing comes in the form of detailed
conversations with students that come forward, and also teachings that
operate on the same basis. The teachings mentioned here cover all of the
principles, but whilst traditionalists may not appreciate the step-by-step
approach to teaching a student the principles of writing, the effect is that
it allows students to obtain the basic skillset quicker, upon which they can
develop advanced skillsets.

The open-door policy comes into effect again when, after receiving
their ungraded feedback on their *formative* work, the cohort can continue
to question their development with their tutors. Ultimately, developing a
supportive environment is a constitutive element of the students' development, without which the following will not be accepted.

PRINCIPLE II: SIMPLICITY

Focusing on writing now more specifically, understanding this 'gap' that
students coming from FE must cross is vitally important. It is important
not only because of the different skillsets required, but because of the *perception* of the different skillsets required. For many students, their thinking
is that an Undergraduate degree (or the equivalent) will be the final location of their formal education. If that is the case, there is a likelihood that
a student may be of the opinion that one must operate in a sophisticated
and excessively complicated manner in order to *belong* at that level. It is for
that reason that the next principle – *simplicity* – is developed very early on
in the development of the cohort.

To foreshadow a principle which will be described later, the *identity* of
a writer is a fundamental component to consider. What is meant by this is
that it is very rare that work produced in FE (and in earlier levels) will ever
be read by somebody other than the examiner of the work.

In HE, there is a potential that this is less true (work could be published in Student Reviews etc.), but considering the aims of HE mean that writer/reader dynamic *must* be impressed upon the cohort immediately; if the aim is to train for skills which will be useful in the marketplace, then enveloping an inherent incorporation of the understanding that work *is to be read* is of vital importance. What that does is change the dynamic within the mind of the writer, and for students who are entering HE and looking for guidelines, that dynamic provides for a number of useful practices.

To facilitate the incorporation of that principle, *simplicity* is key. Whilst I do not want to be too colloquial, there will be many practitioners reading this who can recount similar instances of examining work that contains the usage of words which are clearly unfamiliar to students, and which clearly came about as the result of using the in-built thesaurus in the word-processing software. Whilst the aim here is not to encourage the usage of only simple language, there is a need to make clear to a cohort that the effect of not doing so can be detrimental. What is optimal is that the cohort seeks to *understand* the words they are using and, more importantly, *why* they are using them where they are.

Teaching Tip
To help impress upon students that simple and well-used language is more effective than sophisticated but poorly used language, think carefully about the way that you talk in a lecture. If students hear lecturers use sophisticated language, they firstly might not understand it, but secondly they will presume that this is what is expected of them in their writing.

The importance of this principle, however, is that it allows for the cohort to develop a varied skillset at a certain pace. Some students will be comfortable with more sophisticated language, and might go on to work in careers where it is expected and needed. However, most students will not and therefore it is important to encourage students to communicate effectively rather than use 'fancy' language incorrectly.

PRINCIPLE III: DECONSTRUCTION

In order for the cohort to develop beyond the so-called 'surface-level' and towards the 'deeper-level' knowledge, there needs to be an incorporation of the process of *deconstruction*. A simple way to transmit this to the student is the application of the word 'why?' What this does is impress upon the cohort the need to examine components of their practice which may be taken for granted. This has the associated benefit of developing a process of careful scrutiny and the adoption of the importance of process (a principle which will be discussed later).

In providing, say, a lengthy quote which needs to be 'discussed' or 'critically evaluated', the actual aim is to provide the cohort with a vehicle within which they will obtain this necessary skillset of *deconstruction*. During the teachings, the cohort is encouraged to ask 'why?' when assessing every point, every sentence, and indeed every word; for example, 'why does the quotation use a question mark there?', or 'why does the author of the statement order their points in that manner?'

What this does is twofold: it allows for the cohort to carefully examine a piece of data, but it also begins a process which becomes the blueprint for this and future works. Examining data carefully is a key skill which is directly translatable to almost all professional appointments, and this ties in directly to the concerns held by the marketplace about the skillsets obtained by students during their time within the HE sector. However, it is not enough to just do this; this concept of translatability must be directly addressed and impressed upon the cohort if it is to be effective.

For a student studying accountancy, for example, there may be a difficulty in understanding why taking this approach with the answering of an essay question may be of benefit to them in their future careers. What needs to be discussed is that the act of deconstructing relates directly to a cohort's particular field, so that for an accountant the skill of reviewing new and difficult data and being able to deconstruct it so that a more palatable analysis can take place will be of crucial importance for their time in the field of accountancy.

Teaching Tip
The approach of deconstruction can also be used in helping students to understand an assessment question. In a lecture students can discuss the question together, breaking down the question into simple steps.

They can then start to structure their assignment by thinking about the different areas that they will need to write about, and what will fit into the different sections such as the introduction and the conclusion.

PRINCIPLE IV: PROCESS

There are indeed many advantages to teaching the process of deconstruction, but perhaps the biggest advantage is that it simultaneously leads into the next principle, and that is *process*. In my experience, many students in the first year in HE struggle to know where to start, with the self-directed experience allowing for many opportunities and pathways to travel along but the student struggling to choose.

There are a number of procedures which are used within FE, but quite often the process is provided for, meaning that the requirement in HE to develop one's own pathway can be quite daunting (particularly when we return to an earlier point about the vastly different cohorts within HE in the modern era). To alleviate this pressure and, in truth, anxiety, the art of deconstruction feeds nicely into the beginning of a process which becomes the blueprint for the cohort's written development. In applying the notion of 'why?' to a question or statement, what the cohort is actually doing is developing a set of initial research questions which has the effect of, often unbeknown to the student, actually starting the writing process.

In my experience, some students have difficulty with knowing how to locate research and, more importantly, the right research. To assist with this, the cohort is exposed to navigating databases which, when combined with the practice developed through deconstruction, allows for the process to actually begin.

To demonstrate this process to the cohort, I describe 'two pyramids' which illustrate the process in a simplistic manner. The first pyramid (the research pyramid) demonstrates the composition of research pieces, with textbooks being represented by the bottom layer of the pyramid, and research articles and focused books being represented by the upper levels of the pyramid; this has the effect of diagrammatically explaining to the cohort that they should be aiming to build a foundation to their research, but ultimately should be aiming to ascend the pyramid and utilise focused works for their own analyses.

The second pyramid (the process pyramid) represents their writing process, and at the bottom layer there is the initial deconstruction phase. Once that phase is completed, the student moves up the pyramid to answer these simplistic research questions with the use of textbooks (the two pyramids correspond to each other).

After this level, the student is instructed to create a new set of research questions, as they are now more informed than at the bottom layer of the pyramid. To answer this new set of research questions, the student must now seek to move up the 'research pyramid', with the result being that the student is now much more informed and ready to ascend to the next level of the (process) pyramid, which is to plan the work.

During the teaching, the vital importance of effective planning is meticulously impressed upon the students, and perhaps the most important part of those teachings is that the plan and the writing of the piece represent only a fraction of the entire process. Once that plan is produced and the research collated efficiently, the student then reaches the peak of the (process) pyramid and is ready to write the work.

Teaching Tip
It is important that this process is not transmitted in a manner which suggests that it is only applicable to writing HE-level assessments; it is not. Rather, if transmitted correctly, the process becomes a blueprint for everyday life, as well as professional life, with the sentiment of rigorous and efficient preparation followed by informed execution being translatable to almost every instance.

If the pyramid approach is communicated effectively I have found that the level of engagement or 'buy-in' increases significantly as the cohort realises they are being trained for far more than they can see. This mechanistic process can become a foundation for increased efficiency, which has the potential to start a process where positive results lead to further engagement with the process. Developing this ideal in a cohort at this vital stage in their lifelong development can – and has had – extraordinary results.

PRINCIPLE V: IDENTITY

It was touched upon earlier in the chapter, but the concept of work being produced to be read is of vital importance to the cohort's development. It is often only after the completion of a certain suite of training that an individual internalises the skillset or position they were training for – for example, a student studying History often only realises they are becoming a Historian once they complete their training.

However, a question to be raised is what may be the effect if that student were to realise that eventuality while they were completing their training? Perhaps that question cannot be answered, philosophically speaking, but there is a translatable sentiment that can be used in training a student to write more effectively. The final principle offered here is *identity*, and what that describes is the process of empowering students to believe they are writers, not just students.

To achieve this, I have used the work of Erving Goffman, an extraordinarily influential sociologist/philosopher who developed key works surrounding the concept of 'performance'. This philosophical concept of 'performance' is impressed upon the cohort to reimagine their role as 'students', so that now preparing to write an essay becomes preparing for a performance. Simultaneously, the act of writing now becomes a 'performance' with an audience which must be considered.

Teaching Tip
Encourage students to think of someone reading their work. Think of the
reader coming to the work eager to read and to learn. Has the student's
writing met the needs of the reader?

This development of an identity has a number of associated benefits.
Perhaps the most important one is that it quickly allows the students to
settle into their new environment, providing the cohort with a purpose for
their actions. Also, the actual act of writing becomes a more considered
journey, with advice such as 'read your work out aloud to yourself'
contributing to this shifting mentality that the 'performance' must be
witnessed.

On this basis, it becomes much easier for the teacher to put in place
fundamental developmental elements that are required, like a recalibration
of the use of grammar for example; grammatical fluency is acquired at
a young age and then, unless one forces themselves to, is rarely engaged
with again – it is crucial that this is done in the early stages of HE, and
the development of the 'performance' sentiment easily allows for this (a
crude analogy that is often used is the similarity between doing this type of
basic work for a greater purpose, and a professional boxer running every
morning).

CONCLUSION

These principles do not operate alone, and form part of a consistent and
cumulative approach which has a predetermined goal in mind. It was
discussed from the outset that the HE sector is being forced to adapt, and
how it adapts will have a demonstrable effect upon those who come into
contact with it.

In incorporating into the very fibres of the approach within HE the
understanding that the increased marketisation of the sector has brought
so many different people to HE institutions, there exists the possibility
to create lasting skillsets which will be of benefit to many, not just the
student. This is, of course, not to say that this does not already take place
within HE institutions, and similarly the principles offered here do not
represent the only approach HE practitioners should take; in fact, it is
quite the opposite, with the flexibility and diversity of approach being one
of the most important aspects to the sector.

However, whilst the principles have been defined in this chapter as
relating to the art of writing they offer so much more than that. They
have been designed to offer the particulars of a mentality, which sees the

students' development put at the very centre of what an HE teacher does. There are many pressures upon HE teachers in the modern era, but the honour of being able to assist in so many people's development needs to be, and should forever be regarded as, the most important. To that end, the principles contained within this chapter offer just one approach that will allow for that honour to be met.

SUGGESTED FURTHER READING

Goffman, E. (1990). *The Presentation of Self in Everyday Life*, London: Penguin Books.
Kotzee, B. and R. Johnston (2011). '"Can't string a sentence together?" UK employers' views of graduates' writing skills', *Industry and Higher Education*, 25 (1), 45–52.

PART III

Enhancing Teaching Practice

9. Getting the most out of large group teaching

Caroline Elliott and Jon Guest

INTRODUCTION

Many have predicted the end of the lecture, but it remains one of the most common ways of teaching students at university. What are some of the advantages of large group teaching?

- It gets all the students together and helps to build a sense of community.
- Being part of a large crowd can generate a sense of excitement and feeling of a shared or memorable experience.
- It provides timetabled opportunities to see the module leader/ lecturer who may be an academic 'star'.
- Having one person discuss a concept ensures a level of consistency.
- Students may feel more confident about attending large classes as opposed to feeling more anxious about the potential for personal attention in small group teaching.
- It is a cost-effective way of delivering a module.

CHALLENGES TO LARGE GROUP TEACHING

Many academics believe the main purpose of lectures or large group teaching is to disseminate large amounts of information. One of the most popular responses of those reluctant to change is the belief that traditional lectures are the only way of covering large amounts of material. However, there are a number of issues with this approach.

- Limits on concentration and processing capacities. The human brain cannot absorb large amounts of information in 50-minute or 2-hour intensive sessions. Students' attention tends to fall significantly after 20 minutes, unless they are particularly interested in the subject material. One potential reason for falling attendance at traditional lectures is that students start finding them an ineffective way to learn.

- Reliance on passive learning. If the objective of the lecture is to transmit large amounts of information then students have to sit quietly, listen and take a few notes. However, it is widely accepted that people learn more and gain a deeper understanding when they have to do something meaningful with the material rather than simply listening to somebody else trying to explain it very quickly.
- Sending the wrong signals. Trying to cover large amounts of information in class may signal to the students that surface learning and memorising material will enable them to perform well in the assessments. It may also indicate that everything they need to know is covered in class and so deters independent study.
- It is impossible to cover the whole syllabus even in a fast-paced 'slide and talk' lecture.

An alternative approach is to discuss less material in class and include more student activities. These activities should enable the students to engage with and apply the material so they develop a deeper understanding. The greatest challenge with this approach is to develop a shared understanding of (a) what is not discussed in class and (b) how this material should be studied. Students must clearly see the role played by large group teaching and how it fits in with the other learning activities in the module, including independent learning. Effective signposting of self-directed study is very important; if students believe that everything they need to know is in the lectures, they will perform very poorly.

In this chapter, we discuss how to start the first lecture of a module before outlining strategies to settle students down at the start of any lecture. We go on to discuss a number of activities that can be incorporated into large group teaching sessions. We then look at teaching technologies that are widely used in large group settings, namely the use of visual aids and lecture capture. Finally, we discuss how to end a session.

THE FIRST LECTURE

The first lecture of any module can be daunting, but remember that the students may also be nervous, especially if they are first year undergraduates and new to higher education. Act confidently even if you do not feel it and remember to project your voice. Even if you hate the sound of your voice when amplified, consider using a microphone to ensure that everyone can hear you and be aware that there may be students with hearing difficulties that rely on you using a microphone even if they do not tell you explicitly.

Teaching Tip
On entering the lecture theatre for the first time check with the students that they are in the room waiting for your class rather than, for example, Biology 238.

STARTING LECTURES AND THE PROBLEM OF LATE ARRIVALS

Lecturers have to address a number of issues at the beginning of each large group teaching session. These include:

- How to start a class in a way that takes into account students arriving at different times and some turning up late.
- How to stop students talking so the class can begin.
- How to start the class in a way that will capture and stimulate interest.

Students drift into lectures over a 5–10 minute period. They are typically chatting with their friends and the conversation usually continues when they find a seat. The initial noise in the lecture theatre can be loud and often rather intimidating for relatively inexperienced lecturers. There are usually late arrivals.

One immediate problem is how to stop the students talking and signal that the class is about to begin. For many years, I made an announcement along the following lines:

'Okay everyone, quieten down it's time to start.'

Unfortunately, it often had very little impact on the noise level in the room so I typically ended up repeating the same thing on a number of occasions with each repetition getting ever louder. I found the whole process rather unsatisfactory as it took a number of minutes to quieten the class down so the lecture could begin. Once the noise level had subsided, the first slide usually included a number of intended learning outcomes for the session.

On reflection, many of the intended learning outcomes were written in rather formal/educational language and unlikely to stimulate much interest amongst the student body in the presentation to follow.

The following are a number of different approaches I have tried and found to be far more effective.

- Displaying a photo or data chart that has some relevance to the topic for the class. The photo/chart also has an accompanying question such as 'What do you think the chart is illustrating' or 'What relevance does it have for this module'.
- Playing a short video clip for a couple of minutes that relates to the class i.e. a short extract from a news report. The Box of Broadcasts is a very useful source for video clips (https://www.jisc.ac.uk/box-of-broadcasts).

The displayed images capture the students' attention as they walk in the room and they start talking about issues that are relevant to the lecture. Also reading out the question on the slide when the majority of students have settled down is an effective way of signalling that the class is about to begin. After some in-class discussion based on the student responses, the lecture moves on to introduce the aims for the session, linking these to the initial discussion.

Displaying photos, charts and video clips is a way of trying to stimulate students' initial interest in the subject. However, many students are more strategic learners. They will only attend and engage if they see the direct relevance of the material for the assessment. Therefore, an alternative approach is to begin the lecture by displaying a question from the previous year's examination or coursework. It is important to communicate clearly to the students that this is an actual question used in a previous assessment.

Some staff might object that this is 'teaching to the test' but I think we have to be pragmatic about what motivates many of our students.

Another alternative is to begin the lecture with a question and use interactive polling software to collect and display their responses. The use of interactive polling is discussed later in the chapter. The question could relate to (a) the content of the previous lecture; (b) the work you expect them to complete before attending class; or (c) their opinion on a particular topic or issue. It is interesting to re-poll opinion questions at the end of the session to see if the lecture has an impact on students' views.

Whatever type of question is used, an initial question helps the class to settle down and engage with the lecture. It is also important at the beginning of the class to illustrate where the lecture fits into the module as a whole.

Teaching Tip
Try to vary the way you begin each class to keep it interesting and appeal to different types of learner.

WHAT HAPPENS DURING THE LECTURE?

As previously discussed, it is important to be realistic about how much material students can effectively absorb and process in a lecture. When planning a class, there is a danger that academics will focus more on what they are going to do rather than on what they expect the students to do. The reverse should be true. The key to a good lecture is to get the class actively involved in meaningful learning activities and to encourage two-way communication. What methods can we use to do this? How can we make large classes more dialogic as opposed to monologic?

Ask students questions in ways that both encourage and enable them to answer. Asking students questions plays two important roles. It gets them to engage with the lecture material and in the process improves their understanding of the material. It also provides the academic with feedback on how well the audience is following the presentation. In the early weeks of a class, it is important to build up students' confidence. Hence, initially ask questions that anyone can answer, such as examples of a simple concept or theory. For example, when introducing the concept of product differentiation, I will ask students what flavour of crisps, type of cereal they prefer etc. If the cohort is internationally diverse, ask for examples from their home countries. Similarly, if students have undertaken short periods of work or longer business placements ask for examples from their industry experience. I also ask for examples of news stories relevant to the topic under discussion. This encourages students to keep up to date with current business affairs, for example by reading *The Economist*, *The Financial Times*, *The New York Times* etc.

Time restrictions often mean we can only solicit a couple of answers at most to any particular question. It might also be difficult to hear students' responses. Finally, there is also a danger that when questions are asked aloud in a large lecture theatre that the couple of answers will always come from the same small group of very confident students. Ideally, we want to encourage everyone in the room to attempt the questions to maximise their learning whilst also providing a more representative feedback on how well the class understands the material. This is an area where interactive polling technology (sometimes referred to as student or personal response systems) can really help.

Interactive polling technology is a quick and effective way of asking many students a question to which they can all reply by using an Internet-connected device such as a smartphone, tablet or laptop. Many of the most popular polling tools such as Socrative, Poll Everywhere and Mentimeter have free versions that have less functionality than the paid versions but can still be useful in large group teaching. It is possible to ask different styles of questions such as short answer, numerical and multiple choice. Some of the polling tools enable the questions to be integrated into existing PowerPoint presentations. The tutor can also decide whether to display the student responses anonymously or not.

Teaching Tip
Avoid presenting the responses on the big screen for a couple of minutes. Check the answers on the computer screen at the front of the lecture theatre and delete any offensive or inappropriate comments before transferring the display to the main screen.

There are further ideas about how to use interactive polling technology for multiple choice questions in a separate chapter of this book.

ENCOURAGE STUDENTS TO ASK QUESTIONS

Try to create an environment in the lecture that encourages students to ask questions. Even if a question seems silly, try to hide your true feelings. If you are dismissive and make it clear to everyone in the room that you think it is stupid, it will deter others from asking in the future. In reality, only the most confident are likely to speak in front of hundreds of their peers. If a student does ask a question, it is highly likely that other people in the room will not hear it clearly. Therefore, it is also important to repeat it aloud so that everyone can make sense of your answer.

Teaching Tip
Using one of the polling software packages, set up an anonymised free text answer option at the start of the lecture and leave it running for the whole session. This may sound complicated but can be easily done with many of the software packages. Invite the students to text any questions they have during the class and stop the lecture every so often to respond to those that they have sent. Inviting questions in an electronic and anonymous manner increases the chances of getting more responses from a more representative sample of people in the room.

ENCOURAGE NOTE MAKING RATHER THAN NOTE TAKING

Note taking is a passive activity where students simply write down what the lecturer says. Note making, on the other hand, is a far more productive activity. This is where people try to make sense of the material, i.e. by questioning, evaluating and applying. It is an active process and requires more cognitive effort. Students will simply not have time for note making in fast-paced lectures. Note taking may also be limited and the comments impossible to understand shortly after the class has finished. To encourage note making, periodically stop talking and give the class a couple of minutes to summarise what you have been presenting. Ask them to compare summaries with their neighbours and add any useful points.

PLAYING GAMES

It is possible to play some games/experiments even in very large lectures. This usually involves some volunteers taking part whilst the others in the room observe and record their actions and decisions. The learning benefits are maximised when the students who are simply observing the game actually have to do something with the results they are recording. The use of short classroom games is discussed in more detail in Chapter 23.

GIVING BREAKS

Given the limits on the ability of most people to concentrate for a whole lecture, they may learn more if you give them a five-minute break. Some students may use this time to give their brains a complete rest and check social media on their mobile phones. Others will take this opportunity to ask either their neighbours or the lecturer questions about the material they are struggling to understand. You could formalise this process by displaying a slide along the following lines: 'Reflect on what you have learned and read through your notes. Compare your notes with your neighbours and ask them any questions about the material you think you do not fully understand.'

Some students may feel uncomfortable about walking to the front of the lecture theatre so ask them to raise their hand if they have a question so you can walk over to where they are sitting.

Teaching Tip
Make an informal contract with the students. Tell them at the beginning of the class that if they focus on the material and do not become distracted by social media that you will give them a break after 20/25 minutes.

Use an online countdown timer when including an activity in class. The sight of a large clock counting down on the screen helps to keep students focused on the task. This will also help reduce noise levels during the activity. Keep referring to the clock during the activity.

LINKS TO ASSESSMENT

If you advertise a class as a revision lecture, attendance increases dramatically. Why is this? As we discussed earlier, many students are strategic learners who only attend and engage if they see the direct relevance of the material to the assessment. Making the relevance of all lectures for assessments as clear as possible will increase attendance and engagement.

USING SLIDES/VISUAL AIDS

See Chapter 12 in this book for more advice on creating effective lecture presentations. Here, we restrict ourselves to a few practical tips to avoid 'Death by PowerPoint'. First, do not feel pressured to include all the material on slides. It is fine to have gaps that you fill in with the students. These gaps may be examples, numerical workings or the development of diagrams. It can be really beneficial for students to build up the technical material gradually alongside the lecturer. The best way to do this is using a visualiser. If the lecture is recorded using lecture capture (see below) then the material on the visualiser will also be recorded, but crucially students are likely to be able to see material projected on a visualiser much better than if a lecturer tries to write on a black/white board.

Second, avoid having too much text on any slide and keep slides simple. Slides can provide prompts to you as a lecturer but should not be relied upon by the lecturer or student as a record of everything said. Avoid multiple types of animation as this just looks tacky. Also, guard against creating too many slides. We have all sat through presentations where the presenter rushes at the end and flicks through multiples slides that the audience has no chance to read.

Nevertheless, there are advantages of using slides. Sometimes a picture can be much more memorable than a sentence of text (but do not use pictures for the sake of it). Similarly, slides offer great opportunities for embedding hyperlinks to short films and examples – again ways of ensuring that students remain engaged.

Teaching Tip
To demonstrate that there is more to the lecture than just the content on the slides, it is useful to turn the presentation off at various points during the

session. This is easy to do by simply pressing either the letter 'B' or 'W' on the keyboard during a PowerPoint presentation. This blanks the screen – pressing 'B' sends the screen black while pressing 'W' sends it white. Pressing the same letter once again returns the screen to the PowerPoint presentation. Turning off the presentation is an effective way of signalling to the students that you really want them to concentrate on what you are going to say for the next few minutes.

THE USE OF RECORDED LECTURES

Increasingly, universities are installing lecture capture facilities whereby lectures are recorded so that students can watch the recordings after the class. Research indicates that there are a number of potential advantages of offering these recordings (Elliott and Neal, 2016). Students can use the recordings to go over material that they found difficult in the class, if they became distracted in class, and may use the recordings to build more extensive sets of notes than they were able to take in the class. The recordings can help with revision, and may be of particular value to international students and students with special learning needs. However, critics argue that class attendance is negatively affected and that students become less concerned about keeping up with material throughout a module, with the erroneous view that catching up will be easier with lecture recordings available. Nevertheless, currently an increasing number of universities are requesting that lecturers use lecture capture technology. Hence, below we offer a few tips to ensure that lectures are recorded as effectively as possible.

Familiarise yourself with the technology in advance. It seems obvious but learn to what extent you have to start and stop the lecture recording, whether there is the facility to pause a recording, whether you need to be concerned about where microphones are positioned etc. Also, get into the habit of repeating student class input as microphones may be positioned to pick up the lecturer's voice but not those of students. Do not point at a whiteboard as it is likely that it will not be clear on a recording where you are pointing. Similarly, use a visualiser rather than writing on a black/white board if you want handwritten text to be legible on the recording. Crucially, if students can watch recordings after class then think of giving them reasons to come to class. Hence, the use of questions, class discussion, games and experiments are all ways of encouraging students to attend classes that will be recorded as the experience of them is never as great 'second hand' when students cannot participate but only watch the previous participation of others. This way lecture recordings will be a complement to lecture attendance rather than a substitute.

Finally, there is an additional potential benefit of recorded lectures as we can view recordings of ourselves as lecturers. We are likely to be our own toughest critics, and however excruciating the experience may be, we are likely to learn what we do right and wrong from watching recordings of ourselves lecturing. Hence, we may discover that in fact we rattle change in our pockets, constantly frown at our students, speak too fast or too slow etc.

THE FLIPPED CLASSROOM APPROACH

Increasingly university lecturers are adopting a flipped classroom approach whereby material that traditionally would have been introduced in the lecture theatre is made available to students in short films in advance of classes. Class time can then be devoted to exploring concepts and theories in more detail, discussing extended examples, or considering more advanced applications of the material covered in the films.

THE END OF THE CLASS

It is always important at the end of the session to find time to summarise the key points and signpost what the student should do after the class. However, it is difficult to plan lecture time accurately. It often takes longer to explain and discuss material than we anticipate. If you find yourself running out of time, it is not a good idea to rush through the last five to ten slides in the last couple of minutes. Covering all the slides you originally planned might make you feel better but the students are unlikely to learn very much. If you start rushing, they will simply lose interest and start packing up their bags. Try to judge the most appropriate point to stop introducing any new material while leaving enough time to summarise the key points effectively.

Teaching Tip
If you are running out of time and want to skip over a number of slides to get to the last one in your presentation, simply type '99' on the keyboard and then press enter. Typing any number equal to or greater than the total number of slides in the presentation will have the same effect.

CONCLUSIONS

Ultimately, enjoy the opportunity that lecturing affords to engage with a large group of students, to inspire them, to interact with them, to hear their experiences and examples and possibly to make them laugh. If you enjoy it then there is a much greater chance that they will too.

SUGGESTED FURTHER READING

Elliott, C. and D. Neal (2016). 'Evaluating the use of lecture capture using a revealed preference approach', *Active Learning in Higher Education*, 17 (2), 1–15. Reprinted in *Teaching College Economics*, ed. P.W. Grime, part of the International Library of Critical Writings in Economics (2018), Cheltenham, UK and Northampton, MA: Edward Elgar Publishing.

10. Storytelling as a technique for teaching

Sudeshna Bhattacharya

The day starts early for Kabir, less traffic means he can get to the depot quicker. They don't pay for your time until you collect the packages from the depot. It is a bit more than minimum hourly wage, so in many ways that is better than the cleaning job closer to home. He has two children at home, 4 and 6 years old and his wife stays at home to care for them and his elderly mum. The rent is high, but the flat is good, light and airy. Not that he gets to spend much time there, however it calms his nerves to know they are safe. It is hard on one income, but they get by.

Yesterday it snowed a little, the roads are icy, and he was prudent and recently changed the tyres on the van anticipating the turn in the weather. If only he had foreseen the icy drive leading to that house on the incline, he broke his leg delivering the package . . . No driving, no wages, the savings are thin, the rent in arrears . . .

What happens now . . .

INTRODUCTION

I used this story for a lecture on insecure employment contracts and in particular the gig economy. An economy that our students participate in, whether it is as consumers being driven through the city streets or as employees riding with delicious merchandise strapped on their backs. To them the gig economy has brought opportunities; however, the agency it provides to them is not everyone's story.

In management education, very often the abstraction of social and economic theory can mask the real tensions that exist. A skilfully told story can bring to light the assumptions buried in apparently unproblematic linear reasoning. Storytelling allows us to present a vantage point of multiple perspectives, which lends itself to critical thinking. This is particularly true when studying subjects such as insecure employment contracts, environmental sustainability in business, all of which present complicated systemic links to wider society.

Storytelling is not new, it has a long history in human existence. Stories are narratives with plots, people and characters that can be full of meaning. Good stories have the ability to capture and engage, very often eliciting emotional reactions in the reader. While some stories may be pure fiction, others, like those told by Steve Jobs at his commencement, are inspired by actual events. It was thought that technology and evidence-based science would see the demise of storytelling within academia or even business for that matter. Yet the evidence is clear from a quick search on Amazon where the term 'storytelling' results in 26000 books, a substantial proportion relating to business as a sector in general.

The aim of this chapter is to examine and explore the role of stories within the context of teaching and learning in Higher Education (HE) in the UK. I start with the work of Professor Yiannis Gabriel who has written extensively about and taught using storytelling within HE. Then I draw from my own practice to illustrate the various functions a story can play both within and beyond the classroom.

But before I can start to discuss the particular tools and techniques, I take you back to my own guru who encouraged my interest in storytelling in the classroom. As a young PhD student I sat in one of Professor Gabriel's classrooms and he conducted an entire lecture on consumption in society through a series of eighteenth- and nineteenth-century paintings. Time was fluid in that space of two hours that seems to slip away, and I came out with a multifaceted view of consumerism that still sticks in my memory and decisions. Arches of consumption he called it. This is how I view engagement within the classroom, lectures that are more like experiences that impact us and stay with us.

I start with one of his stories that beautifully illustrates, through a story, the value of storytelling as a technique for teaching and learning (see Box 10.1).

Here we see how stories are an important way in which we connect to each other. These stories carry messages of knowledge and the narrative is one of the oldest forms of transmission between humans. So the fact that we use it within the context of the modern lecture theatre is no surprise. It is rather warming to be part of this continuity of human history of communication.

Teaching Tip
Always use stories that you know very well. There needs to be a good flow to the storytelling, rather than a hesitant retelling.

BOX 10.1   EXAMPLE STORY 1

A few years ago, I was stuck in Denver's international airport due to a storm brewing in the American Midwest. At one of the airport restaurants, I was overhearing the conversation of four pilots, like me stranded due to bad weather and waiting for their flights to resume. And guess what they were talking about? They were each describing the most dangerous escapes that they had had while flying their planes in bad weather. In these stories, the planes, 747s, 727s and 757s, were not just flying machines but characters with distinct personalities, likes and dislikes that required special and careful handling. Listening to such scary stories was the last thing I needed just prior to taking off, but it taught me many things. Clearly, each pilot was competing with his peers in recounting a more dangerous situation and a more brilliant escape. At the same time, however, they were all sharing knowledge, knowledge about particular weather conditions, knowledge about different planes, and knowledge about different risks. The pilots were what we refer to as a community of practice, learning from each other's experience through the medium of storytelling.

STORIES WE BRING TO THE LEARNING SPACE

Now I move our focus to the classroom, in particular to the introductory story of *Kabir*. It brings to life the subject of insecure employment contracts and opens the floor to more students as they can relate to the issue through the concrete example of the story. Therefore for some the story elicited anger, as they felt empathy for the protagonist. However, another group took the more rational economic view about labour costs and profits and the role of short-term contracts in creating competitive advantage. This expanded the discussion further as other students reflected on the cost to society and whether that diminishes the return from the competitive advantage. Still others raised ethical questions on part of the organisation.

   Time took on a fluid quality, like that time in Professor Gabriel's classroom, and we were left with 10 minutes at the end to collate our ideas and finish the class. That 2-hour lecture slot had involved only ten slides, but at the end the students left feeling more awake and maybe a bit melancholic at 11am . . .

Teaching Tip
A short emotionally charged story used within the classroom setting can be very useful to get the students interested. Later, a longer article, written in the same story style, can help to populate the details of the issue. This I find motivates the early interest that later translates to references to academic studies.

STORIES INSPIRE STORIES: STUDENTS' REFLECTIONS

Students have their own narratives and they can find voice through the stories that you bring to them. One such story was about careers within the media and broadcast industry in the UK. The source of this story is a small subsection of the journal *Work, Employment and Society*, where they have this special allocated section for stories from the workplace (see Box 10.2).

This story was discussed in class, however unlike the first short story, this was a paper that they were asked to read before they came into class. This particular career story was told by a woman in the broadcasting industry and resonated with a lot of students across both genders. Significantly, it seemed that female students who had previously not spoken in class found their voice through this story. It was an uncomfortable story and some of them came out with their own stories of gender differences faced at work and their own fears regarding their careers. Given this was a lecture on critical issues in HR, the content of the discussion directly lent itself to HR policies around recruitment, diversity and talent management. However, it is important to have a strategy for handling these discussions motivated by stories. Given the emotionally charged environments stories can create, a pre-planned learning outcome is useful to manage the learning. For this, I specifically use board plans, and the next section provides a description of this method/technique.

BOX 10.2   EXAMPLE STORY 2

Although I didn't realize it at the time, the mentoring was especially important as I was not hugely confident and, although I clearly had great drive and potential, I was pretty clueless about how to get ahead. Because I was freelance, I knew I always had to set up the next job. Looking back, I think I was pretty naive – I thought that because I was bright, hard-working and good at my job, the next job would come fairly easily. But that wasn't the case at all. Once, early on in my career, I wrote to every single independent production company in the region – I got just two replies: one saying they'd gone out of business and the other offering me the chance to sit in and watch an edit. What happened next was a classic case of making your own luck – a chance encounter and chat over a coffee break led to a permanent job in the newsroom at the other major regional broadcaster. But I should have made more use of my time to network: I didn't hustle for jobs with key producers in my field of science, environment and history – I was too embarrassed to do that as it seemed too presumptuous. I was hopelessly unstrategic. I knew what I wanted to do – to write and present my own specialist factual programmes – but never once planned how to actually get there and never thought to ask for advice, either.

From an organisational point of view: retaining talent, policies and their impact on different groups of people, employee engagement.

For the individual student: thinking about factors that will play a role in your careers. Thinking of careers as journeys with different priorities at different points, learning to craft careers.

Figure 10.1   Predetermined board plan for recording student discussion

TOOLS AND TECHNIQUES: BOARD PLANS

As an example, Figure 10.1 above is a board plan used for the 'woman in broadcasting: career story' illustrated in the previous section. A board plan is a rough plan drawn up in advance that links the story to the general themes of the issue, relevant for the lecture. As students feedback to the class their thoughts and interpretations, the ideas can be recorded on the white board roughly following this plan.

Having this predetermined plan for the white board helps to get maximum learning from the story. Further, students who contribute to the discussion feel empowered as their voice is heard and recorded. This further builds students' confidence and voice. Finally, it becomes a learning and teaching resource as students usually want to take pictures of the white board in addition to their own notes.

Teaching Tip
For most lectures where I have used a story that encourages a discussion, I take a picture of the white board and upload it to the virtual learning environment. Also, the lectures with stories are linked to assessment, so that students can draw upon them in their essays/exams/portfolios. This links to the issue of critical engagement which is discussed later in the chapter.

CASE STUDIES AND STORIES: ARE THEY DIFFERENT?

In many ways case studies and stories are very similar, and in practice are often used interchangeably within the classroom. The main distinguishing characteristic is the emotional involvement that it elicits in the person that is listening to it. Stories always have a narrator recounting their experience and expressing emotion. This serves to engage the student through encouraging empathy, which becomes a way for them to understand a different perspective.

Going back to the opening story of Kabir, working as a delivery driver. The particular characteristics of his family life and financial situation allows the student to see a different kind of worker in the gig economy. They start to appreciate that the lower (or rather the near absence) of entry requirements means that very often those that are most vulnerable in society will be drawn to this sector. The family condition provides the student a window to what vulnerability looks like, and they begin to appreciate what insecure contracts mean, namely the particular features of such contracts; for example, being paid only for the hours they work (excluding travel to work) or the absence of sick pay. They begin to have a more vivid view of what it means for a vulnerable young family.

No amount of theory would have made as much impact as this little story did; it helps the student truly understand the dynamics of the theory. This provides them with a much-needed tool to engage in critical analysis, which very often is difficult for students to understand in the abstract.

STORYTELLING AND CRITICAL ENGAGEMENT

My throat is sore trying to explain in the last few weeks before the essay is due that you need to critically engage with the content. Please don't just describe to me what a gig economy looks like, I need to see that you understand the different facets of the same.

> Students: Does it mean we have to list the advantages and disadvantages of the gig economy?

> Me: (Silently in my head visualising myself tearing my hair out) No that would just mean more description.

Stories are my saviour. This is when I started to use more stories in the classroom. I refer to the story of Kabir. I explain, use the example and think about the different dimensions. On one hand the gig economy is brilliant, providing Kabir with an opportunity to earn money for the family to have a comfortable, safe life. He only arrived in the country a few years ago, escaping war and a failing economy back at home. Yet the nature of hourly paid work in insecure contracts can have risks that those who work within it can't mitigate. So who has responsibility here?

The story provides the string they can use in the essay, because the term critical engagement in the abstract doesn't necessarily make sense to all, especially within our classrooms in HE where we have more international students who haven't necessarily worked with such forms of assessment. They don't have an equal point from where they start. The stories can also act as equalisers to a certain extent as they are tools that those with no experience of essay writing can draw upon to construct their arguments.

WHY DO STORIES MATTER?

Stories are powerful because:

1. The narrative in the story help us make sense of our experiences, especially when these draw us outside routines and habits. Therefore through the story we can bring the wider context into the classroom.
2. Stories enable us to learn from the experiences of other people and to share our experiences with others. Within the classroom, they can be an excellent technique to encourage engagement.
3. Stories encourage an emotional response and influence hearts and minds, making it more likely the students will engage with the content.
4. Stories can be effective triggers of change.
5. They are vehicles through which we construct our individual and group identities; and sustain our bonds to our communities through shared stories.

CONCLUSION

In conclusion, stories can be a useful method of engaging the student body both within the classroom (through lectures) and outside the classroom (through assessment or reflection logs). Stories are quite flexible and can be used across a range of disciplines, which is part of their appeal for teaching and learning. Finally, the main points that I consider when choosing and using stories are:

1. The story is uncomfortable, it instigates emotion and thought.
2. Having a clear plan before the lecture for organising thoughts from the discussion.
3. Links to the assessment are useful.
4. Have a mixture of short stories and longer stories within the curriculum of the module.

5. Stories can provide an excellent tool to explain process and nuances of critical engagement.

SUGGESTED FURTHER READING

Eikhof, D.R. and C. York (2015). '"It's a tough drug to kick": a woman's career in broadcasting', *Work, Employment and Society*, https://doi.org/10.1177/09500 17015601859.
Professor Yannis Gabriel has spent a majority of his academic career using storytelling as a practice in both research and teaching. His blog (http://www. yiannisgabriel.com) is a useful resource for developing storytelling-related techniques for the classroom.
The journal *Work, Employment and Society* has a separate story section where true accounts are presented in short 3000-word articles. It is a very useful resource for stories as the front of the paper makes useful links to the literature and the story is then written from the perspective of the protagonist, usually in first person. The special section is called 'On the Front Line'.

Thought 5

Geetha Ravishankar

The following is an example I use to help motivate my class on (quantitative) research methods and introductory maths. It is also one that fits well with other theory-based principles modules in first year economics. The example is based on the Independent Commission on Banking's (2011) final recommendations to improve the stability and strength of the UK banking system in the wake of the financial crisis. I specifically reference the following aim of the report: 'means a banking system that is effective and *efficient at providing the basic banking services*' (italics added for emphasis). In lectures, I start by giving students a couple of minutes to think about how such efficiency can be identified. What do we mean by efficiency in the context of banks? How can we measure such efficiency? What sort of information would we need?

Students typically identify cost control as an important element of efficiency offering a natural segue to discussing cost and production functions. This can be linked directly to theory covered in other modules (namely microeconomics), thereby helping to highlight the interconnectedness of the various modules they take. With advanced classes, we move on to cost functions directly, but for introductory classes we begin with the idea that costs are allied to production. So I ask students to think about how we characterise production for a bank. For example, what are the inputs and outputs? Most readily identify loans as outputs and labour as an input. With a few prompts, we identify assets and deposits as further inputs. They have thus intuitively identified a rudimentary production function, albeit verbally. I then demonstrate how this verbal information can be summarised using the f(. . .) mathematical notation, as follows:

$$Loans = f\,(deposits,\ total\ assets,\ labour)$$

Again, depending on the level of the programme, we can then move on to formalising the function, for example using a Cobb–Douglas production function. I would follow this by showing students the data that is needed to operationalise the estimation of the function. The question then is one of determining the precise relationship between each input and output (for example, the magnitude of change in loans from a given change in deposits assuming the other inputs don't change), which modules taken further on in the programme will cover. I stress that understanding why and how functions work is the first step to being able to use them in answering such questions later. I then preview the results of empirical research into the banking efficiency of the UK, thus showing the policy relevance of the same.

Throughout this empirical demonstration I explicitly state that the aim is to understand the intuition and make the link with real data and issues. The challenge in this is in simplifying the presentation so that students are not overwhelmed with the data and maths involved. When this is achieved, the informal feedback I receive is that it helps makes the maths seem less abstract.

REFERENCE

Independent Commission on Banking (2011), http://webarchive.nationalarchi
ves.gov.uk/20120827143059/http://bankingcommission.independent.gov.
uk/ (accessed 30 August 2018).

11. Experiential learning: use of business simulations

Clive Kerridge

不闻不若闻之，闻之不若见之，见之不若知之，知之不若行之
Tell me, and I will forget. Show me, and I may remember. Involve me, and I will understand.

Attributed to Xun Kuang (Chinese Confucian philosopher, 312–230 BC) in Book 8, ch11 of the *Xunzi*, by Liu Xiang ca. 818 AD

INTRODUCTION

Most of us aim for some variety in our teaching techniques, not least by involving our students in active learning processes, complementing the familiar didactic pedagogies. Examples are problem-based learning (PBL) and the recently in-vogue flipped approach, both of which contrast with traditional subject-based learning (SBL) approaches.

In this chapter, we will focus on experiential learning and, specifically, on the use of business simulations. Feedback from our students, consistent with published research, confirms that such simulations are liked by many students – engagement levels are often high. They are applicable for different levels and varied class sizes; work well with mixed cohorts (subject disciplines and/or cultural and language mixes); and can be conveniently embedded into assessment regimes. Through them, students gain valuable insights into the multidisciplinary nature of business decision-making and entrepreneurship. Good business simulations can be fun and memorable too – for instructors as well as students.

After introducing 'serious games', we will look at key features of experiential learning pedagogies, before considering why and how simulations are used to enhance learning and to develop management skills. Maintaining a focus on the intended beneficiaries, from time to time we will insert relevant quotations from our students. Towards the end of the chapter, we will consider choosing appropriate simulations and offer some guidance on what not to do!

WHAT ARE 'SERIOUS GAMES' AND 'SIMULATIONS'?

Simulations feature in numerous professions and situations, notably health care (medical students' cadavers!), aviation training (flight simulators) and meteorology (weather forecasting). They provide the opportunity to develop learning through a simulated 'real-world' situation in which actions can be taken in a low-risk environment. With the advent of computing and digital capabilities – notably video gaming – simulations have become more sophisticated and have been applied in various learning and training applications across management education.

As a student told us:

> 'As the simulation progresses, it feels more realistic and because you engage in the process, you actually learn more.'

Similarly, the adoption of more active learning pedagogies in HE has encouraged use of digital games and simulations that positively impact learning goals. In business schools, 'serious games' and 'gamification' are increasingly being incorporated into programme curricula. In this chapter we focus on business simulations, sometimes called 'simulation games'.

Before we go further, a small health warning. The prevalent digital technologies, particularly video, provide us with great opportunities to deliver content in eye (or ear) catching ways. This is mostly but not wholly good news: there is an attendant risk of us becoming providers of 'edutainment', focused on student engagement but divorced from the learning objectives.

WHY EXPERIENTIAL LEARNING?

The education literature confirms that *learning by doing* positively affects knowledge retention (for example, Sousa 2017) and also soft skills development. As that example opening quotation implies, the perceived advantages of experiential learning, whether facilitated or through self-discovery, are well recognised through history; for example, the apprenticeship concept. The best-known recent exponent of experiential learning as a pedagogy is David Kolb, originator of the Experiential Learning Cycle (1984), in which the role of reflection is an essential element that takes the learning beyond mere experience (see Figure 11.1).

Although an in-depth analysis of the nature of learning is beyond the scope of this chapter, based on Bloom's Taxonomy of learning and considerable subsequent research, such as Loon et al. (2015), in the context of

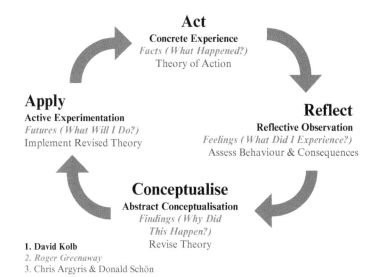

Source: Compiled by Andrea Corney; www.edbatista.com/2007/10/experiential.html.

Figure 11.1   Experiential learning cycles

business simulations we can consider the three types of learning: affective, cognitive and behavioural.

1. Affective learning, i.e. feelings. This is manifested in student engagement with the subject matter and tasks, when conducting simulations – all the more so when these are collaborative and involve role plays.
2. Cognitive learning, i.e. knowledge. Measuring the development of cognitive learning is notoriously difficult. Many believe that deeper cognitive learning is facilitated by the intensity of study and higher levels of student engagement that are seen with experiential learning and training.
3. Behavioural (psychomotor) learning. Again, there is evidence – from both instructor and student viewpoints – that behavioural learning is also enhanced. This is particularly so when (a) teamwork forms a significant part of the simulation, and (b) a simulation runs over an extended period of hours, days or weeks, requiring and enabling students to develop and adapt teamwork skills such as cooperative task allocation, negotiation and compromising for collective decision making.

'I think companies like people that have experience, and this is as close to experience as you can get.' (Student feedback)

Perhaps unsurprisingly, there is increasing evidence that business simulations, particularly those involving collaboration and group working, help develop employability skills. This reinforces the feedback from students who have commented upon how they were able to use their simulation experience to advantage in job interviews, assessment centres and for working in project teams.

WHEN TO USE A SIMULATION?

One example might be in a module in which there is already a structured basis of relevant academic theory and tools; for example, through lectures and readings, before using and applying these in a simulation. For instance, a strategic management module may consider theory for positional analysis and for developing strategic options, then use a simulation in which students are encouraged to consider scenarios and make decisions on choices for implementation. Even better, after doing so there can then be an opportunity to reflect on the reasons for – and wisdom of – the choices that were made.

More generally, simulations can be used within scheduled classes or off-campus, even for those that involve group working. Many proprietary business simulations can be run wholly or partly online, though arguably the most effective for HE are those that include an offline component but require more than just iterating numeric choices. Hybrid simulations may involve choice and data input online but with the associated researching, discussion and decision-making taking place offline, for example in meetings. Similarly, there are opportunities for synchronous or asynchronous working – both within cohorts and in relation to the roles and contributions of the instructors/facilitators and their provision of guidance and feedback to students.

ANOTHER WARNING: NO TUTOR ABDICATION!

There are a wide variety of commercial and in-house business simulations. These can make a tremendously positive contribution to the success of a module or programme; however, this rarely works without significant tutor/facilitator input, even for the more sophisticated simulations that provide online feedback. Much of the added value will derive from *our* input, before, during and after our students engage in the simulation.

BENEFITS FOR WHOM?

'Instead of writing boring things on a piece of paper, this is more interactive and more "out there". You've got decisions to make, you've got ideas to put forward. We just feel that we are in a real business environment, so it's nice to do!' (Student feedback)

As the word 'simulation' implies, students get quasi-practical experience and can extend their perceptions about commercial and management processes, be they marketing, operations, accounting and finance, HRM, ethics and CSR, strategic management, etc.

Simulations are not just about developing subject-specific knowledge; students' feedback and reflections affirm their appreciation of the opportunity to develop soft skills, such as communication, negotiation, compromise and even conflict resolution, especially when working cooperatively with others, for example in 'management' teams that need to take decisions, based on what may be imperfect data. The significance of empathy and the need for adapting behaviour to accommodate personality or working styles are also often commented upon.

These learning benefits are not restricted to our students. Instructors' involvement can also be at a deeper level than for seminars and lectures, enabling better understanding of students' needs and idiosyncrasies but also reinforcing or extending our subject knowledge as we, like our students, consider scenarios and alternatives.

WHICH TYPE OF SIMULATION TO USE?

There is an enormous range of available simulations and many are doubtless being developed right now. Some are standardised, others bespoke to a programme or its students' needs. Some involve purchase of individual or institutional licences; some are 'paired' with a textbook or a case study; some are developed in-house as an embedded part of a module. A number of business simulation developers also design and adapt them for companies and professional organisations – and similar tailoring can be made for education customers too (see Table 11.1).

An element of competition is often a significant contributor to student engagement. However, many students are already well versed in playing online games, through consoles or via phones and tablets. Most are played individually, though varying degrees of collaboration and cooperation are also inherent in some of the more sophisticated multiplayer video games. A risk is that the business simulation gets considered as just another game,

Table 11.1   Categorisation of the main simulation choice criteria

Choice criterion	Options	Associated factors
Duration	Short; medium; long (multi-component)	May vary from just a single class session through to a sim conducted over several days or even weeks
Participation	Individual or group/collaborative	Self-teaching conducted individually, for example driving tests or flight simulators; team-working, enabling development of soft skills for example, for employability
Measurement	Qualitative and/ or quantitative; 'numbers driven'	Metrics may vary, depending upon complexity; multicomponent simulations may involve several for example, be composites of financials and non-financials
Competition	'Market place' or parallel competition; non-competitive	In 'marketplace' simulations, choices and decisions taken directly affect the other 'players', for example pricing of products or investment. Even if independent of other players, a leader board system is often used
Online/offline	Online; offline; or hybrid	Vary from an online video game style, to mainly offline; to hybrids, for example meetings but data input
Feedback	Interactive or via instructors/peers	Automated and/or available online; interim or formative feedback with peers/instructors

Source: Kerridge (2018).

for which the primary objective is solely to attain the best score or reach a higher level. This is notably so for numbers-based simulations that permit several attempts – students can be very adept at 'gaming' the game by doing multiple iterations!

Teaching Tip
Choosing as to whether a simulation is wholly online and numbers-driven, or whether it ought to involve more qualitative choices and offline work, should be dictated by the needs of the module and the learning outcomes that are involved.

For group working, a key element of the simulation may well be enabling students to develop team-working skills, including the ability to bring different views to the table but work through to effective, collective management decision-making. That will likely involve significant time and energy in offline working and meetings, albeit eventual decisions and related data may be input online.

ENSURING SIMULATIONS WORK WELL FOR YOUR STUDENTS

Some simulations are fairly self-explanatory or intuitive and work well with little or no instructor involvement. However, most business simulations benefit from – perhaps even need – significant input, for example; outlining key principles (of how the simulation works) and specifying intended learning outcomes; identifying useful tools or sources of help and guidance; assisting with in-game guidance (which may be about team working or useful sources of reference), maybe offering some challenge.

Simulations will rarely be of value if they are not linked with the associated learning disciplines and desired outcomes. Although much learning derives from the experience of doing the simulation activities, it is the associated reflection (as in the Kolb learning cycle) that reinforces the cognitive and affective learning in particular. Tutors and instructors can play a key role in encouraging and directing students to reflect on their experiences, both during and after playing simulation games.

There is a myriad of alternatives, varying from free one-hour online self-study games to rich multi-component simulations with well-developed context/story and multiple variables. Some university departments have developed business simulations for their own use, for colleagues or for commercialisation; for example, INSEAD's celebrated Markstrat. Several companies have developed suites of business simulations that focus on particular disciplines: strategic management, or marketing and branding, or operations and supply chains; finance and accounting; technology and IP exploitation; etc. Based on proprietary algorithms derived from many trial iterations (and doubtless considerable student/customer feedback), these rich simulations usually charge licence fees on an institutional or per-user basis.

Teaching Tip
Clearly, the programme/module discipline will be a factor in determining which sort of simulation to select. But you need to consider several other factors too:

- *Is it too dense/difficult (or too superficial) for your particular student cohort?*
- *Does it require and benefit from group working (and if so, what sizes for the groups)?*

- *Is it just numbers-driven (adjust prices or capacity investment; measure profit, expenses, balance sheet value, etc.)?*
- *Is there scope to evaluate more than just financial numbers/returns, for example; CSR, customer satisfaction, etc.?*
- *Does it synthesise management decision-making?*
- *Will there be an opportunity to debrief and for students to get feedback to reflect upon?*

ASSESSMENT AND FEEDBACK

Often the decision to choose a simulation will be based on if/how an assessment can be integrated. An example is by giving marks in relation to simulation performance, for example; achievement of valuation or an aggregate profit. For many simulations this can be automated. More often assessment will relate less to the quantitative performance and more to the standards of analysis, discussion and reflection on why and how choices and decisions have been made. This coaxes students to follow a true experiential learning cycle. What often works well is to have simulation performance contribute to some of a final mark or grade (thereby helping motivation) but having the lion's share of marks associated with the critical evaluation and reflection.

In some instances, simulations are run directly for programme credits: for example, LD's Business Management Experience simulation is run over five weeks, often for 10 credits, at several UK business schools. Well-designed simulations do not require instructors to spend their time inputting decisions and data, so are eminently scalable – even for very large student cohorts.

Teaching Tip
Feedback during a simulation can be very valuable and helps maintain student momentum and confidence. Interim results and a leader board enhance the competitive spirit [don't underestimate the extent to which this contributes to engagement!].

Feedback intrinsic to the simulation can make valuable contributions both to the stimulus and enjoyment from a simulation and to the attainment of learning outcomes. Experiential learning needs to incorporate a strong reflective element if it is to be effective (Kolb, 1984). Simulations, if well designed and well engaged with, provide ample opportunity for that valuable reflection.

BARRIERS TO GOOD SIMULATION USE

As with much in life, unrealistic expectations can be the source of disappointment and disengagement. So it is with simulations: some may be too complex (particularly if there are tight time constraints); too numbers-driven (tempting iteration rather than decision-making based on relevant principles); too susceptible to knowing/finding 'correct' answers; and some may excite at first but have trouble maintaining momentum.

Furthermore, research evidence (for example, Lean et al. 2006) identifies three resource-related barriers: insufficient time within a structured module or programme; availability of funds; and availability of relevant skills, notably in tutors/ instructors. None of these should be trivialised but each can be ameliorated or overcome.

The most prevalent barrier, however, tends to be instructor inertia. Most good business simulations require facilitation to get optimum student experience and benefit. Thus tutors/instructors need to invest time and energy to understand how the simulation works and how it contributes to achieving module learning objectives. The return on investment is usually high – and commensurately rewarding – but it does merit that pre-game planning and investment.

BENEFITS FOR COLLABORATION

> 'The simulation is good because in the future you must work well together, you cannot work by yourself, so good communication is very important to your teamwork.' (Student feedback)

Simulations played in teams offer various benefits to the participants, including all three types of learning specified in Bloom's Taxonomy (Biggs and Tang, 2011), notably the behavioural (psychomotor) and affective learning which are more difficult to engender with traditional teaching and learning techniques. The higher levels of engagement (and more time spent involved with the subject matter) also influence cognitive learning.

There is evidence (for example, Simpson and Kerridge, 2019) that simulations are particularly effective for mixed nationality, cross-cultural student teams – minimising the linguistic obstacles to learning for international students and narrowing their attainment differentials versus domestic/home students.

For students starting out in a new module or programme cohort, simulations can also act as effective 'icebreakers', encouraging interactions within and between teams.

Employers frequently comment on difficulties in recruiting graduates that have developed skills at effective group working and can contribute well to project teams. This is most apparent when it comes to collective decision-making; balancing differing opinions and views, data vs intuition, short-term vs medium/longer-term benefits, etc. In many university programmes, there are few opportunities to engage deeply in such activities, even though these may be core elements in subsequent employment roles. Students experienced in simulations can put that learning (and associated confidence) to good effect in job interviews and employer assessment workshops.

WHAT NOT TO DO!

Yes, we can certainly share some tips about what not to do too:

Teaching Tip
- *Don't overdo the use of simulations: like any good teaching techniques, they should be used sparingly – the greatest value is likely to be within the variety of a blended learning pedagogy. So, for a programme, by all means embed simulations in several modules BUT not in them all.*
- *Don't expect students to 'just do it', without good explanation of aims and objectives or good guidance on the mechanics of how the simulation operates: do signal benefits but also set reasonable expectations.*
- *Don't forget that your instructors/facilitators need some instruction of their own before starting. If they have poor or superficial understanding of the simulation, this will inevitably impact on students' performance and enthusiasm too. Ideally do a 'dry run' of the simulation for new instructors.*
- *Don't choose generic simulations that are easy for staff to manage but offer little challenge or benefit to students – we should be providing an opportunity to build and develop business skills such as project management, scenario analysis and evaluation of priorities.*
- *Don't be intimidated by the 'inconvenience' of learning to use simulations as new teaching tools. Our own positive experiences indicate likelihood of a very good return on your investment of (really not so much) time and effort.*

EXPERIENTIAL LEARNING SHOULD BE FUN TOO

'The simulation is exciting and completely different from other modules *and makes us feel what it is like working in a real company.*' (Student feedback)

Much of the above has been about the rational, learning-related reasons for trying more simulations in class. However, please don't lose sight of that other key feature: it is often fun!

CONCLUSION

In this chapter, I have tried to spare you a lengthy consideration of experiential learning theory and mechanics – though there are many good journal articles and books based on research evidence. In our 'real world' of HE teaching and learning, we recognise that student engagement is often the principal differentiator associated with 'successful' modules and programmes. Use of a business simulation can be a significant contributor to that higher level of engagement – do try it and enjoy it!

SUGGESTED FURTHER READING

Biggs, J. and C. Tang (2011). *Teaching for Quality Learning at University*. Maidenhead: Open University Press.

Kolb, D.A. (1984). *Experiential Learning: Experience as the Source of Learning and Development*. Englewood Cliffs, NJ: Prentice Hall.

Lean, J., J. Moizer, M. Towler and C. Abbey (2006). 'Simulations and games: Use and barriers in Higher Education', *Active Learning in Higher Education*, 7 (3), 227–42.

Loon, M., J. Evans and C. Kerridge (2015). 'Learning with a strategic management simulation game: A case study', *International Journal of Management Education*, 13 (3), 227–36.

Simpson, C. and C. Kerridge (2019). 'Enhancing the teamwork, leadership and negotiation skills of international students on a business simulation module'. Submitted for publication.

Sousa, D.A. (2017). *How the Brain Learns*. Thousand Oaks, CA: Corwin, a Sage Publishing Company.

Zhang, C. and N. Kyriakidou (2012). *Learning Theories and Practices*. In M. Butler and E. Rose, *Introduction to Organisational Behaviour*. London: CIPD, pp. 108–56.

Thought 6

Kris Lines

Last year, I was preparing a lecture when I was suddenly struck by how close my office was to the location of one of the leading, some might say infamous, cases in the law of economic loss. Indeed, that specific case was going to form the central focus of the lecture that following week. I knew every detail of the case, having taught it for the past decade, but even though the location was only a couple of minutes' walking distance away, I had never visited that street before. That afternoon I set out with my phone and camera.

It quickly transpired that the factory in question shut 30 years ago, but despite this inconvenient revelation I could still stand very close to the original incident and reread the case transcript. In doing so, it made me reflect on whether I viewed those same facts differently now that I was a part of that environment. No longer did I have to paint an abstract picture in my mind, now I could see the street signs and walk past the other industrial units. While ultimately this trip did not change my mind as to the correctness of the verdict, it certainly made it easier to remember the details of that case when I presented it.

On the way back, I wondered out of curiosity how many other cases (infamous or unreported) had taken place in this vicinity? Perhaps more importantly, I also reflected on whether the physical world could, or indeed should, be an important tool for learning. Such an approach to learning should not just be limited to negligence law, or to geographical locations, but rather could be extended to tangible artefacts and indeed all business subjects. For example, would a student who had never sampled a Jaffa cake view the infamous VAT decision any differently once they had eaten one?

Does handling an object, or visiting a landmark, actually cloud the issues and introduce more subjectivity and emotion into what should be clinical decision-making? Or does an appreciation of the physical world add another (softer) dimension to learning?

In the end, I decided that that choice should be left to the individual students. Not every student might wish to expand their horizons (or navel gaze) into the past. Indeed, engaging with the physical world brings with it inherent cost implications, whether monetary or time-based.

In the end, I did produce a glossy self-guided map for those students interested in how their local area interacted with the legal landscape, but it was for formative rather than summative interest only. Now, where did I put those Jaffa cakes . . .

12. How to do a confident presentation
Chris Jones

INTRODUCTION

Over the years I have been to many business research conferences across the world and have often wondered why the quality of a number of academic presentations I have viewed are so unengaging. Business academics spend many hours in the classroom, often delivering lectures to hundreds of students. They also spend substantial periods of time watching colleagues present their work in internal seminars or even assessing students based upon the quality of their presentations for a specific piece of assessment. So what on earth is going on? Doing a presentation to an interested audience is one of the most important and exciting aspects of being an academic.

In my view, at least 75 per cent of presentations I go to leave me feeling frustrated – not knowing what the presenter is trying to achieve, not understanding the key message and making me question my own intellect because the presenter has left me in a state of confusion. I doubt I am alone in thinking this. Very often, I also observe academics in the lecture theatre and feel the same way. Hence, the aim of this chapter is to outline what makes a good academic presentation for a group of students you are currently teaching or for an audience of leading scholars, at an academic conference for example. Hopefully my thoughts will be useful to scholars of all ages and levels of experience but I guess my focus will be on providing useful tips for early career researchers or colleagues interested in taking a teaching route in Higher Education (HE). I would also like to think that the key messages I make are applicable to all scholars worldwide as classrooms do not fundamentally differ across borders.

DEATH BY POWERPOINT

The first thing you need to consider when doing a presentation is what piece of software you are going to use. But hold on – actually, let's backtrack somewhat – do you even need to use a piece of software at all?

When I was an undergraduate student at the University of Leicester in the late 1990s/early 2000s (yes, I am old enough to have paid a tuition fee, albeit a small one), the finest lecturer I ever encountered was a man called Bob Borthwick, an academic in the Department of Politics. My major was in Economics but during the first year we could choose electives in American Politics and Political Theory. At that time there was no lecture capture, no PowerPoint, no technology at all. Put simply, Dr Borthwick would sweep into the large lecture hall with some notes tucked under his arm (perhaps written 20 years ago!). He would then stand at the lectern and deliver an impassioned lecture about a topic that he seemed to have an encyclopaedic knowledge of. He clearly knew his material and students sat there mesmerised, hurriedly writing copious notes to track what he was saying. The lecture hall was packed throughout the term and if I could go back in time and watch any of my lecturers again it would certainly be him. Recently, I bumped into a fellow Leicester alumnus at a restaurant. He too had studied Politics and I leave it to you to work out the first name mentioned.

Another story that can be told is of the now late and great Nobel Prize-winning economist Milton Friedman. Whether you agree or disagree with his political views you can only marvel at his ability to explain economics to a mass audience, as shown by his famous documentary 'Free to Choose'. Although anecdotal, past students of his have told how Professor Friedman would often walk into class unprepared with a newspaper. He would then choose a story from within the newspaper and students would then discuss the economics behind the article. Hence in many ways, Friedman was engaged in a type of problem-based learning with his students. According to Robert Lucas – one of Friedman's students and another Nobel Laurate – Friedman's classes were built around concrete cases (see Cord and Hammond, 2016) and points of discussion that led to proposed actions. Questions were discussed and the class would end up with answers:

> We needed to restate the issue in the language of economics, as a question about equilibrium quantities and prices, about supply and demand. This was the common feature of all the problems, but of course each specific problem requires its own specific treatment. What to emphasise? What to set aside as second order? So we would reformulate the problem and work out some answers, usually diagrammatically, on the blackboard. Of course, Friedman held the chalk, and these discussions were guided and dominated by his intellect. But he was always receptive to questions, and listened closely; giving his full attention to the one student he was engaged with at the moment, never playing to the gallery, responding with questions that served to keep the focus on substance. The discussions involved complicated issues of fact and logic, and each step was considered and debated until everyone was satisfied (or pretended to be). Friedman's goal was not simply to replace the authority we were questioning with his own authority – though that would have been easy for him

to do – but to equip us to identify the needed economics and apply it correctly ourselves. (Robert Lucas, cited in Cord and Hammond, 2016)

As both of these cases illustrate, academics have impact, just like the best high school teachers that taught you in the past – you remember them. Notably in this context, their ability to captivate an audience had nothing to do with the technology at hand. This leads us to the first key tip:

Teaching Tip
You don't need software (PowerPoint) in order to deliver an engaging presentation.

IF YOU REALLY MUST USE POWERPOINT

Okay, I know what you're thinking – Dr Borthwick and Professor Friedman lived in an HE world with no Facebook, YouTube, Twitter, Instagram, laptop computers or mobile phones that have significantly more computing power than the first Apollo Space mission to the moon. They also didn't have to worry about the UK National Student Survey and the Teaching Excellence Framework. It would perhaps be an incredibly risky approach to turn up to a lecture or academic presentation these days without a written presentation. So if you really must, you are going to have to choose a piece of software. I would imagine there are plenty of options available, for example Prezi is now becoming much more popular but usually business and management academics will utilise PowerPoint or a simple PDF. These are easy to use and can be created quite quickly. As with any learning tool, learning to use it well is essential and a skill in and of itself. Used badly and it is to the detriment of your students. I myself use PowerPoint. This is my advice:

1. Work out the time of your presentation and try and have one slide to use for every four minutes.
2. As you become more experienced reduce the quantity and comprehensiveness of your slides.
3. When teaching a 40- to 50-minute lecture, you really shouldn't be using more than 12 slides. The only exception to this tip is for early career academics that are new to lecturing.

Teaching Tip
You don't actually really know something, until you have taught it!
Hence, for new lecturers if you are still not completely in tune with the material, in particular if it is not your area of expertise, then use a few

more slides in case you lose yourself. The slides can act as prompts to get you back on track. As you become more experienced, you should reduce the number of slides and reduce the amount of content presented on each slide.

4. Use a nice background to your slides and make the slides interesting to the viewer. For example, if you are teaching economics, then make the slides dynamic. You may be using diagrams to illustrate an economic theory; use the animation tab in PowerPoint to build up the models from start to finish. Furthermore, if you are using a standard introductory textbook, the publisher may even be able to provide you with these diagrams for free, saving you time. The same logic applies to other areas of business and management. Students will be better focused if the slides are gradually built up in front of them in contrast to a slide that is full at the outset.

    Many people are visual learners so use diagrams and pictures as much as possible. One way that I like to start the lecture might be to put a picture on the screen and ask the students to discuss what they see. I do this when discussing the phenomenal economic growth rate of China over the last 25 years (see Figure 12.1). I put up a before and after picture of Shanghai to illustrate this. Then after that you can outline the learning outcomes for the rest of the session.

5. If you have to, use bullet points, but use them sparingly. Try not to overload the slides.

6. Do not include big chunks of text. The audience is there to look at you for most of the time, not your PowerPoint. It is important not to over-clutter your slides, try to use them to clarify the key points to your audience and develop them to help you keep on track.

7. Integrate short and relevant video clips into your presentations if possible.

    These days it is very straightforward to integrate video material into your lectures. My advice would be to try and break up your lectures with these but only by using short clips that last between one to five minutes. This gives students a breather and allows them to hear another voice. It is also very straightforward to integrate these into a PowerPoint presentation.

HOW TO DELIVER

The next part of this chapter really is the important bit. Once you have created your presentation slides, if you can't express your thoughts to the audience you will have failed. You won't have captivated your audience and

Figure 12.1   Shanghai: before and after

they will go away frustrated and annoyed that you have wasted their time. Or instead, they will have spent the time during your presentation looking at their phone/iPad/laptop and completely ignored what you have just told them. Hence, delivery is key.

So how do you go about delivering your presentation? This is my advice but it is important to note that you will get better with practice over time. Academics can often be characterised as having more introverted personalities. Whilst undertaking their PhD, researchers often spend much time alone – crunching data or working in a lab. There is only a limited amount of time available to teach and it is hard to do teacher training whilst you are writing up your thesis. So very often when new academics become teaching active or start presenting papers at conferences they are not very well trained to perform well in this new role. I myself hated the idea of doing a presentation. I shied away from them as a student (I remember just skipping a tutorial because I had been asked to do one) and would often find myself blushing and embarrassed. I was horrified when my former line manager asked me to teach a class in front of 200 people. But I gave it a go and in the end it worked out quite well.

Teaching Tip
It is very likely that you have more knowledge than your audience. Even if you don't feel confident make sure you appear confident.

This really is crucial. If you do not know the content of your presentation it is very likely you will project uncertainty and so the audience will not find you credible. In order to build confidence in yourself, use visualisation techniques prior to your presentation. Wayne Rooney, the famous Manchester United, Everton and England footballer, revealed in an interview that since he was a young boy he would lie in bed the night before a match and imagine himself scoring a wonder goal. He would then take that mental preparation into the game the following day. He was fairly successful and there is no reason why you can't adopt a similar approach.

Teaching Tip
Practise your presentation!

If you can visualise the presentation in your mind, why not actually practice it for real in front of colleagues or family members? Although this might seem awkward at first, usually family and friends will put you at ease and give you honest and critical feedback. Furthermore, they might ask you to return the favour.

The next few tips are fairly obvious and self-explanatory. Most readers will have seen them before but they shouldn't be glossed over. Some people lack confidence and find it hard to project their personality. It is really important that you try to get over your fears. Most audiences want you to perform well and it is extremely unlikely that you will face hostility. If you do face hostility, try not to be combative in return. Be polite and agree to disagree. Hence, speak very clearly, not too fast (easy to do when nervous) smile and look people in the eye. Try your best to get off to a good start by preparing your opening line and have a strategy for dealing with difficult questions. It is okay if you can't answer a student's question. Ask them to clarify what they are asking as this gives you more time to work out the answer. If you still can't answer, tell the student that you will get back to him or her with the correct answer and some further reading.

Teaching Tip
Speak clearly, use good body language, use the space provided, smile and look people in the eye.
Try your best to start well. Start with a story.
Have a strategy for dealing with difficult questions.

If you manage to achieve these tips the chances are you will have done so because you are relaxed and have stuck to your core message. Not everyone finds it easy to relax, some people simply can't keep still, but if you can do this it will put your audience at ease and create a calm environment.

Teaching Tip
Connect with the audience in your presentation and try to show your personality with passion and humour.

Connecting with your audience is crucial. Hopefully the audience has chosen to be there so make sure you meet their demands for an enjoyable and engaging experience. Again, use your personality. Try to use a bit of humour if you can. Obviously this does not come easy to some people but one thing you could try is to speak to some of the audience before the presentation/lecture. Get to know some of them. This will put you at ease and enable you to crack a few jokes. Self-deprecation often works quite well.

One thing I also do is to try and involve the audience in the presentation. Not so long ago at a conference presentation I wasn't particularly well-prepared, so instead of the audience asking me questions I put the ball in their court and asked them questions. You could do the same with your students. If you are teaching in a large lecture theatre to hundreds of students, trying to connect with your audience will actually keep them awake. I often cold-call students. This keeps them on their toes and keeps them awake but over time it allows you to build rapport. If your lecture spans two hours, during the half-time break go and chat to the students. This will build their confidence and make them more likely to contribute in the class.

Teaching Tip
Watch or listen back to your presentation in order to reflect on what did and didn't go well.

One thing that worked very well for me when I started lecturing was listening to my own lectures via recordings. At the time, lecture capture was in its infancy so I used a Dictaphone. I realised that my Birmingham accent didn't actually sound that bad and that what I was saying actually came across quite well. But by listening back I was also able to be self-critical and it enabled me to determine how I could improve. Nowadays, you can also watch lecture-capture recordings, giving you an opportunity to assess critically your body language and how you move around the room.

Teaching Tip
As you gain more experience, the nerves will disappear and you will actually enjoy it!

Lastly, and this isn't really a tip, as you gain increasingly more and more experience you will no longer feel nervous, the blushes will go away, you will find it easier to prepare and you will actually enjoy being asked difficult questions. There are some exceptions to this, for example a job interview or a conference panel, but sometimes nerves actually allow you to perform much better and those nerves will quickly disappear once you get into the flow.

CONCLUSION

So those are my tips for a successful academic presentation. The list I have provided is not exhaustive. I'm sure you can think of many other pieces of useful advice. I have no doubt though that if you follow some of these tips it will allow you to be successful and turn academic presenting into an enjoyable experience.

Good luck!

SUGGESTED FURTHER READING

Cord, R.A. and J.D. Hammond (eds) (2016). *Milton Friedman: Contributions to Economics and Public Policy*. Oxford: Oxford University Press.

Thought 7

Caroline Elliott and Jon Guest

A WAY TO AVOID CLASSES BEING INTERRUPTED BY MOBILE PHONES

In Chapter 9 a benefit of students having mobile phones is high-lighted, namely that lecturers can ask questions to which students respond using their mobile phone. This can keep students engaged and can add an element of fun to the class. However, more frustrating is when a student's mobile phone goes off in the class, often result-ing in much rummaging in bags to switch off the offending phone, students becoming distracted, the lecturer possibly losing their train of thought, and so on.

As an economist I have always believed in incentives. Hence, at the beginning of every new set of lectures or seminars that I teach, I now always tell students the same thing. I tell them that I will never be angry if a student's mobile phone rings in class. However, if a phone does ring then all the other students get to decide whether the student whose phone rang brings chocolates, sweets or biscuits to the next class for everyone. I promise the students that the same rule applies to me: if I forget to switch my phone off and it rings, I would have to similarly bring in the snacks as a forfeit.

If a mobile rings, the students are delighted to identify whose phone rings and they are happy to encourage the bringing in of the forfeit. Even in a very large group the cost of the forfeit is small, the students appreciate the opportunity to have a chocolate, sweet or biscuit and very quickly students remember to switch their mobile phones off before class starts. Ultimately, very few sweet forfeits ever have to be brought in.

13. Making teaching relevant for the business student

Kathy Daniels

INTRODUCTION

In an edition of the Channel 4 programme *The Great British Bake Off* the presenter Sandi Toksvig was talking about her school days. She commented that she had spent weeks trying to understand logarithms and then, once she had managed to gain the necessary understanding, she had never used them again. Why, she asked, had anyone ever thought that she needed to know about logarithms?

I have seen this questioning of 'Why am I learning this?' echoed in a recent television programme comparing children having a grammar school education against those being taught in a comprehensive school. A number of children who were not achieving at the level which was expected were simply asking why they should learn various topics. Why did they need to understand chemical equations? When would this knowledge ever be of any use?

I am sure we can all look back at our school days and think of things we learnt that were never any practical use to us. We probably found the things that we thought would be useful to be of more interest, and we probably engaged more with the learning experience when we could see that there was some point to the learning. So, what does this tell us about our approach to teaching students in a business school?

SHOULD WE TEACH INFORMATION THAT MIGHT NOT BE USEFUL?

Teaching adults, who have chosen to be at university and who have chosen to study business, might be a very different experience to teaching in a school with children who are being forced to study topics that do not interest them at all. However, University students are still very keen to know whether the information that they are being taught is useful.

The difficulty here is the definition of 'useful'. Is information useful because it can immediately be applied to a work situation that the student might encounter, or is it useful because it challenges the thinking of the student and broadens their horizons?

I was recently asked to go and talk to a group of work psychology students. They were studying a module about personal development, and there had been some debate amongst them about the different responsibilities that an employer has to an employee and a self-employed person. That had led to some confusion over the definition of an employee and my colleague, who was leading this lecture, had asked me to go along the following week to explain the legal definition of an employee and some of the recent, headline-grabbing cases that there had been on the topic.

When I went into the lecture I introduced myself and explained what I was going to talk about. Immediately, one student asked if the material I was about to teach would be in the end-of-module exam. When my colleague confirmed that it would not the student asked why it was being taught if it was not being examined!

This instrumental approach to learning has become very prevalent amongst students who are often working in a part-time job alongside their studies. They are time-poor and therefore they only want to spend their time learning what is essential. So, should we teach information that is not obviously useful?

My argument is that our teaching should be a mix of giving students information that they need to be successful in the work that they are going to do in a business setting, and of challenging them to think more broadly and to broaden their horizons. Yes, covering the set material is important but we should also help students to debate and argue and to develop critical thinking.

However, we also need to ensure that students understand the purpose of what we are teaching. This might mean that we are sometimes saying that the purpose is to broaden their horizons and to get them to think. If we think that this is important then we should have no hesitation in telling students that this is what we are doing.

Teaching Tip
Tell students if something is going to be examined, but also tell students when something is not going to be examined but will aid their deeper understanding of the topic.

HOW DO WE MAKE IT CLEAR THAT INFORMATION IS RELEVANT?

If we are going to argue that everything that we teach is relevant, either directly or indirectly, we need to make sure that students understand how it is relevant.

At the start of each lecture we traditionally tell students what the learning outcomes are for the session. We should also tell students how they might use the information that they are about to be taught, and therefore why it is relevant.

For example, when I am teaching employee relations I do a lecture about trade unions. Many students will never work in an organisation which is unionised, so it could be argued that this information is of limited relevance to the majority of the class. So, I start the session by talking to students about the purpose of representation. Why do employees need someone to represent them in their discussions with their employer? Is the need for a representative a sign that the employment relationship has broken down in some way?

Having discussed some of these questions I then explain to students why it is relevant to discuss trade unions. It is relevant because understanding why people feel the need for representation gives us an insight into their relationship with the employer. If we understand the employment relationship we can hopefully improve it and then we can increase productivity. This is essential information for anyone who wants to work in business. (I also point out that students do not know where they will work throughout their whole career, and they might well be in a unionised environment at some point and need to understand the dynamics that go with this.)

Teaching Tip
I would suggest that we need to start all of our lectures by telling students why the information that they are about to study is relevant, and how they might need to use the information in their future career.

APPLYING MATERIAL TO PERSONAL EXPERIENCE

Another useful technique to help students understand why teaching is relevant is to ask them to reflect on their own working experiences and to apply the material to that. Most students have some work experience, whether this is an internship/placement, a part-time job or some voluntary work that they have engaged in.

For example, I often find that the topic of employee engagement can become a rather false hope and unobtainable ideal. If we focus solely on the theoretical concepts we can start to convince ourselves that it is easy to engage employees, and everyone will be engaged. Students can then become rather sceptical about the topic – it all sounds too easy to produce a workforce that is totally committed to a high level of achievement.

To overcome this I ask students to think about someone in an organisation where they have worked who they would categorise as being engaged, and someone they would categorise as being disengaged. Why do they think that there were these different levels of engagement? Working in small groups students list out the factors in two columns:

- Contributes to engagement
- Contributes to disengagement.

Once we have those factors listed we then move on to look at the theory of employee engagement. Typically this fits very well with the factors that the students have listed, and they start to understand how the theory works in reality.

We can also think about why employee engagement is relevant. Having debated the theory we go back to the people that the students chose to reflect on. If they had been a manager in the organisation would they have wanted to influence the employees to make them more engaged? What positive impacts would the increased engagement have had on the organisation? This is relevant to the student, because when they are managers they will need to understand how to improve engagement to achieve the positive impacts that they have identified.

Teaching Tip
It is important to remind students that personal experience is limited. It is not a well-structured piece of theoretical research. However, it is a useful way of understanding a topic before exploring the theoretical concepts.

APPLYING MATERIAL TO SOMETHING TOPICAL

Another approach to make learning relevant is to link it to something that the students know and understand. For example, when I teach about leadership I always start the lecture by asking students to think about a leader that they respect, and a leader who they do not respect. I encourage students to think outside of the business setting, maybe choosing a football manager or a leader from a sector that they find particularly interesting.

Having identified the leader I then ask students to list out the factors that make the leader successful or unsuccessful. Then, in small groups the students are asked to put the information together to describe the leadership styles of their chosen leaders, and to critique the styles.

We then move onto the theory. For example, I might explain the autocratic, democratic and laissez-faire leadership styles. Do the leadership styles that the students have described fit with the styles that the theorists have identified? Does the critique that fellow researchers have made of these styles fit with the critique of the students?

Having done this we then think about the implications of working with a different type of leader. We look at subordinate styles, and students are challenged to think about their own subordinate style and how they might clash with a particular style of leadership. If, in the future, they are in a role where they are clashing with their line manager could they use the information that they have just been taught to understand the situation better and to adjust their behaviour? We also think about the style of leadership that the student currently has (albeit most students are still at the early stages of developing their own style). What are the strengths and weaknesses of the approach that they are using to leadership and what might they want to change? These debates make the material relevant.

APPLYING MATERIAL TO THE REAL WORLD

Another approach I have taken in my employee relations module, which has been particularly well received by students, is to ask them to follow the news. Each week they have to come to the lecture prepared to answer the question:

What has happened in employee relations this past week?

They are expected to come to the lecture with examples of industrial action that has occurred, redundancies that have been announced, new jobs that have been created, individual disputes that have hit the headlines or developments in employment law. I then use the first part of the lecture to listen to what they have to report.

Students find this very useful because they start to see the variety of issues that are arising in the business world. However, most importantly, they start to see why what they are learning is relevant.

For example, recently there was industrial action announced at a relatively small local manufacturing organisation. One student reported this at the start of the lecture. We had recently studied the Trade Union Act 2016, and I had taught the students about the changes to the law – that a ballot for industrial action now has to have at least 50 per cent of those eligible to vote casting a vote for it to be valid.

Having reported the industrial action I then asked the students what legislation the trade union representing the employees in this organisation would have had to follow and what this required them to do and not do. This was an excellent opportunity for them to revise what I had taught them, and to check their understanding. I then asked them about the 50 per cent rule. Given the very real situation that we were considering, did they think that the 50 per cent rule was fair on the organisation and on the employees? Was it too severe or too lenient? This reinforced their learning about the legislation, but also gave them the chance to see how legislation changes impact on the way that employees and employers operate.

INTEGRATING CONCEPTS TO HELP UNDERSTAND THE REAL WORLD

Another important way of making students realise the relevance of the material that they are learning is to help them to understand how the various aspects that they are being taught link together. If the student has found one particular topic less relevant, or less interesting, they will still be able to value the information if they can see how it fits into the 'bigger picture'.

This became very evident when I was teaching discrimination legislation and we got to the topic of harassment. I taught students the law about harassment, and then we moved on to discuss some cases of harassment which have gone to the Employment Tribunal, and thought about the reasoning behind the judgments.

There was one case which caused a lot of debate, where a manager had made one ill-advised comment to an employee, and that had been found to be sufficient to be defined as harassment. We applied the legal definitions to understand the ruling of the Employment Tribunal but then linked back to the material that we had learnt many weeks earlier about leadership. If an employee is being harassed is there an abuse of power by the leader? If we are going to reduce the possibility of harassment occurring in an organisation do we need to understand leadership behaviour? The law gives a punishment when the law is broken, but it does not stop harassment occurring.

We also linked to work that we had studied about the culture of an organisation. We debated whether harassment is more likely in some organisational cultures (and also had an interesting discussion about whether harassment is actually seen as acceptable in some cultures). We then discussed whether the harasser should receive a disciplinary warning, or whether dismissal is the only appropriate punishment.

At the end of that lecture we had linked together several topics. As I summarised at the end of the lecture I pointed out to the students that there is a need to understand topics broadly to really be able to explore what is happening.

Teaching Tip
Something which might not seem particularly relevant when explored on its own takes on a much more important relevance when applied to the bigger picture.

MAKING ASSESSMENT RELEVANT

Having made a big effort to make it clear why the material being taught is relevant it seems appropriate to conclude the teaching of a module by making sure that the assessment is relevant. There are a number of ways that this can be achieved:

1. Give work-related scenarios to address
   When I set coursework for employment law I write a series of ficti-tious case studies. For example, one assessment I wrote was a series of emails that a Human Resources Manager had waiting for her when she returned from annual leave. The students had to take on the role of that HR Manager and write the answers to the five emails. One such email was:

   Email: From the Administration Manager
   Angelo keeps making errors, and this is now becoming a problem. Today he has made a number of inputting errors which mean that 25 customers have been sent the wrong orders. I now have the cost of recalling all those orders, sending out the right orders and dealing with the complaints. He has been with us for 6 months now, and the problems keep occurring. I plan to dismiss him this afternoon, is that a problem?

   It is quite possible that students will receive an email just like this at some time in their future, so practising the identification of the relevant law and the reasoning behind the answer that they would give is useful for them, as well as being an assessment of their performance on the module.

2.   Linking assessment to real organisation situations
      A colleague of mine, who teaches learning and development, asked
      students to identify an organisation which had a particular issue
      that needed addressing. It could be any organisation of the student's
      choice. For the assessment the student had to analyse the issue, iden-
      tify the learning and development needs and then propose a solution
      using appropriate learning and development interventions.
      Again, a real situation that students might face in their future career.

Teaching Tip
Using work-based scenarios in assessments helps students to see the relevance,
because they can see how they would use the information that they have
learned in a real situation that they might face. It also helps them to develop
the skills of critical thinking, both in their academic studies as they debate
the relevant theoretical concepts, and in their future work as they learn how
to identify the best answer to a problem.

CONCLUSION

If students see that what they are learning is relevant they are more likely to
see the value in their learning, and to engage with the learning experience.
Putting in place opportunities to apply learning to business situations
helps achieve the goal of relevant learning, but there is also the need to
explain to students why something that they are learning is relevant.

SUGGESTED FURTHER READING

Breen, R. and R. Lindsay (2002). 'Different disciplines require different motiva-
    tions for student success', *Research in Higher Education*, 43 (6), 693–725.
Kember, D., A. Ho and C. Hong (2008). 'The importance of establishing relevance
    in motivating student learning', *Active Learning in Higher Education*, 9 (3).
Kember, D., A. Ho and C. Hong (2010). 'Characterising a teaching and learning
    environment capable of motivating student learning', *Learning Environments
    Research*, 13 (1), 43–57.

14. Problem-based learning

Chris Owen

INTRODUCTION

In the current context in higher education, teachers need to adopt approaches that are engaging and fun and which will give students an excellent learning experience. Problem Based Learning (PBL) is an approach to teaching which is different because it involves the whole person. PBL is a philosophy of teaching that can be used at any stage of the student journey from first year to final year, and the only constraint on its application is the imagination of the teacher. PBL originated in medical education, but has been applied in many different educational settings. The essence of PBL is giving students a real-life problem to solve. The role of the teacher becomes facilitative, supporting the students to acquire and apply the necessary knowledge to solve the problem. Key to this is a change in the role of the teacher.

In a traditional student/teacher relationship (see Figure 14.1 below), the teacher is the expert and their role is to impart their expert knowledge to students. In terms of assessment, the teacher provides the questions, the student provides the answers and then the teacher marks them. In a

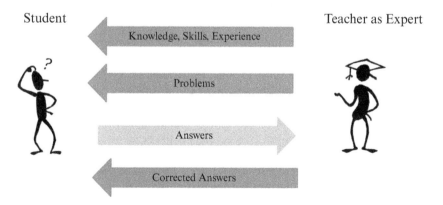

Figure 14.1   Picture of traditional teacher/student relationship

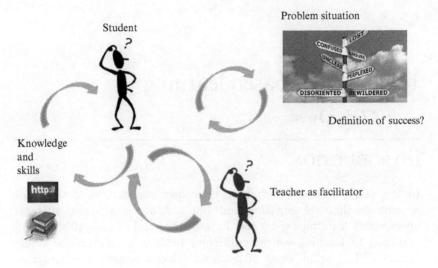

Figure 14.2   Picture of PBL teacher/student relationship

PBL context (see Figure 14.2), the student and the teacher both face the problem together. The teacher doesn't necessarily know any more than the student about how to solve the problem. What the student can do is investigate and gather the knowledge, skills and information necessary to solve the problem presented to them. The role of the teacher in this context is to be a facilitator, to support learners but also to challenge them in the appropriate way.

WHY IS PBL REWARDING FOR STUDENTS?

Problem solving can be fun. Effective problem solving requires students to demonstrate several personal qualities such as curiosity, creativity, perseverance, organisation and resilience. Real-world problem solving (as opposed to textbook problem solving) can be very rewarding to students and solving a problem with a practical application can be more satisfying. Problem-based learning involves students taking risks, but in a relatively safe environment compared to the real world. Students get to try ideas out, to experiment and to engage in practical activities. Problems can be designed to involve interacting with others, either as customers or participants in the designed activity. Interacting with other people can be very rewarding for students as it gives them the opportunity to practise interpersonal skills such as persuasion, influencing, listening etc. Sometimes the unexpected may happen, or things may go wrong. Students may experience the ups and downs and emotional rollercoaster of dealing with many challenges. Often at the time they may not be enjoying the activity, but, in reflecting on the challenge, they report that they have found it very rewarding.

WHY IS PBL REWARDING FOR STAFF?

PBL is a deeper form of learning and doing PBL with students brings many rewards. First, there is the opportunity to work with students on helping them solve the kinds of problems that they will meet in their careers when they leave university, thus helping them to acquire directly relevant employability skills. Second, it is rewarding as an educator to build deeper relationships with students where you move beyond the provision of knowledge and content and into a coaching role where you are helping students to develop their skills and competencies and their confidence in their ability to be creative and to lead, for example. Finally, PBL can also stretch the teacher out of their own comfort zone. This is because students will often push the boundaries of the problem and come up with innovative solutions which challenge the knowledge and skills of the teacher. Thus PBL can be a great learning opportunity for the teacher as well as the students.

WHAT KINDS OF PROBLEM ARE SUITABLE FOR PBL?

Any problem is potentially a candidate for problem-based learning or at least may be the catalyst for defining the appropriate problem. Experience has shown that the following are useful characteristics when selecting and designing a problem for students.

Real world – this is the opportunity to move away from the textbook approach. Choose a problem or a challenge that exists in the real world, where students can and will see the results of their actions and solutions. Are there problems in the local environment or in the university that students can help solve? Are there local organisations that need help with something?

Practical – choose a problem that involves designing, making and doing something. This is a chance for students with a practical orientation to shine, and an opportunity for all students to develop their practical skills alongside their intellectual capability.

Non-prescriptive – find a problem that has many potential solutions, where there is the opportunity for students to be creative and to explore different solution alternatives. Development of the creative side of students is a key capability here.

Complex – it is important that the problem is sufficiently challenging and complex. This is a fine judgement as we don't want the problem to be too difficult or off-putting, but it needs to be hard enough to motivate students to work at solving it.

Relevant – where possible, choose a problem that the students will see is relevant to their future careers, lives and employability. This will help with engagement and motivation.

Engaging and fun – try to select a problem that is fun to work on. This is of course subjective, and students and lecturers will differ as to their definition of fun! One way to do this is to design enough flexibility into the task that students have a lot of discretion in how they go about it, thus giving them the opportunity to shape it.

EXAMPLES OF PBL

One example of a PBL project is a charity challenge project for final year students on an undergraduate business degree. Students are placed in teams of four or five and challenged to raise as much money as they can for a chosen charity inside a 24-hour period. The 24-hour period must take place within a 2-week event window towards the end of a 12-week term. Students are given £50 seed money to fund the event. There are no other constraints placed on the students, they can organise any type of event, choose their location and their target audience. Student groups are required to submit an event proposal form in about week six of term to ensure that their event is feasible and safe. Various support services across the university provide advice and guidance to the students on organising events, complying with local procedures and in particular making sure that health and safety rules are complied with.

Over the years, students have carried out a range of events raising anything between £100 and £5000 for their chosen charity. Some examples of events and amounts raised are given below in Table 14.1. The challenge develops the students' capabilities in a number of areas including creativity, stakeholder management, marketing, planning, communication and fundraising.

Table 14.1   Examples of student events

Event concept	Details of event	Indicative amount raised
Young leaders networking day	A networking event was organised where inspirational young leaders and entrepreneurs with a national reputation were invited to speak. The event was advertised and promoted amongst the university, the wider alumni network and the local business community. Attendees were requested to register to attend the event, although the event was free. At the event itself, people were invited to make donations to the chosen charity. The event was very well attended and a significant amount was raised for charity.	£2000
Charity abseil	A team organised a charity abseil down the side of the tallest building in the university. Fifty people paid for the opportunity to have this experience after which they received a photograph and a signed certificate. Key challenges of this event were the health and safety challenges and obtaining the necessary permissions from the building owner and the university for the event. The event went smoothly and was enjoyed by everyone who participated.	£5000
Wine tasting evening	This team approached a wine supplier and invited them to run a wine tasting evening. The evening was hosted by a wine expert from the company who was able to explain the details of the wine and its provenance and vintage. The evening also involved some light food and snacks. Attendees were charged a nominal fee for the evening. As part of the evening, boxes of wine were for sale. The wine supplier donated a percentage of their takings from the evening to charity.	£250
Street food festival	Students organised a street food festival in the university grounds. Local vendors were invited onto the premises and were asked to donate a percentage of their takings from the day to the chosen charity. The main challenge of the day was to organise the logistics of getting the vans on site and complying with the relevant health and safety requirements. Marketing via social media along with locating the event in a strategically favourable location in terms of footfall led to a successful event with a large amount raised.	£850

PREPARING STUDENTS FOR PBL

It is necessary to do some preparatory work with students before embarking on delivering PBL. In the first instance it is important to explain to them how PBL differs from conventional forms of learning. That said, this difference shouldn't be overemphasised to avoid raising unnecessary concerns. It's better at this stage to emphasise the benefits and rewards of taking part in the PBL experience. Students are always interested in how they are going to be assessed. In introducing PBL to them, the method and rationale for assessment should be explained. Often, this will be different from the way that they have been assessed previously.

Teaching Tip
For PBL, we are often interested in a mix of assessment measures, some of which are outcome measures, i.e. they measure the success of the problem-solving endeavour, and some of them are process measures, i.e. they measure the effectiveness of the problem-solving process.

PBL does require a certain level of support from the teaching staff. The journey that the students will go on will involve ups and downs, and they are in unfamiliar territory, so will require an enhanced level of support during this process. The nature of the support is also slightly different from that which is conventionally provided. The support required in this context is closer to coaching than conventional teaching. Teaching staff in this situation are required to supply skills and knowledge to students but more in a 'pull' rather than a 'push' manner. This means that the students identify the gaps in their knowledge and skills to tackle the problem and then staff provide seminars and sessions targeted on these required topics. In addition to this, some of the support requirements required can be more practical and to do with navigating the processes and bureaucracy of the University. This support can sometimes be provided by support staff from within the university (see below).

PREPARING THE UNIVERSITY FOR PBL

PBL is a different approach and it is worth ensuring that you have the support of key management in your endeavours. This is partly a pragmatic issue, you need their support in terms of funding and perhaps the additional level of teaching support that may be required. However, you also need their support for the overall approach and philosophy. For example, the assessment approach tends to be different and may need explaining and justifying. Building support for PBL can also be achieved by managing the PR around this activity, taking opportunities to publicise student successes in the university media, but also where appropriate with related media. Over time, the PBL activities can become a differentiator for the university and the department, an example of how students are engaging with the wider community and making a difference.

For PBL to be successful it is necessary to do some groundwork with university stakeholders to get their support and cooperation. It's worth putting some time and effort into this because it will save time and problems further down the road. Exactly who you need to contact will vary depending on exactly what you intend to do, but with the Apprentice Challenge example, which involved organising and delivering events, we needed to contact the following stakeholders for the reasons given below in Table 14.2. These are just examples – the stakeholders that you need to manage will depend on the nature of the activities that you plan to carry out.

In addition to these internal stakeholders, you may have external stakeholders. For example, in the case of the Apprentice Challenge, we have a number of charities which we have supported and in some cases we have built up a long-term relationship with them. In addition to managing stakeholders, it is important to understand the local environment in which you plan to carry out PBL. Understanding the context and the local

Table 14.2   Stakeholder support

Stakeholder	Support provided
Security	Gaining permissions for events. Advice on various aspects of event management, including booking and securing venues, managing visitors from outside the University, providing security if required for events, coordinating with other events taking place on campus.
Estates	Advice and guidance on the whole event management process. Managing external contractors and providers on campus. The provision of necessary services; heat, light and power. Management of open-air events.
Health and Safety	Advice and guidance on carrying out risk assessments for events. Advice on how to manage and mitigate the risk of events.
Catering	Advice and guidance on events that involve the provision of food and drink. Managing the relationship between on-site and off-site provision of food and drink.
Marketing	Advice to students on how to market their event and how to use social media.

bye-laws that apply is essential for success. Otherwise you run the risk of accidentally falling foul of local arrangements and upsetting people unnecessarily!

Teaching Tip
Funding is a key consideration for PBL. Depending on what you decide to do, there will almost certainly be a need for some funding to support the activities.

PREPARING COLLEAGUES FOR PBL

PBL can require additional levels of support depending on the exact nature of the problems that you challenge the students with. It is worth building a team of colleagues over time who you can work with and can provide support to these kinds of activities. In the first place, you will need to invest a little time in finding colleagues that you can work with in this way. Some colleagues will find a more natural affinity with this teaching philosophy, and you will need to identify those like-minded individuals you can work with. Spend time working with these colleagues to explain to them the benefits of the PBL approach. In addition to academic teaching staff, it can be useful to also identify colleagues in support and administrative roles who are interested in getting involved in these activities.

CHALLENGES OF PBL

. . . with Students

Although PBL has the potential to be fun and engaging for students, for some of them it can be nerve-racking and raise anxiety levels. They are being taken outside their comfort zone and away from the familiarity of conventional forms of learning and assessment. The real-world problem solving aspect that makes it so appealing can also be threatening if students are concerned about their own ability to perform in this context. This can particularly be the case in the final year where students are concerned about their overall degree grade and they may have several assignments due at the same time. Given these concerns, it is important that the students are given the appropriate level of support throughout the process to ensure that these concerns are properly managed.

As with any team-based activity, students need support in working together effectively as a team. The first step is to ensure that teams are assembled in a balanced way. It is often better to assign students to teams rather than letting them choose their own teams. This better reflects the world of work where they will often need to work with new people from a variety of backgrounds and develop this ability as a vital skill.

Teaching Tip
Effective team working doesn't just happen, it needs support and nurturing. One approach that can work is to deliver weekly input sessions to the students on different team-working topics, for example a set of topics could look something like this:

- *Team development process*
- *Setting a team charter*
- *Appointing a leader*
- *Setting and achieving goals*
- *How to be creative*
- *Managing your time*
- *Dealing with conflict.*

It is important that students understand that it is normal for problems to occur during team activities, and that they need to develop the language to talk about these issues with each other and to learn how to deal with them in a mature way. There are critical moments in PBL where teams need a nudge to move them in the right direction.

Supporting problem-based learning in a team context requires skilful and patient facilitation. The facilitator needs to provide just the right balance of support and challenge to the team. They need to observe the team and help quieter and less outgoing team members be heard. Problems with teams can escalate and if not dealt with early can become very difficult to deal with later on.

. . . with the Institution

Without wishing to generalise, universities can be both conservative and bureaucratic. They can unintentionally discourage innovation and risk taking. Depending on your local context, the environment may be more or less welcoming of PBL in terms of leadership, culture, processes and procedures and the local learning and teaching assessment climate. A key consideration is resourcing. PBL can be quite a resource-intense approach to teaching, so will only succeed if support exists to provide this. All these factors will have a bearing on the relative ease or difficulty you will face in introducing PBL approaches. That said, many institutions have embraced PBL because they recognise the benefits and it has become a mainstream approach in many places. If you are working in one of these institutions, then you will be able to draw on the support of local like-minded colleagues. If, however, you are more of a pioneer of PBL, then you will need to test out the support of leadership and perhaps be prepared to build support for your efforts over a longer time frame. Either way, the point here is to be sensitive to the local context within which you are operating.

THEORETICAL BASIS OF PBL

In PBL, which originates from medical education, students are presented with complex, ambiguous problem situations. Importantly, they do not have the knowledge to deal with the problem, part of the challenge for them is that they need to identify and gather the necessary knowledge to tackle the problem (Savin-Baden, 2001). PBL is not without its challenges as it departs from traditional 'teacher-student' models of teaching. There is a higher degree of ambiguity and students may initially struggle to adapt to this new way of teaching and learning (Klunklin et al., 2011). Evidence from research suggests that some students may be concerned about fairness and consistency (Landeen et al., 2013). Some students may be distrustful of the process of skill development and the workload (Jay, 2014). As a group teaching method students may be concerned about face saving and rapport (Robinson et al., 2015). There is some evidence that PBL improves students' transferable skills and engagement (Carvalho, 2016) and can help with career readiness for business students seeking careers in consulting (Akpan, 2016). PBL has been used to teach undergraduate students about sustainability (Brundiers et al., 2010), logistics (Alvarstein and Johannesen, 2001) and Six Sigma (Miller et al., 2016). A detailed review of PBL is contained in Savin-Boden and Major (2004).

CONCLUSION

It is important that business schools prepare students for the world of work and the challenges that they will face on graduation. PBL provides an additional approach to teaching students which is rewarding, engaging and meaningful. It can supplement other teaching methods in developing students' competencies and skills in a real-world context. If done well, it can bring significant benefits in terms of achieving deeper student engagement and satisfaction. PBL presents some challenges to the teacher and these have been described as well as some potential ways of dealing with them. PBL can be fun for staff as well, giving an opportunity to work with colleagues across the university to provide a deeper learning experience for students.

REFERENCES

Akpan, I.J. (2016). 'The efficacy of consulting practicum in enhancing students' readiness for professional career in Management Information Systems: An empirical analysis', *Decision Sciences Journal of Innovative Education*, 14, 412–40.

Alvarstein, V. and L.K. Johannesen (2001). 'Problem-based learning approach in teaching lower-level logistics and transportation', *International Journal of Physical Distribution and Logistics Management*, 31, 557–73.

Brundiers, K., A. Wiek and C.L. Redman (2010). 'Real-world learning opportunities in sustainability: From classroom into the real world', *International Journal of Sustainability in Higher Education*, 11, 308.

Carvalho, A. (2016). 'The impact of PBL on transferable skills development in management education', *Innovations in Education and Teaching International*, 53, 35–47.

Jay, J. (2014). 'Problem-based learning – A review of students' perceptions in an Occupational Therapy Undergraduate curriculum', *South African Journal of Occupational Therapy*, 44, 56.

Klunklin, A., P. Subpaiboongid, P. Keitlertnapha, N. Viseskul and S. Turale (2011). 'Thai nursing students' adaption to problem-based learning: A qualitative study', *Nurse Education in Practice*, 11, 370–74.

Landeen, J., T. Jewiss, S. Vajoczki and M. Vine (2013). 'Exploring consistency within a problem-based learning context: Perceptions of students and faculty', *Nurse Education in Practice*, 13, 277–82.

Miller, K.E., C. Hill and A.R. Miller (2016). 'Bringing lean Six Sigma to the supply chain classroom: A problem-based learning case', *Decision Sciences Journal of Innovative Education*, 382.

Robinson, L., A. Harris and R. Burton (2015). 'Saving face: Managing rapport in a problem-based learning group', *Active Learning in Higher Education*, 16, 11–24.

Savin-Baden, M. (2001). 'The problem-based learning landscape', *Planet*, 4, 4–6.

Savin-Boden, M. and C. Major (2004). *Foundations of Problem-based Learning*, Maidenhead: Oxford University Press, McGraw-Hill.

Thought 8

Alison McPherson

Sometimes when we give students group work not all of the groups work together as well as we might hope. One area that often causes issues when groups of students work together is where some students feel that others in the group are not contributing as much as they are. This is referred to as social loafing and concerns the tendency for some individuals to reduce the amount they do to complete a task when they are in a group. The size of the group allocated to the task will play a part in this, i.e. the larger the group the greater likelihood that social loafing will occur. The outcome is often conflict in the group, less productivity and poorer quality work.

Social loafing happens in the workplace as well as the classroom, with the same negative consequences. Student employability is important and we need to ensure graduates leave us with skills that enable them to flourish and succeed in their working and their personal lives. Building in group work to our modules will help this happen but how can we maximise their learning from and enjoyment of these experiences?

To improve the student experience of working in groups I use the following guidelines:

- Teach the class about social loafing and effective group working tips before you break them into groups.
- Keep the group size small, 3–5 members is best and resist pressure from students to let them work in bigger groups.
- You can let the groups choose their own members. Very occasionally there is a student that isn't invited to join a group. If this is the case then I will intervene and help them find a group to join.
- During the session on social loafing get the groups to draw up a 'contract' between themselves which specifies how the group should work together and guidance on what to do if things

150

start to go wrong. I often provide them with a template to follow. If students have been allocated to groups rather than self-selected then the contract becomes even more important.

- Build in some team-building activities to improve the group cohesion before they start on the main task. These activities can be fun too!
- Encourage the groups to formalise and record the split of tasks between themselves.
- Suggest they include in their contract a mechanism for resolving conflict within the group before asking for the lecturer to intervene.
- Build in an opportunity at the end for them to conduct a review of how the group worked together. What worked well, what could have been done differently or more effectively? If the students' studies haven't already covered the concept of the reflective practitioner then encourage them to look at and use a model of reflection such as Gibbs's (1988) reflective cycle.

Collaboration helps students build key skills for the workplace, but group work will only facilitate this if the task you give the group is well thought through and tailored to their particular needs and the required learning outcomes.

15. Teaching students struggling because English is not their first language

Pieter Koornhof

When teaching to students to whom English is a foreign language, a variety of difficulties may arise, not just in terms of actually understanding the content being taught, but also because of cultural differences, all potentially contributing to a sense of isolation. This chapter discusses and reflects on some of the potential problems that may arise in this context and how the author has used their knowledge and experience to solve and/or pre-empt them. Tips on how to make one's teaching more accessible are discussed, along with a reflection on the intersection between language and culture. Advice on how to adapt teaching materials and assessments is also provided.

INTRODUCTION

As a lecturer in South Africa I developed my teaching ability in a context where the majority of my students spoke English as a second (or often third) language. Aside from this, I, along with many of my colleagues, was not necessarily a native English speaker. Whereas I have always considered myself as fluent in English, I have had the odd occasion where things get lost in translation, including in the classroom! As such, I have become very mindful of the role and importance of language. If one is not attuned or empathetic to this aspect, it may become a significant barrier to education. This could in turn manifest in poor grades, a diminished student experience, or lower student retention and feedback – all of which are unnecessary and can be addressed in a proactive manner. Given the high number of international students at UK universities (especially in postgraduate programmes), effective management of this aspect could have a significant impact on the reputation of a university.

In this chapter I reflect on some of the advice received and practical steps I have taken to assist students that struggle to either understand or express themselves properly in English. I am mindful of the resource demand on universities and staff, and have therefore focused on advice which can be implemented relatively simply and with little to no cost implications. These include ways to adapt both your teaching activities and your assessments in order to be more accessible not only to foreign language students, but students in general, which I believe could assist both young and experienced lecturers in improving their teaching.

BE PROACTIVE AND INCLUSIVE

Being a foreign language speaker may have a significant impact on a student. Whereas for some the whole experience may be different and exciting, for others it can create intense feelings of isolation or alienation. As such, it is important not to underestimate the effect that merely speaking a different language may have on a person. My experience has been that a key factor in determining whether international students fall into the former category has been the extent to which they feel welcome – not only within the place where they are studying, but also within the programme. As a lecturer, you cannot necessarily create a sense of community on your own, but you can contribute to this within the context of your programme.

One of the best ways of doing so is by taking an interest in the composition of your cohort. First, identify whether there are any international students within your class. This should be relatively simple to do, and also need not take a lot of your time. Second, once you've identified how many international students there are, enquire as to what their language proficiency is. Again, this information should be relatively accessible as most international students would likely have had to complete some kind of language test. Having this information at your disposal allows you to identify which students within your module may be at risk, which allows you to be proactive in assisting them from the start. It is also sensible to make yourself both aware of and acquainted with the language support structures within your school or university. Language support structures can also be beneficial for lecturers in other ways, such as helping to ensure that your notes or teaching materials are presented in simplified English, affording it a higher likelihood of accessibility and understanding.

I have found that the time required to take the above steps is far outweighed by the positive effect it tends to have. By equipping yourself with this knowledge you can easily reach out to students pre-emptively, offer to help them and also ask that they indicate how you can help them in other ways. This will help you develop a rapport with your international students. Not only will it help them feel more welcome, it may also go a long way towards developing a reputation that you are an accessible lecturer, something which is usually a key aspect with regard to student feedback.

BE MINDFUL OF THE INTERSECTION BETWEEN LANGUAGE AND CULTURE

From 2015 to 2017, South African universities were driven to a standstill because of ongoing student protests. Whereas the initial protests related to student fees, they quickly moved on to tackle wider issues relating to the student experience. A chief concern was the fact that the higher education culture, teaching activities and classroom activities were dominated by a Westernised, Euro-centric approach that students felt alienated by, and that they had had enough of. These protests were widely reported, and although they were traumatic for lecturers it was clear that they were equally so for the students involved in them.

What living through the student protests – not to mention teaching and examining, often at personal cost – taught me is that, whereas a difference in language is a very apparent barrier to education, there are other, more nuanced variables which may also have a significant impact on the student experience. I would argue that something which is closely related to language is culture, and the fact that a foreign student is removed from their culture may also have a further alienating effect. Furthermore, managing cultural differences between individuals may, as the above example shows, become quite tricky.

In reflecting on what transpired during the protests, it struck me that, in the context of the classroom, a lecturer may inadvertently lose the attention or respect of students because of how they say and do particular things. Not only could this result in poor feedback, it also impacts on the students' willingness to learn and be taught by you. Whereas this wasn't the cause of what transpired in the South African higher education environment, a lack of empathy and understanding likely contributed to exacerbating the situation.

Whereas the problem described above can be overcome through hard work, taking steps to manage this risk before it manifests is the most sensible approach.

Teaching Tip
I have found through experience that the best approach is generally not to be overly sensitive, but rather to be mindful of difference in culture and how this may influence students' approaches to particular topics.

Although it may be painful to do so, it is often beneficial to reflect on one's own innate biases and culture and how this may affect the way you teach and the examples you use in class. How I have used this to my advantage is by being open and honest, providing students with a meta-phorical snapshot of my life and making the odd self-referential humorous comment relating to my teaching (especially when I make a mistake). I believe this humanises me, makes me more relatable, and allows me in turn to ask students to share relevant experiences and examples from their perspective. This not only enriches the overall classroom conversation, but also provides lecturers with new examples for future classes. By constantly engaging with students in such a manner, you also receive feedback about whether your teaching is accessible to students, allowing you to refine your methods over time. Admittedly this strategy may not suit every personality or institution, but it does serve to illustrate one possible way of making yourself more relatable and your classroom an inclusive space. It would be well worth the effort to reflect on other ways in which this can be achieved.

SUPPLEMENT YOUR TEACHING MATERIAL

There may be instances where a foreign language speaker is quite capable in conversational English, but when faced with the highly specialised and/ or academic language of a particular profession they may nonetheless struggle. When teaching to foreign language students there is always a risk that there may be a disconnect between what is being taught in the classroom and how the student is able to comprehend and consequently communicate this information. This, in turn, may manifest in a lack of understanding, an unwillingness to contribute to class discussion and, in the worst case, poor grades and student feedback.

Over the years I have been exposed to novel ways of diminishing this impact, many of which have made me a better lecturer. One particularly simple yet effective solution that a colleague of mine used (while teach-ing a class on human rights), was to make copies of the relevant human rights charter available in various languages. This not only made the core substantive content of the programme available to each student in their mother tongue, it also was used as a striking example to then start discussions on rights within the charter (such as those of human dignity and equality). Some disciplines may have comparable textbooks in other languages, and key concepts or arguments may be explored in foreign journals. In the case of law, you will often find policy papers, model laws or conventions in more than one language. These may not always be appro-priate, but nevertheless it may be sensible to do some research on what is out there. Colleagues who speak other languages may also be willing to help, provided you help them in a similar fashion.

In addition to supplementing your prescribed material, you can also adapt your own notes and materials in order to increase accessibility. As mentioned earlier, converting your notes to simplified English would increase the likelihood that it is understood by a foreign language speaker. In most disciplines there is also an unintended benefit of the use of simplified English, namely it strengthens your ability to explain complex concepts in an accessible manner. This is a skill which is not only beneficial for you, but it is also a skill that can be conveyed to your students (especially those in the professions where they are at times expected to relate their specialised knowledge to a lay person).

Teaching Tip
The use of infographics to convey certain concepts or processes may not only make your presentations more visually striking, but also help students who are more capable of visually processing information, resulting in a net benefit for not just foreign language students.

DEVELOP ASSESSMENTS THAT MINIMISE LANGUAGE DEFICITS

Just like your teaching materials can have a significant impact on student performance, the choice of assessments used (as well as how those assessments are presented) may turn an otherwise accessible programme into a negative experience for a foreign language speaker. Imagine you are attending every lecture and contributing to class discussions only to be faced with a final exam that seems utterly detached from what has been presented. This, under normal circumstances, would be a failing of proper curricular alignment, and most would agree that it needs to be rectified. When dealing with foreign language speakers, these aspects may become even more exacerbated. As such, it is important to bear in mind the impact of language when reflecting on how you assess content.

Similar to how you can use simplified English for teaching materials, it is an equally good idea to adopt this practice when drafting your assessments. Doing this not only reduces the risk of a foreign language student misunderstanding a particular question but also reduces ambiguity. Additionally, the time pressure that accompanies traditional written examinations may become a barrier to proper assessment if a student is also facing other difficulties such as language. Unless the nature of the subject requires this pressure in order for it to be accurately assessed, it is sensible to consider using assessments where more time is granted. A written exam can easily be switched with a take-home variant with very little effort or time investment from a lecturer, and in my experience tends to produce answers of a much higher quality.

Teaching Tip
Providing ample opportunities for formative assessment by discussing exam questions in tutorials and having students submit questions for feedback will also help students who are struggling across the board.

Something I have done for both coursework and take-home exams is craft questions that explicitly have more than one potential point of view or solution. I then actively encourage students to work together in discussing the questions and have them ultimately choose a particular point of view for their individual answers. This allows students who may be struggling in expressing themselves to be assisted by other students which in turn not only helps develop their confidence but also allows for the marketplace of ideas to continue outside of the classroom environment. Certain disciplines (law, politics and philosophy being obvious examples) lend themselves to such an approach quite easily, though I am sure there are ways of adapting this method to other subjects. You can also consider experimenting with alternative assessments such as the creation of video presentations to create a similar effect.

CONCLUSION

As I have tried to show above, the problems of someone who is struggling with English may manifest in a variety of ways. It may not even initially be clear that the student's language is hampering their education. Because of this, there is no single quick-fix solution or trick that can address this nuanced issue. I am also mindful of the fact that the advice presented herein may not be applicable to all disciplines or teaching styles. These solutions were developed following my own exposure to the advice and practices of lecturers, both as a student, and later as a colleague. At the very least, I hope that it provides some inspiration for other lecturers when reflecting on how best to address these issues on their own terms.

SUGGESTED FURTHER READING

Carroll, J. and J. Ryan (eds) (2005). *Teaching International Students: Improving Learning for All*, London: Routledge.

Dove, L. and N. Bryant (2016). 'Law in translation: Challenges and opportunities in teaching international students in business law and legal environment programmes', *Journal of Legal Studies Education*, 33 (2), 263–91.

Macgregor, A. and G. Folinazzo (2018). 'Best practices in teaching international students in higher education: Issues and strategies', *TESOL Journal*, June, 9 (2), 299.

Makalela, L. (2018). '"Our academics are intellectually colonised": Multilanguaging and fees must fall', *Southern African Linguistics and Applied Language Studies*, 36 (1), 1–11.

Roberts, D. (2017). 'Higher education lectures: From passive to active learning via imagery?', *Active Learning in Higher Education*, 20 (1), 63–77.

'Teaching International Students: Pedagogical Issues and Strategies', *University of Michigan Center for Research on Teaching and Learning*, available at https://bit.ly/1J01vRu (accessed 4 April 2019).

Warwick, P. 'Ten Tips for Teaching International Students', *HE Academy Website,* available at https://bit.ly/2jBAuz8 (accessed 4 April 2019).

16. How to teach students from a range of different countries

Uche Ogwude

INTRODUCTION

You are into the first few minutes of giving a cohort their first teaching session. So far, everything seems to be going swimmingly. You have introduced yourself to the class, given an exemplary speech regarding the module's structure, format, assessments etc., and have pointed out to the class the session's learning outcomes from your dutifully prepared cutting-edge teaching materials. As you launch into the first topic of the day, an internal surge of confidence assures you that this is going to be a fun and rewarding experience for both you and the participating students. As the session progresses, you dutifully ask for feedback on the taught topic from the students – and this is when you remember (or re-remember!) that the cultural nuances of the individual students may colour the way they both interpret your request for feedback, and the way they give you said feedback. Consequently, as you face the class with your PowerPoint clicker weighing leadenly in one hand, you realise that you will have to devise an effective way to navigate the often treacherous waters of inclusively teaching this culturally diverse body of students. And quickly too!

If you teach in a UK university, the odds are that you have, at one time or another, faced a scenario similar to the one just described. The last few decades has seen a marked increase in the number of international students that attend institutions of higher education in the UK. Though the inclusion of these students from different countries has brought an enriching presence to our classrooms, it has likewise widened the definition of inclusive teaching for us teachers. Although I consider myself a fairly reflective teacher, there have been several occasions in my teaching career that have seen me at a near loss on how to handle the nuances presented by a culturally diverse classroom. In this chapter, I shall employ a reflective presentation of three case studies based on my personal experiences of teaching cohorts that have a varied mix of students from different cultures and countries. The case studies will: highlight common problem scenarios

I have encountered in my teaching practice thus far; the underlying reasons that create potential problems within those scenarios; what I did to adapt my teaching and learning activities as an active experimental response to those identified problems; and what the outcomes of my experimental responses were. It is my hope that sharing my personal tribulations and triumphs will provide the reader with some additional insight into how to tackle, and grow from, the challenge of inclusively teaching students from a number of different countries.

'WELCOME ONE, WELCOME ALL' – THE ART OF ACTIVELY RECOGNISING INTERNATIONAL STUDENTS

The very first teaching session I delivered was a first year undergraduate module in statistics for business students. I had gone into the classroom that day determined to make the subject matter accessible and engaging, and to that end had come armed with a portfolio of carefully crafted real-world scenarios to aid the teaching and learning process. About halfway through the session, however, I noticed that the class was effectively split into two groups: one that vocally engaged me in dialogue, and one that did not. After the first few weeks of observing this recurring pattern, I decided that the scenarios I had developed were not as fit for purpose as I had originally assumed. I went back to the drawing board, came up with new teaching materials and activities – and saw absolutely no change in the status quo. At my wit's end, I finally decided to directly ask them what the issue was. I knew (almost instinctively) that a blunt inquiry during the teaching session could potentially cause embarrassment and would most likely not yield favourable results, so I bided my time, and discreetly requested that three of the non-responsive students stay behind a few minutes after the class. As the class was emptying, I asked if everyone was getting on well with the module, and if they were satisfied with the way the sessions were progressing. After a few minutes, the grievances came tumbling out. One particular statement struck me at the time: 'You speak too quickly, and not just you. You all do. And we feel shy speaking.'

After that conversation, many things came into clear focus. The lack of engagement I had seen was not caused by the quality or alignment of the teaching materials, or the relative difficulty of the taught subject matter of statistical methods. The lack of engagement was, for the most part, a product of my failure to identify and address the inherent differences that occur in a cohort that has a large number of international students in it. I had been so focused on potential flaws in my teaching and learning activities that I had neglected the obvious. Even though I had been an international student myself, it had never really concretely occurred to me to place that cultural difference high on my list of teaching priorities. Over the remaining session of the module's run, I counteracted the observed problem by engaging in new proactive activities that I will now discuss.

One of the first changes I made was to cultivate what I call 'the soft art of active recognition'. Being an international student can be a daunting experience that can be eased by the simplest of gestures. For example, by taking pains to smile each time I made eye contact, I was eventually able to get a few of those previously silent students to contribute the odd sentence or two. I also began to take an active interest in the students themselves, and soon found that I could weave some of my teaching scenarios around cultural references that they were familiar with. So, for instance, before a session, I would do some homework on, say, the well-known Chinese actress, Gong Li, and then in class discuss the correlation between her appearance in a film and the film's financial success as a way to explain the statistical concept of dependent and independent variables. I found that taking pains to incorporate aspects of what was familiar to them into my teaching activities not only actively included the international students into the teaching sessions, but also broadened my horizons and enriched my teaching practice. The feedback I got from the student cohort was a testament to how effective this teaching tool was; I was told that I made them feel welcome, and that my teaching was 'broad' and 'interesting' (their words!).

Incorporating familiar cultural references in my teaching was one facet of the tool I used to ensure that the international students in my sessions were fully included in my teaching activities. A second facet was my active recognition of potential language barriers. One major reason behind the silence of international students is the fear of potential embarrassment they might suffer if they make what they perceive to be grammatical blunders in front of their colleagues. I got around that problem by doing two things: first, I openly and repeatedly reminded the class that no one has a perfect grasp of any language, and that a university learning environment is meant for holistic learning for everyone, lecturers included. Second, I made optimal use of the student's mobile phones. I find that all students find information faster if you ask them to check for additional information on their phones. Because most international students have translators built into their mobile phone web browsers, pertinent information is passed along faster if the students spend a few minutes on their beloved phones ferreting it out themselves. Apart from the advantage of passing information, asking the students to use their mobile phones in class gave them a strong measure of agency in their learning, dramatically increased their engagement in the sessions. As an illustrative example, if I wanted to explain the term 'probability' I would ask the entire class to check out the word on their phones. That way, the international students get to use their phones to translate the word without me potentially embarrassing them by painstakingly explaining what the word means.

I have used this art of active recognition in almost all my sessions thus far, and I find that it works well regardless of the taught subject matter, or the composition of my classes. The students integrated much more demonstrably with their domestic counterparts (especially when they volunteered to give extra information on a familiar cultural reference used as an example in class), and the entire cohort was all the richer for its mixed nature.

Teaching Tip
By acknowledging the international students, but not unduly pointing them out, I have been able to include them much more effectively than I did in my first weeks as a teacher.

'BUT WHAT ABOUT US?' – RECOGNISING THE VOICES OF THE DOMESTIC STUDENTS

The art of active recognition works well in fostering inclusivity because it pulls the international students' presence into the very fabric of well-designed teaching and learning activities. This learnt art, however, only truly works if care is taken not to neglect the domestic students in a mixed cohort. But why exactly? How do domestic students feature in the inclusion of international students? In my experience, I have found that the first few weeks determine the social dynamics between the domestic and the international students in a cohort. Often I find that international students paired or grouped with domestic students tend to withdraw into themselves. While actively recognising the international students helps greatly with this, there is also the potential attendant danger that the domestic students might feel neglected. If this happens, the tone of the classroom session would change, and that change will ultimately affect the international students. I will now present a case to illustrate this point.

A few years ago, I had a colleague who confided that he was having problems with getting the international students in his strategy class to fully engage with the session's activities. After I had eagerly suggested my then nascent theory of active recognition to him, he said he would try it, and would let me know how things turned out. Afterwards, he told me that the domestic students in his classes felt the sessions were gradually becoming all about catering to the needs of the international students, and so he had to consciously find a workable balance. When I heard this, I did some reflection, and came to realise that I had unconsciously placed emphasis on the learning experience and not explicitly on the need to accommodate the international students. I made sure to use cultural references that were familiar to the international students, and also used cultural references that were familiar to the domestic students; I made sure I spoke slowly during the teaching sessions, but I prefaced this by telling the entire class that I would try to speak that way because I was aware that I was a fast talker; concisely put, I performed the art of actively recognising the international students without antagonising the domestic ones. By openly focusing the nuances of active recognition on the session itself and not on the students directly, I was able to achieve a functional optimal balance.

As I mentioned in the previous case study, one of the measures I use to evaluate the efficacy of my modified teaching approach to international students is the feedback I get from them. It is important to note, however, that I have also gotten feedback from domestic students who appreciate the expanded cultural references used to deliver teaching outcomes.

Teaching Tip
Inclusivity, if well executed, allows for an altogether richer teaching and learning experience for students and teachers alike.

'ASSESSING YOUR ASSESSMENTS' – DESIGNING TRULY INCLUSIVE ASSESSMENTS FOR CULTURALLY DIVERSE COHORTS

Let us assume you actively recognise the international students in your cohort, and you also take care not to alienate the domestic students amongst them. If you do not add a careful consideration of your session's teaching assessments to your toolkit, you would be missing an important leg in the tripod necessary for effectively supporting and including international students. So, how exactly should a teacher assess his/her assessments to ensure that they are truly inclusive? What are the things and nuances to look out for? I shall mention a few of the practices that have worked well for me in this regard.

The first practice I employ towards developing and delivering inclusive assessments is attention to necessary supplementary teaching materials. This practice has two fronts which I shall discuss in turn: supplementary teaching materials focused on class sessions, and supplementary teaching materials focused on assessments and exams. I have already mentioned how I employ the use of mobile phones in the classroom. I have personally found this practice to be a godsend. If, for example, I am about to deliver a lecture on corporate governance, I would put a slide that says 'San Lu milk in China and Enron in the USA'. I then ask the students to spend a few minutes reading up on the case. The international students can privately read any necessary translations they need, while the domestic students (who in all probability would be weary of the oft-cited Enron case) get to learn something new about Chinese firms.

Another potential bugbear facing teachers revolves around getting students to read up on learning materials like case studies before class sessions. To achieve true inclusivity in this regard, I design my learning materials to have the essential information presented as succinctly as possible. This both provides the students with concise useable information aided by optimally placed infographics, and continuously hones my skill in transferring information as efficiently as possible. If a module I am delivering has, for example, case studies built into its teaching and learning activities, I always make sure I have simplified versions of the case study on worksheets that I distribute to the entire class before the activities begin. This way, any student that was initially intimidated by the original case study can put something down from the gleaned worksheet (and this works for both international and domestic students).

When it comes to supplementary teaching materials focused on assessments and exams, I always work from the first principle. This means that when I design any assessment, I always factor that I may have international students taking that assessment.

Teaching Tip
All students require a firm level of alignment between a module's teaching and learning activities, and its assessments.

With international students, these expectations are even higher because of the potential additional (language) barriers they may face. Consequently, the costs of getting this crucial alignment wrong are higher as well. As a result, I make sure that I design a module's assessments with the same pared down, direct 'feel' as I employ in the construction of the module's learning activities. There are little things that a conscientious teacher should always consider like (a) making sure that the criteria in an assessment brief are clearly, directly and simply worded, and/or (b) that the questions in an exam paper are as direct and to the point as possible. These seemingly small gestures have a massive impact in the way international students engage with assessments, and they also help expand the reflective boundaries of a teacher's philosophy on practice.

Most institutes of higher education here in the UK allow for foreign dictionaries to be made available to students during exams; unfortunately, most students are not made aware of that fact until rather late in the learning process. Reminding students about the resources made specifically available to them by your institution not only helps settle their minds and increases their confidence about any upcoming exams, it also helps demonstrate that your institution values the unique presence that they bring with them. These unspoken gestures of consideration in the end speak much louder than colourfully written passages in a marketing brochure ever could.

CONCLUSION

In this chapter, I have shared my experiences with inclusively teaching international students in UK higher education academies. I have shown how actively recognising international students during class sessions dramatically increases their inclusion into designed teaching and learning activities. I then went on to emphasise that active recognition has to be executed in a manner that does not alienate the domestic students in a taught cohort. Finally, I mentioned the need to design assessments in a fashion that facilitates the effective inclusion of international students.

Two more issues are worth noting in closing. First: there is no silver bullet for dealing with issues as nuanced as these. Because each cohort is different, you as an effective teacher have to adapt and mould these three suggested principles to fit whatever particular teaching circumstances you find yourself in. I have been fortunate enough to teach many classes with very large numbers of international students, but I still find myself having to spend the first few weeks of every teaching session in a constant state of adaptation. I always reflect on my teaching both during and after sessions, and this helps me greatly with the calibration process. Asking questions like 'What worked today? and 'What could have been better?' always helps shift the needle of my teaching practice in a positive direction.

The second issue worth noting is this: if I chose to share all the gaffes, mishaps and blunders I have encountered in my continuous struggle to inclusively teach international students, this chapter would have ended up looking very different indeed! As a teacher, you will always meet challenges that baffle and frustrate you. You could put 110 per cent into striving for inclusive teaching, and end up with one, two or more students that find your efforts lacking. I find that a good way to maintain a positive optimistic mindset/spirit about this topic is to approach it from the perspective of self-reflection and development. Doing this has allowed me to continuously strive towards improvement, and has also given me the ability to accept the occasional failures that I subsequently reflect upon and use as growth opportunities.

SUGGESTED FURTHER READING

Arends, R. and A. Kilcher (2010). *Teaching For Student Learning: Becoming an Accomplished Teacher*, New York: Routledge.

Ball, S., C. Bew, S. Bloxham, S. Brown, H. May, P. Kleiman, et al. (2012). *A Marked Improvement: Transforming Assessment in Higher Education*, 1st edn, York: Higher Education Academy.

Biggs, J. and C. Tang (2007). *Teaching for Quality Learning at University: What the Student Does*, 3rd edn, Maidenhead: McGraw-Hill/Society for Research into Higher Education and Open University Press.

Bloom, B.S. (1956). *Taxonomy of Educational Objectives: The Classification of Educational Goals*, New York: David McKay Company, Longman.

Brown, G. and M. Atkins (1988). *Effective Teaching in Higher Education*, London; New York: Methuen.

Carroll, J. and J. Ryan (2005). *Teaching International Students: Enhancing Learning for All*, London: Routledge.

Macgregor, A. and G. Folinazzo (2018). 'Best practices in teaching international students in higher education: issues and strategies', *TESOL Journal*, 2, 299–329.

Marangell, S., S. Arkoudis and C. Baik (2018). 'Developing a host culture for international students: What does it take?', *Journal of International Students*, 3, 1440–58.

Moon, J. (2000). *Reflection in Learning and Professional Development: Theory and Practice*. London: Kogan Page; RoutledgeFalmer.

O'Farrell, C. (2010). *Enhancing Student Learning through Assessment: A Toolkit Approach*, 1st edn, Dublin: Dublin Institute of Technology.

Race, P. (2007). *The Lecturer's Toolkit: A Practical Guide to Assessment, Learning and Teaching*, 3rd edn, London; New York: Routledge.

Thought 9

Matthew Olczak

Sometimes it can be extremely useful to provide students with a short video containing annotations and an accompanying voice-over explaining the material covered. The ShowMe app (https://www. showme.com/login) provides a great free (or for a small monthly charge for the premium version including increased cloud storage) way to easily produce such videos from the office or at home. For example, as illustrated by the below screenshot in Figure T2, I have used this app to produce videos to go through the solutions to mathematical problems and draw accompanying diagrams.

Via this app such videos can be recorded on an iPad using the built-in microphone and a low-cost stylus for the annotations. Useful features include options to vary the colour and style of the annotations, erase parts of the annotations and the ability to add fresh pages of content as you move through material. Furthermore, the videos can be recorded in bite-sized segments by pausing the recording whenever you choose to do so.

Figure T2   Example solution to a mathematical problem

Once the recording is complete, it is then very straightforward to upload a link to the video onto the programme Virtual Learning Environment or webpages. Students can then watch the videos in their own time on any Web-enabled device. Furthermore, students are able to pause and replay sections of the material as they see fit and this can help them to see clearly each of the steps involved. I believe a key benefit of providing support to students in this way is that it is flexible to accommodate students with varying mathematical abilities and approaches to practising problems. Overall, it provides a great way to support student learning and aid their revision. Evidence from my teaching shows that the students make considerable use of such videos and the feedback has been extremely positive. More generally, there would seem to be a wide variety of settings in which such videos could provide extremely useful complements to face-to-face classes, lecture-capture recordings and other online resources.

17. Teaching small groups

Alison McPherson

INTRODUCTION

Whilst the prospect of teaching a small group of students sounds delightful to many lecturers and teachers it can, and does, present its own challenges and in this chapter I will consider, based on my personal experience, what some of these challenges are and what can be done if they arise.

First, let's consider why you might have a small group. It may be that you are delivering a module on a programme which doesn't recruit large numbers or perhaps delivering a seminar or tutorial to a small number of students who are part of a larger cohort of students. In either situation the tips and techniques that work will be the same and, whilst many of these are effective in any teaching situation, I will look at them in terms of how they relate specifically to teaching small groups of students. The aim of this chapter is to give some tips that have worked for me and are applicable across cultures and contexts.

BUILDING A POSITIVE RELATIONSHIP WITH YOUR STUDENTS

Due to the nature of my subject (I'll let you guess what I teach as you read through the chapter!), I have been fortunate to teach small groups of students at both undergraduate and postgraduate levels. I have found that in small groups I have been able to get to know the individual students much better than in larger cohorts. This opportunity to build a more personal bond with the students has enabled me to be more flexible and tailor the sessions to meet the particular needs of individuals in the group whilst not losing sight of the needs of the whole group. Students really appreciate this much more personal interaction and this brings me to my first tip.

Teaching Tip
At the first teaching session greet every student at the door and welcome them individually to the class.

As you greet each student ask them their name. You can then use their first name in class when you need to; for example, to thank them for a contribution they have made. The individual will be made to feel special, the class will be impressed, and also studies show that hearing our name in a noisy room makes our brain pay attention!

Teaching Tip
Use a memory aid to help you remember student names. For example, link their name to someone famous or someone you know who has the same name. Repeating their name back to them or asking them to spell it can also help us to remember. Exercising our brain in this way is good for us too!

The introductory session with the small group is an opportunity to start to build rapport and let the students get to know you and your style and approach. It is important to use the first session to discuss and establish boundaries for behaviour, theirs and yours! What rules will there be for latecomers, mobile phone use, eating, drinking, treating others with respect, and any other standards you expect? What are their expectations of you and what commitments can you give to them? With a small group it is much easier to get all of the students to input into what they expect, both from themselves, their fellow students and you, their teacher. Establishing these ground rules, with the students' input, early in the programme or module allows you to refer back to them whenever you need to.

Teaching Tip
Make sure you get the students actively involved in setting rules and boundaries for the teaching sessions through discussion or interactive technology in the first session you have with them.

INDIVIDUAL DIFFERENCES

In small groups, differences in an individual student's behaviour may be more 'visible' to you and other students. As stated earlier, the small group gives you much more of an opportunity to understand your students' individuality than when they might be lost in a sea of faces in a large lecture theatre. I know that students differ from each other in many ways and cultural differences will play a part, but I have found one area of individual difference is particularly relevant here because it has a direct impact on student behaviour in groups and influences my approach to teaching. It is the difference between 'introverted' and 'extroverted' students.

An in-depth discussion of personality is not for this chapter, nor would it be useful to use labels to stereotype students, but thinking about some differences between individuals will help you to create learning experiences that work for all students. In some ways I have found that small group teaching can provide the more introverted students with a better learning experience; they feel less daunted and overwhelmed than they would be in a larger group and are therefore more likely to contribute to discussions and activities. However it also means that for some students it is less easy to hide.

Whilst psychologists might debate the finer points of introversion and extroversion, what I have certainly experienced as a teacher is that some students are less likely than others to ask or answer questions in class, appear less likely to participate in class discussions and seem to need more time to reflect than their colleagues. Yet, frequently, these 'quiet' students produce written work for assessments that is at least as good as other students. For those who are interested I have suggested a TED talk to watch (see Suggested Further Reading) which is both amusing and educational and offers an insight into this area.

Introverts are not necessarily shy. They spend more time thinking before they speak out and may prefer to interact with smaller, rather than larger, groups of people.

Teaching Tip
Watch for these introverted students early in the module, they will be the students who come up to you at the end of the lecture, or who email you with questions, seemingly a preferred option to asking you in front of the whole group.

MAKING IT WORK FOR ALL STUDENTS

If your group is particularly quiet you may have a group with more introverts than extroverts. If you are an extroverted teacher then quiet classrooms might not sit too comfortably with you. Extrovert teachers are more likely to enjoy, and expect, noise and activity as evidence of student engagement and learning but a group of introverted students quietly concentrating and completing their tasks are just as likely to be engaged and learning and can be just as rewarding to work with as a teacher.

Teaching Tip
Build in (even) more opportunities for (even) smaller group work and take the
opportunity to walk round and interact with each student on a one-to-one basis.
You might need to check their progress or see if they have any questions more
frequently as they will wait to be asked whereas the more extroverted students
won't wait, they will tell you!

With a small group, where students are predominantly more extroverted, the challenge might be to keep students focused and to keep the session on track to meet the learning objectives or outcomes.

Teaching Tip
Group activities and interactive debates and discussions are usually much
more engaging for all students and we all know that there is much evidence
that points to the importance of social learning in education.

However with a group of more talkative and participative students it might be more difficult to stop the conversation and regain their attention.

Teaching Tip
At the start of the activity stress to the students that there are strict time limits
and that sticking to them is important.

You may need to project your voice more to gain their attention when it is time to bring the whole group back together again. One very highly rated and effective teacher used to use the opposite tactic and lower his voice and this worked for him, however a whisper may not be heard over the sound of the hubbub; I have tried! A loud noise such as a clap of the hand or a whistle may work. I sometimes use a countdown clock or timer with an alarm and project it onto the screen.

Whatever your technique, with the more boisterous groups don't be surprised if you need several attempts to bring all of the students back. Some less experienced or less confident teachers and lecturers are sometimes tempted to recommence the session regardless while a few students are still engaged in talking to each other but it will do more for your credibility and the future behaviour of the students if you avoid this. I assertively make it known that there is a clear divide between when students are expected to engage and discuss the content with each other and when they need to pay attention to you. This is another point to cover when you are discussing boundaries in your introductory session! One useful technique suggested in assertiveness training is to repeat an instruction over and over again until it is heeded. I have used this and it works for me.

Teaching Tip
Use an attention-seeking technique to bring the group back together and don't restart the lecture until everyone is attending. Remembering students' names will be useful here!

In reality most groups of students will include a mixture of introverted and extroverted students and an issue that may arise here is where some students are more participative and talkative than others. In small group teaching it should be much easier to ask students questions and to facilitate a discussion around a topic but in some cases you might find that it is the same student or a few students who always respond to you and enter the discussion. Here you have to make a judgement about whether these students are becoming too dominant in the group and not allowing other students the opportunity to speak.

Teaching Tip
If the vocal student or students stay on topic then their contribution is often helpful and you can always draw in the quieter members of the group by asking for their views on what has been said.

Doing this also subtly draws attention to the other members of the group that the opinions of quieter members are also of value. Through careful observation it should quickly become apparent if the student is uncomfortable with this but often they will respond positively with a constructive contribution and their reaction often signals that they are pleased to contribute.

Teaching Tip
If they have no contribution to make or seem to be fazed by this approach then I consider it best to leave them and not keep asking. For some more introverted students being put 'under the spotlight' can be very uncomfortable.

Extroverted students may contribute a lot more to discussions. I never want to be rude or undermine these students but sometimes they will deviate from the focus of the session and take the discussion off at a tangent. Proponents of student-centred learning, which I am, place the teacher as a facilitator of learning and students as active participants in their own learning. However my view is that does not mean that I cannot be directive on occasions when it is for the good of the whole group. In the past I have found myself in a situation where one student has been so vocal and side-tracked the discussion to such an extent that I have noticed the other students starting to get irritated.

Teaching Tip
If you need to politely interrupt the student, ask other students for their thoughts, and point out that whilst their contribution is interesting the group needs to get back on topic. Again, assertiveness techniques help here!

The student-centred or learner-centred approaches have moved us away from the model where the student is a passive recipient of knowledge as in a traditional lecture. Although such approaches are also effective and to be encouraged in larger groups, they are practically much easier to manage in small group teaching.

A small group of students can be split into even smaller groups (I recommend groups of three) and given a task to prepare which involves researching and learning about a topic which they then are required to teach to the rest of the group. Whether you deliberately mix the quieter students with the more vocal ones or leave students to choose their own groups is up to you and will depend on your context.

In these groups I often find that the quieter, more reflective students fulfil an important role, just as in life and work generally. For example they often do thorough research and their reflective nature will often help the group produce a more in-depth piece of work. I have also found that introverted students are just as likely to volunteer to take the teaching role and this may be because they feel more comfortable when they have their material prepared, know what they want to communicate and are in a supportive environment. Depending on the group I will sometimes specify in the task brief that each member of the group must take a turn in conducting the teaching session. This shouldn't be too threatening for students in a small group.

I have had the pleasure of sitting through some great sessions where students have put considerable work into researching a topic and been very creative in the way they have taught it to the class, and feedback from students about this approach is invariably positive. The British Psychological Society article suggested for further reading (see link below) states that students who spend time teaching others show improved understanding and retention of knowledge overall.

Much attention is given to the flipped-learning or flipped-classroom approach and learning by teaching fits well into this category. In flipped learning students gain a basic level of knowledge and understanding of a topic before class. The teacher's role is that of facilitator and coach and the students, through collaborative activities and peer learning, deepen their understanding of their topic.

Teaching Tip
If you use the learning by teaching method you should always be prepared to fill in the gaps if students miss anything important out of their sessions as it is still important that the content is covered.
Put plenty of good quality reference material onto the e-learning platform and guide the students to the material they should use in their preparation.
You still need to facilitate these sessions and avoid overusing it as a technique as students might get bored.

CONCLUSION

Small groups mean that more students can be given the opportunity to participate in a wider range of activities and will feel more comfortable about doing so. But we mustn't forget that there are some students who are shy and lack confidence and in small group teaching these students may not be able to hide as they can do in larger lecture theatres. As I indicated earlier we need to be alert to these students and not put undue pressure on them to participate and engage. If we do the danger is that they will stop attending. Our students, whether introvert or extrovert, should be able to build on their individual strengths while they are with us and, as the article listed in further reading about extrovert and introvert leaders argues, there are many strengths shown by introverted leaders which organisations need.

And finally – yes, one of the subjects I teach is psychology.

SUGGESTED FURTHER READING

Farrell, M. (2017). 'Leadership reflections: Extrovert and introvert leaders', *Journal of Library Administration*, 57 (4), 436–43, Library, Information Science and Technology Abstracts, EBSCOhost, viewed 22 August 2018.
Jarrett, C. (2018). 'Learning by teaching others is extremely effective – A new study tested a key reason why', Research Digest, *The British Psychology Society*, https://digest.bps.org.uk/2018/05/04/learning-by-teaching-others-is-extremely-effective-a-new-study-tested-a-key-reason-why/ (accessed 4 May 2019).
Little, B. (2016). 'Who are you really? The puzzle of personality', TED2016. https://www.ted.com/talks/brian_little_who_are_you_really_the_puzzle_of_personality (accessed 4 May 2019).

PART IV

Technology-Enhanced Learning

18. Technology-enhanced learning activities and student participation

Bahar Ali Kazmi and Umair Riaz

INTRODUCTION

Does technology-enhanced teaching have the potential to improve student engagement? This chapter reflects on this question and provides two examples of technology-enhanced learning activities that can produce an active learning environment. The chapter serves as a practical guide for those who are already utilising virtual learning environments (VLEs), as well as inspiration for those who are reflecting on the potential of VLEs for teaching and active learning.

One of the tested ways of improving student satisfaction is to increase and enhance student participation, involvement and engagement in learning activities (Trowler and Trowler, 2010; Hennig-Thurau et al., 2001; Kotze and Plessis, 2003). Robust though this method may be, it is hard to put it into practice. The practical challenge stems partly from the current market-driven policy environment which tends to promote passive learning (Naidoo et al., 2011). Partly it originates, our experience tells us, from the variations in class size, age, gender, student learning experiences, and operational ease and excitement (from a student perspective) of engaging with learning activities.

Active learning assists students with higher-order thinking, which is central to achieving deep learning (Bonwell and Eison, 1991; Gibbs, 1992; Hanson and Moser, 2003; Scheyvens et al., 2008). The real task, hence, for us as teachers is to reimagine ways of using new learning technologies in designing and structuring curriculum, creating and patterning learning activities, planning assessments and providing feedback. Surely, the scope of this chapter is limited, and it is not intended to provide a template for designing a teaching programme or a module. Nonetheless, below we provide two examples of technology-based learning activities which we have successfully used to produce an active learning environment. Before we look into these examples, we would highlight that the aim is to highlight the use of technology-enhanced learning activities, focusing mainly on

177

VLE technology to increase student participation in the class and not on the use of social media. The examples clearly show the potential of technology-enhanced teaching and learning to improve student engagement.

The first example details the method of using online quizzes to build students' knowledge of accounting techniques, while the second example describes the method of using wikis in classroom sessions for teaching reflexive writing. Together they make it evident that the technology-enhanced teaching is a valuable tool for improving student participation in the learning process, as it can be used for a range of learning activities, i.e. from testing basic knowledge to developing critical and reflexive writing skills.

AUTOMATED DEVELOPMENTAL QUIZZES

Because of the 12-week timeline of a teaching period we often see learning as a linear process. Each lecture builds on the contents of the previous lecture. To put it differently, we move from simple to complex ideas. We assume that the learning of complex ideas needs a scaffolding of simple ideas. This way of developing knowledge is useful for the students of accounting who need to master the basics to perform complex accounting tasks. Our experience suggests that this is a useful method of building and assessing incremental learning related to accounting techniques. It is particularly a valuable tool to observe the performance of those students who do not have prior knowledge of accounting techniques. Below we briefly describe the process of setting up and conducting the systematic online quizzes.

We have established a set of online quizzes for a postgraduate 'Financial Accounting' module. The aim is to improve students' participation in classroom sessions and to build incrementally a scaffolding of basic accounting techniques needed to perform complex tasks. Between 60 and 70 students attend the module in each academic year. The in-class teaching resources and the associated supplementary readings for each week are used to draw the questions for online quizzes.

Each weekly quiz includes between 6 and 8 multiple choice questions which students can access online (Kahoot's website). Each student is given a weblink to log on to the website by using their mobile device to answer the questions by clicking on one of the options provided. The correct responses are then shown at the end of the session to the students for reflection.

Teaching Tip
Occasionally we withhold the results and repeat the same quiz which enables our students to reinforce their knowledge about accounting techniques.

Evidence suggests (Brothen and Wamback, 2004; Johnson and Kiviniemi, 2009), and our experience confirms, that online quizzes motivate students to complete assigned readings; increase participation in class discussion; and improve their performance in summative assessments. The adoption of developmental online quizzes as a formative learning activity has enabled us to engage students in collaborative learning activities such as group projects and classroom discussion.

Teaching Tip
We have observed that many students are positive about the process of feedback as they get to know their results instantly.

The feedback also encourages the students to participate in discussions and reflect on their individual and collective learning. More notably it facilitates those students who are, for various reasons, finding it hard to raise learning issues in lecturing sessions.

A set of developmental online quizzes is a valuable method for constructing steady formative learning environments for the students, often helping them to prepare incrementally but constantly for their summative assessments. It has enabled us to monitor the progress of the students and to identify learning gaps which require attention and action. The successful automation has also helped us with managing time efficiently. Based on our experience of designing a set of developmental online quizzes and automating it, we conclude with the following tips:

Teaching Tip
- *A set of developmental online quizzes can be used both as a planned (announced) or as a spontaneous (unannounced) learning activity to involve students in discussion and group projects.*
- *As a part of ongoing assessment, quizzes can encourage students to attend the lecturing sessions and enable them to observe the gradual improvement in their collective and individual performance, leading to improved results.*
- *An automated quiz system can make time management efficient, resulting in higher productivity.*

TECHNOLOGY-DRIVEN SITUATED LEARNING EVENTS

Our experience with a VLE shows that it can be used to produce an iterated learning experience which plays a vital role in helping the students to actively link diverse concepts and apply them to describe, explain and solve problems. We have successfully designed an undergraduate module by creating a series of 'doing' sessions which are linked with three or four different lectures and each lecture is linked with at least three 'doing' sessions. For example, we have informed the students that to successfully complete the negotiation game in an international context, you need to draw from the three online lectures on political, economic/legal environment; cross-cultural communication; and alliances/joint ventures. Likewise, to play the international human resources (HR) recruitment game, they were asked to go through the lectures on international human resources management (HRM); cross-cultural communication; and cross-cultural teams. We have accomplished this iterated design by uploading all the lectures and guidance on VLE, prior to the doing sessions. In short the VLE offers an opportunity to transform the classroom sessions into 'situated learning events'. Below we describe a situated learning event which we have organised for our MBA students.

Our new full-time MBA programme includes a core module which aims at helping students to recognise the characteristics of the business environment that hamper or facilitate socially responsible management and to examine, evaluate and design socially responsible and sustainable management strategies, processes and practices. This is an important core module as Corporate Social Responsibility (CSR) and Sustainability have not only become key features of corporate innovative practices, they are also an important aspect of the national and international Higher Education accreditation schemes (AACSB, EQUIS, AMBA and PRME).

The summative assessment of the module consists of a reflective analysis of MBA projects. The students are asked to examine and evaluate their own MBA project by using theories of CSR, sustainability or business ethics. The assessment responds to the learning needs of both aspiring and mature managers as it facilitates them to reflect on their own experience, evaluate and engage with diverse viewpoints, solve problems, and examine the beliefs, assumptions and ideologies that underpin theories and practices of CSR, sustainability and ethics and take ownership of their own learning.

This is a challenging assignment for two reasons: first, it is hard to examine your own lived experience which is a core of reflective writing. Second, we have observed that many students find it difficult to understand the demands of reflective text. Often, they submit an essay with limited reflective insights. The genuine understanding begins with our own lived experience. We only appreciate it when it transforms into a textual representation, informed by the theoretical focus of our learning.

In short, a reflective writing process requires techniques of introspective and retrospective analysis and methods of transforming that analysis into a scholarly text. To meet the needs of our students, we have designed a series of situated learning events (doing sessions) by using wikis. Below we describe its structure.

We have organised the module in a block. This format has allowed us to immerse the students in carefully designed and planned learning activities for seven days. The learning activities include short lectures, workshops, group work, guest speakers and documentaries. The programme typically has 48 contact hours. Each day for seven days, the students are asked to practise reflective writing individually and collaboratively for two hours in classroom sessions. At the end of each session, we provide feedback to the students.

We have used wikis (Blackboard) to organise the reflective writing sessions. According to the Blackboard help page, 'A wiki is a collaborative tool that allows you to contribute and modify one or more pages of programme-related materials. A wiki provides an area where users can collaborate on content. Users within a course can create and edit wiki pages that pertain to the programme or a programme group. Instructors and students can offer comments, and your instructor can grade individual work' (https://help.blackboard.com/Learn/Student/Interact/Wikis). In short, the wiki is a valuable tool to engage students in collaborative writing and it is this potential which we have used for designing and running the reflective writing sessions.

We have created five wikis for the classroom sessions. We have organised them sequentially, i.e. each wiki is analytically linked with the next wiki. The sequence of wikis is designed to enable the students to begin with their personal experience and step by step move to accomplishing a reflective text. Below we provide the sequence.

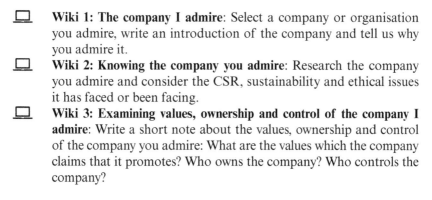

- **Wiki 1: The company I admire**: Select a company or organisation you admire, write an introduction of the company and tell us why you admire it.
- **Wiki 2: Knowing the company you admire**: Research the company you admire and consider the CSR, sustainability and ethical issues it has faced or been facing.
- **Wiki 3: Examining values, ownership and control of the company I admire**: Write a short note about the values, ownership and control of the company you admire: What are the values which the company claims that it promotes? Who owns the company? Who controls the company?

⌨ **Wiki 4: Strategising CSR**: Based on your analysis of values, owner-ship and control, propose a CSR objective which the company you admire can use to formulate its strategy.

⌨ **Wiki 5: Examining the company I admire**: Revisit the wikis about the company you admire and write a short note (4/5 lines) describ-ing a theoretical perspective which may explain their actions, behav-iour or strategies.

We have asked the students to work in pairs and engage each other in critiquing and posting comments. This collaborative process has helped the students to further develop the drafts of the wikis and engage in co-production of the reflective text. Furthermore, we have coordinated the collaborative process and provided instant feedback on the emerging analysis and text. This technology-enhanced situated learning activity has helped the students to learn the process of drafting a scholarly reflective text which they are required to submit as a summative assessment.

CONCLUSION

Student engagement is an essential condition to achieve desired learning outcomes. In developing technology-enhanced teaching for improving student engagement, we need to choose a learning technology that can be supported by the theoretical and practical insights (Lawless and Pellegrino, 2007). It is vital that the technology we will use in creating 'situated learn-ing events' cultivates creativity, social motivation and interaction and enhances curiosity and autonomy. The examples which we have shared in this chapter include collaborative, collective and personalised learning which may persuade less motivated and interactive students to participate actively in their own learning and can help institutions to increase knowl-edge about technology in curriculum activities.

It seems to us that the technology-enhanced teaching can be used to improve student participation and engagement. Increasingly, the new technology-based approaches to education are facilitating teachers to construct an active learning environment in which students actively produce their own learning. Our experience also tells us that technology is a valuable tool to construct an active and self-directed learning environ-ment and may contribute to building confidence and emotional wellbeing among our students. However, it can only produce the desired results if it will be adopted at the institutional level which means that it becomes integral to designing and delivering programmes and modules. If it will be used for some programmes and modules it may not satisfy the students, because they often use the traditional teaching and learning method as a benchmark for comparing the quality of the learning environment.

SUGGESTED FURTHER READING

Bonwell, C.C. and J.A. Eison (1991). 'Active learning: Creating excitement in the classroom', ASHE-ERIC Higher Education Report, Washington DC: School of Education and Human Development, George Washington University.

Brothen, T. and C. Wamback (2004). 'The value of time limits on internet quizzes', *Teaching of Psychology*, 27, 58–60.

Gibbs, G. (1992). *Improving the Quality of Student Learning*, Bristol: Technical and Educational Services.

Guzey, S.S. and G.H. Roehrig (2009). 'Teaching science with technology: Case studies of science teachers' development of technology, pedagogy, and content knowledge', *Contemporary Issues in Technology and Teacher Education*, 9.

Hanson, S. and S. Moser (2003). 'Reflections on a discipline-wide project: Developing active learning modules on the human dimensions of global change', *Journal of Geography in Higher Education*, 27 (1), 17–38.

Hennig-Thurau, T., M.F. Langer and U. Hansen (2001). 'Modeling and managing student loyalty', *Journal of Services Research*, 3 (4), 331–44.

Johnson, B.C. and M.T. Kiviniemi (2009). 'The effect of online chapter quizzes on exam performance in an undergraduate social psychology course', *Teaching of Psychology*, 36, 33–7.

Kotzé, T.G. and P.J. du Plessis (2003). 'Students as "co-producers" of education: A proposed model of student socialisation and participation at tertiary institutions', *Quality Assurance in Education*, 11 (4), 186–201.

Lawless, K.A. and J.W. Pellegrino (2007). 'Professional development in integrating technology into teaching and learning: Knowns, unknowns, and ways to pursue better questions and answers', *Review of Educational Research*, 77, 575–614.

Naidoo, R., A. Shankar and E. Veer (2011). 'The consumerist turn in higher education: Policy aspirations and outcomes', *Journal of Marketing Management*, 27 (11–12), Special Issue: On the Marketisation and Marketing of Higher Education, 1142–62.

Scheyvens, R., A.L. Griffin, C.L. Jocoy, Y. Liu and M. Bradford (2008). 'Experimenting with active learning in geography: Dispelling the myths that perpetuate resistance', *Journal of Geography in Higher Education*, 32 (51).

Trowler, V. and P. Trowler (2010). Student Engagement Evidence Summary. York: Higher Education Academy. Available online: https://www.sparqs.ac.uk/ch/E4%20Research%20and%20evidence%20base%20for%20student%20engagement.pdf (accessed 6 May 2019).

Thought 10

Elaine Clarke

On a postgraduate Global Business Planning module, as their summative assignment students had to write a business plan for an established company planning to enter a new country. The students selected the company themselves and had this approved by the tutor before starting. They were not required to undertake primary research within the company, but any secondary research about the company had to be based on genuine evidence available in the public domain. The scenario of the company planning to enter a new country was fictitious. Students had to choose a country and justify their choice, and this had to be based on a genuine analysis of macro- and micro-environmental factors and the particular sector in which they would be active.

Peer assessment in this case took the form of a work-in-progress review. I also added role play into the mix. Each group of students was to act as a Board of Directors for another group of students, who would be presenting their ideas to the Board before being given the 'go ahead' for the fictitious project. This took place a week before the students had to submit the final written business plan, so that they had time to absorb the comments from the Board and make any adjustments to their plan before submitting it. I was keen not to give them too long in between, so that the experience was still fresh in their minds.

We set up the classroom so that the desks formed a large board table in the centre, and the students who weren't presenting or role-playing the Board, sat around the edge of the classroom to observe.

I had prepared briefing notes for the Board in advance, as part of the assignment brief, and talked to them about the spirit in which they were to ask questions and provide feedback, and about 'throwing themselves into the role' just before the presentations started. They had already decided which role each was to play, for example Finance Director, Marketing Director, Managing Director,

Operations Director and Human Resources Director, although they were told that they did not have to limit themselves to questions related to their area. In most cases, the roles they allocated to each other mirrored the focus each had taken when preparing their own group's business plan.

After the presentation, the Board asked questions of the presenters, having been told that these should be around anything they needed to know to increase their confidence in the presenters' proposals. Students said they found the hardest part was to stay in role. However, once they got over the initial discomfort, most of them entered into the spirit of the task with relish.

Each Board member had a template on which to provide feedback to the presenting group. The template asked for ratings on a number of statements, for example 'You have shown that the country is a viable market for your products', 'You have shown that there is a gap in the market for your products', and so on. Each Board member rated these on a scale of 1 to 5, from 'strongly agree' to 'strongly disagree'. There was a section for open text at the bottom of the sheet, 'The Board needs to see further information on . . .', and 'Further suggestions for improvement'.

The feedback sheets were given to the presenting group at the end of the class, with the intention of allowing the group to enhance the work they had already done before they made their final submission in written form.

19. Cultivating students' digital literacy

Soumyadeb Chowdhury,
Oscar Rodríguez-Espindola,
Ahmad Beltagui and Pavel Albores-Barajas

INTRODUCTION

Business students recognise digital literacy as key to their future careers given the ubiquity of smart technology and the growing emphasis on digitisation across industries and contexts. Technical taught modules such as applications development, simulation, business software systems and information modelling involve more than just clicking commands and learning to code. At a higher level, these modules introduce a way of thinking about and solving problems. As Steve Jobs said: 'Everyone should learn how to program a computer, because it teaches you how to think.' The challenging question stemming from the quotation for teaching technology-intensive modules is, *how do you teach the students to think?*

Teaching students to devise solutions for a range of business problems, and realising them using technology, should help equip them with a combination of technical and managerial skills to contribute in their future workplace. Logical and creative thinking underlie these skills. For example, in the movie *The Martian*, Mark Watney approaches the challenge of surviving on Mars long enough to be rescued. He breaks this problem into smaller pieces, testing solutions for each and using available resources to put them into practice. In this situation, he survives by improvising, overcoming unexpected challenges and being willing to learn and adapt when things don't go to plan. Much closer to Earth, a similar approach can help build confidence and self-organisation – all key attributes that currently employers demand of business graduates.

Imagine you are a business student, with no prior technical experience, studying a module in which you program the computer to store customer information and help the organisation understand customer trends. First, you might perhaps perceive that learning to use technology means memorising syntax and process – analogous to learning a new language. Second, you might focus on searching and writing the solution, without understanding the problem, reflecting upon the needs and its connection to reality. Third, you might be intimidated with the technical elements, aka gobbledygook, which are necessary to implement the solution. Finally, you will want to get it right the first time, so when things go (inevitably) wrong, you may feel either incapable or demotivated. All these will be detrimental for you to realise the value of the module, and will lead to lack of engagement with the taught contents.

Now think about the tutor's perspective. How do you get this student to see that what they are doing is not just learning technology, but creating solutions to problems using technology? How do you get this student to learn to persevere? How do you get them to explore problems, test viable options and generate solutions? Digital literacy demands the ability to understand a problem and devise creative solutions. In this chapter, a model of design thinking is introduced to help business students overcome their fears and cultivate their digital literacy. This model will help to gain a range of skills, which can provide an edge when entering the workforce.

DESIGN THINKING

The term *design thinking* refers to a particular approach to problem solving that works when the problems are ill-defined and ready-made solutions are not available. Basically, these constitute the typical complex set of problems today's business graduates are likely to face in a world slowly being dominated by automation and artificial intelligence. But rather than a complicated, technical and intimidating process, we can view design thinking as what a child does when they encounter something new – test it, see what it does, try to break it and eventually figure out what it could be for, rather than be told how to use it. In the words of Herbert Simon: 'Everyone designs who devises courses of action aimed at changing existing situations into preferred ones.' Building on this idea, our model of design thinking has four key stages – *framing* a problem from a user's perspective; *envisioning* potential solutions to test; *iterating*, without fear of failure and, finally, *implementing* a solution using technology appropriate to the context. A diagrammatic representation of our model is shown in Figure 19.1. Let's look at each of these stages.

Framing

What characterises a good designer is their willingness to define both the problem and the solution simultaneously. This could at first seem counterintuitive for students who might be more used to being given a clearly

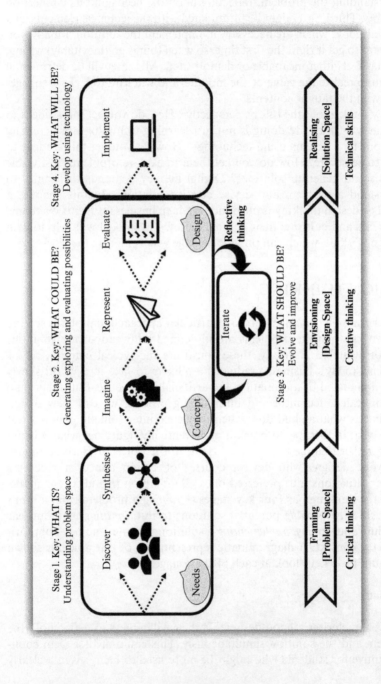

Figure 19.1 A model of design thinking for cultivating students' digital literacy

defined problem and a set of viable solutions to choose from. For example, if a competing company reduces the price of their product, how do we respond? Either we drop the price or raise the quality. This is a problem students can easily solve, but is this the type of challenge that managers will face in a modern, digital workplace? What happens if a competing company decides to do away with their products altogether and creates a digital platform instead?

Teaching Tip
The ability to gain a deeper understanding of the problem and sub-problems corresponding to the context is essential to developing sustainable and viable solutions. But students tend to focus more on the solution, i.e. the end product, rather than the problem itself.

Design thinking helps to understand what it is that customers want. What do they do with the digital platform? What makes them willing to pay for it? This recognises the mindset of the customers, by observing their interactions with technology. Finally, the problem is framed considering the customers' perspective and defines what needs to be created to give customers what they need. The challenge for students is to see that the problem itself needs to be defined. The key question is *What is the problem that we are trying to solve?*

Envisioning

When students have gone far enough in framing the situation and defining the problem, the next stage is to create possible solutions. They don't know whether all the solutions will work but have to try. This might at first seem counter-intuitive. Why not just solve the problem straight away? And again, if it is a problem that can be solved with existing knowledge, this makes sense. If, however, the problem is complex, involving multiple stakeholders, with conflicting objectives and lots of interrelated elements – the type of problem managers face daily – then existing knowledge is unlikely to help.

Teaching Tip
The key to problem solving is to accept that there is no one single and perfect solution that may solve all problems. Often students look for that one silver lining, without realising and assessing a range of potential solutions to a problem.

Design thinking encourages the students to focus not just on *what is* but on *what could be possible*. At this stage, it might mean leaving aside the issue

---

**BOX 19.1   FAMILIAR CONTEXTS FOR ABSTRACT
CONCEPTS**

In a modelling and simulation lecture, students represent physical models in a
virtual form, experiment in different conditions using a suitable technology and
finally propose a solution. Students are often intimidated by the technicalities of
building and testing the virtual form of a model in the computer, and their desire 'to
be the best' implies aversion to risk and failure, which limits their learning experience. To overcome the 'fear of failure' and 'getting it right straight away', models
and simulations are linked to more familiar contexts during class activities. For
example, the students work in groups to describe their experience in a coffee shop
by answering probing questions: where people enter and exit, the tasks involved
such as ordering and payment, how long these take, people behaviour and what
might make these things vary. Groups create sketches to represent these details
and then share these with a neighbouring group to comment. Next, the groups
address the comments by discussing and refining their sketches. There are several
benefits from this process of requiring students to create and debate representations: it encourages discussion between the students in an interactive learning
session; it shows the significance of iterative learning; it helps to move away from
the perception to get it right straight away and avert failure; it helps to develop an
appreciation of the importance of experimenting; and finally, it aids in linking theory
with practice to support decision-making.

---

of *how to implement* a solution. Students require the ability to imagine
possible options and to create representations that can be tested. For
instance, students looking at improving a café service might think about
creating a sketch of how it would look by changing the layout or rearrang-
ing the process using a process map. These representations are not the final
deliverables, but aid in pitching the idea to a potential user and then testing
its viability, before committing time or effort.

Iterating

Generating, exploring and evaluating viable options in problem solving are
very important, but only if we accept that not all the options will work out.

Teaching Tip
*The ability to accept and learn from failure is perhaps one of the factors that
distinguishes those who succeed in business. But this idea is hard for students
to grasp.*

Partly, the challenge lies in accepting that the *idea* may fail but the *individual*, if they learn from what happened, does not. The idea might fail,

but testing it provides additional information to incorporate into the next iteration to improve the ultimate solution. At this point students will start to build a clearer picture of *what should be*. Now, when they iterate – that is repeat the steps in the envisioning stage – there is more certainty about the proposed solutions. Without the safety net that iteration allows, it is natural for students to avoid taking risks. Through this envisioning stage, however, students overcome the fear of failure and develop the ability to learn through iteration, which are essential skills for the workplace.

Realising

So far there has been little mention of technical skills such as learning a programming language, understanding modelling frameworks, and using a simulation software, which students harness through the technology-intensive modules. This has been left until the end of the process employing technology to realise the potential solutions because it is not as challenging as all the thinking that precedes it. What students need is not just the ability to implement the solution using technology, but the ability to interpret, learn and improve.

Teaching Tip
Understanding the problem and the potential solution will make the implementation less challenging and intimidating. However, students often start and delve more into the technical elements.

Having completed the previous stages, the key here is to relate the design to the reality, in this case to understand what a specific procedure means and why it should or should not be used. The task is to translate what has been learned through iterations into the finished product. The key question here is what the final solution *will be* as well as how and why. Learning technical skills is not about mastering the discipline by memorising but instead it is through understanding how the technology can help to organise and translate thoughts into actions.

Student Engagement

The above design-thinking process, which involves teaching technology-intensive modules through more familiar mediums, can help to make the learning sessions less intimidating and more interactive. This approach encourages active learning, which will eventually lead to engagement and enhance student learning experience. The imperative is to help the students appreciate the application of higher-order thinking through metacognition,

---

BOX 19.2   ACTIVE LEARNING THROUGH A PAIR-
PROGRAMMING APPROACH

Students learning to code for the first time tend to focus on the end result, without understanding the process, which is usually viewed as a black box. For example, they look for a sample programme to execute, without understanding what it means and why it is there. To overcome this challenge, a pair-programming approach is used to encourage collaborative learning and help students understand what they are doing – not just get the right result. The session starts by dividing the class into pairs, with each given a distinct program containing multiple errors. Students work like a detective in a crime novel, using critical thinking to uncover the errors (in this context, the culprit). The task encourages them to examine each line of code and, with reference to taught elements, question what it should do. And narrowing down the source of the error leads them to iteratively correct the code – so it becomes natural to try small modifications and test the effect they have. The activity enables students to 'get their hands dirty' with the code, in a collaborative environment and with support from the tutor. There are several benefits stemming from this approach of requiring students to rectify errors in a program by working in pairs: it shows the significance of collaborative learning; it aids the students to harness technical skills by developing a better understanding of the program and its corresponding logic; finally, it helps to develop an appreciation of the significance of iterative learning.

---

problem solving and creativity. Table 19.1 presents a summary of key skills harnessed during each design-thinking stage, and some examples of activities which could be used to increase student interest and engagement.

CONCLUSION

Design thinking offers students and teachers a way of approaching problems and realising the potential solution using technology. The technical skills might at first appear to be the most intimidating challenge from the students' perspective. The real challenges, however, are critical thinking, understanding the context, creative thinking, generating, representing and testing viable solutions, and iterative learning, to refine and improve the solution prior to investing time, money and effort in its implementation. Indeed, any time when the student (or future manager) is faced with a complex technical problem, the solution to which is difficult to comprehend, a design-thinking approach should be used. So, whether creating a new app, deciding on a new product to launch or rescuing an astronaut from Mars, the higher-order thinking skills inherent in a design-thinking approach will always be relevant.

Table 19.1   *Activities to enhance student engagement*

Stage	Skills	Activity
Framing	● Critical thinking ● Observation ● Goal setting	Show students a visual presentation, depicting a situation. Tutor should pose questions to help identify and define the problem. Divide the class into small groups (3–4). Students will share their answers within the group. Next, each group will summarise the discussion and post them through an online discussion forum. Groups will reflect on the posts, which will lead to further discussion in the session. Session will conclude with the tutor reflecting on the discussion and providing a definition of the problem, which has emerged from the exercise.
Envisioning	● Creative thinking ● Problem solving ● Analytical thinking	Divide the class into groups of 3–4. Each group is required to build two towers, one using plastic straws, and the second using spaghetti sticks. Each tower should be built as tall as possible and able to carry the weight of a pen. Provide each group with an equal number of straws and sticks, and one adhesive tape. Groups should spend 25 minutes building the towers, and then spend 10 minutes answering the following two questions: what is the key to building the tallest tower, and what they will do differently if they were to start all over again. Session will conclude with the tutor reflecting on the answers presented by each group and highlighting the significance of 'thinking' before 'doing'.
Iterating	● Reflective thinking ● Experimenting ● Decision making	Give all students time to visit the university cafeteria and then ask them to sketch a process diagram, which describes the business's operations. Next, divide them into groups of 3–4. Each group should come up with a process diagram, which is informed by their sketches. A peer group is assigned to receive feedback, and further refine the diagram. Finally, all the diagrams are posted on a whiteboard, and each group is asked to vote for the one that best represents the

Table 19.1 (continued)

Stage	Skills	Activity
		operations. Session will conclude with the tutor encouraging students to appreciate the importance of consolidating views and refining them through feedback.
Realising	• Technical • Communication • Dissemination	A student is given the image of a common object – a tree, a car, etc. The student is asked to describe the object to the rest of the class, so that they can draw it. Students pair up and discuss their drawings and any differences between them. Then, the tutor shows the actual drawing and discussion is encouraged about any differences in the drawings from students, to highlight the importance of communication and achieving a shared understanding. This activity is suitable for small groups comprising 10 to 20 students, and can be further refined to suit larger groups as well.

SUGGESTED FURTHER READING

Beltagui, A. (2018). 'A design-thinking perspective on capability development: The case of new product development for a service business model', *International Journal of Operations and Production Management*, 38 (4), 1041–60.

Dunne, D. and R. Martin (2006). 'Design thinking and how it will change management education: An interview and discussion', *Academy of Management Learning and Education*, 5 (4), 512–23.

Gustein, A. and J. Sviokla (2018). '7 Skills that aren't about to be automated', https://hbr.org/2018/07/7-skills-that-arent-about-to-be-automated (accessed 22 August 2018).

Knuth, D.E. (2007). 'Computer programming as an art', In ACM Turing award lectures (p. 1974). January, ACM.

Neck, H.M., P.G. Greene and C.G. Brush (eds) (2014). *Teaching Entrepreneurship: A Practice-Based Approach*. Cheltenham: Edward Elgar Publishing.

Newell, A., J.C. Shaw and H.A. Simon (1959). *The Processes of Creative Thinking*, p. 2, Santa Monica, CA: Rand Corporation.

Phan, V. and E. Hicks (2018). 'Code4Brownies: An active learning solution for teaching programming and problem solving in the classroom. In Proceedings of the 23rd Annual ACM Conference on Innovation and Technology in Computer Science Education (pp. 153–58). July, ACM.

Thought 11

Uche Ogwude

'If you want A's, you may have to give Zzz's.'

Early on in my teaching career, I noticed something rather peculiar. Although all modules started off with a relatively enthusiastic student cohort, the run of the semester time almost always saw a rather gradual reduction in the number of students that attended classes. There have been many explanations for this phenomenon.

'The students get lazier as the semester progresses.' 'No, the students just get bogged down with piling amounts of work and then start cutting down on attending classes.' 'Actually, it's the recorded lectures that are to blame. Why would students come to class when they can simply view the recorded lectures online?'

All these explanations seem plausible, but I always felt sure there might be something else, something more mundane, some unrecognised variable that caused this kind of attrition rate in student attendance. A couple of years ago, I had a sudden flash of insight while delivering a seminar of quantitative methods for business students. The session was progressing as it normally had when I decided to give a 10-minute break after the 20-minute mark. Now, this seminar was an hour long, and would usually have been taken as a continuous stretch for about 45 minutes. I noticed that the break did seem to perk things up a bit towards the end of the session, and I made a mental note of it.

That teaching semester ended, the summer holidays came and went, and a new academic year commenced. Armed with a budding theory, I made a point of telling the new cohort (during the maiden session) that the seminars would be an hour long, but would be split into two 20-minute halves with a 10-minute break in between. There were no miraculous exaltations, and no decided gestures of appreciation from the students. I did notice, however, that the number of students that attended all the seminar sessions was larger than the numbers produced by the previous cohort. Of course, no two cohorts are alike, and it was possible that the increased numbers had nothing to do with the increased number of attendees. Still, I thought it was a rather good practice and I decided to keep it amongst the tools of my teaching skills set.

Fast forward to the 2017/2018 academic year. As usual, I mentioned the 10-minute break rule to all the cohorts I was delivering sessions to. Unlike previous years, however, I had resolved to ask the students themselves what they thought about having gap periods during taught sessions. When I did ask, the results were interesting. I was told that the rest periods did not necessarily encourage attendance, but that they ensured that those sessions that were attended were fully engaged in. They also reminded me of the fact that, in most cases, the breaks were spent in informal discussion which they also found useful in a roundabout kind of way. Basically, teaching breaks may not bring students to a classroom, but they definitely help keep them engaged while there.

20. Designing and teaching an online module

Jon Taylor, Richard Terry and Matt Davies

INTRODUCTION

The development and delivery of online learning has become part of the university teacher's role, even if that teacher is primarily engaged in face-to-face teaching. The need to capture the market of students who want to study in a less traditional way has become a requirement of many universities. In this chapter we are going to look at the development and implementation of online materials. The development approach that we are going to follow relates to the ADDIE model of instructional design – a process of Analysis, Design, Development, Implementation and Evaluation.

> ADDIE is also an iterative process, where each phase can suggest improvements in earlier phases. This attribute encourages designers to monitor instructional development and evaluate whether results fulfil learning goals. The model's iterative nature also lends itself to rapid prototyping. A learning model can be deployed, feedback gained from learners, adjustments made at the appropriate ADDIE stage, and the module updated to better match instructional goals. (Mayfield, 2011)

ANALYSIS

This comprises designing an effective online module – an analysis and understanding of what is needed – who are the learners, programme objectives and the delivery environment.

The programme philosophy will dictate what needs to be developed and delivered. This needs to be communicated by the programme director: if the vision is not there, press and participate in dialogue until it is! You will need an understanding of the following:

- Details of expectations at the programme level – the choice of curriculum design approach has a huge impact on resource and support implications – ideally there should be a design rubric for the programme.

- Are there accreditation factors to consider? For example, a requirement for certain types of exam, or certain amounts of synchronous engagement – again the programme director should be guiding here.
- Is there a template that will constrain your pedagogical or technological choices?
- What sort of development timescale is in place? (This can be particularly important where you engage with an 'external' development team – do their requirements for your time fit in with your availability according to other teaching/research demands?)
- What sort of support is available to you (pedagogical, technical, operational)?
- What approval processes will the module have to go through locally; what are your responsibilities?
- Who is your audience? Global audience; part-time? How will this influence their expectations?
- How will success be measured? Student retention rates, satisfaction, pass rates?

What is an Online Module and What Learner Expectations Might we Consider?

Definitions have blurred considerably over the last few years as different blends have appeared. Our own experience of online learning has focused on an environment in which teaching and learning is delivered and facilitated primarily via the Internet. This typically means delivery of learning content and instructions via a virtual learning environment, with learning dialogue primarily occurring asynchronously via discussion boards, wikis etc., and real-time engagement using a virtual classroom. The programme expectations regarding the type of content and engagement need to be understood before development begins if the student is to have even the most basic element of consistency between modules.

Today, online learning within business schools is associated with expectations of flexibility and interaction. The learning design needs to consider who the learners are and to accommodate their needs. While the motivation might be there in your students, empathising with what it is to be an online learner on your programme needs to be explored with them through induction at both the programme and individual module levels, and through setting and understanding expectations of both learner and teacher. Fundamentally, you are creating a learning environment – not just delivering content – and this requires engaging in instructional design to scaffold learning and bring different elements of content and dialogue together.

This will be a Learning Experience for You: New Skills will Need to be Developed

Before you get started, think about your own skill set. An understanding of the programme delivery philosophy, the development process and support available to you should allow you to identify any gaps in your own knowledge. It is likely that the experience will be as much a learning process for you as it is for your students (Debattista, 2018). While you may be an expert in your subject area, you are going to have to consider new aspects in the way you teach and a whole range of available technologies and the principles of instructional design. There is a massive temptation to let the technology take the lead – 'I will use it because it is there' – which is potentially dangerous to the student learning experience, risking overloading students with different 'tools'. We are also in an era where students may prefer and use different digital capabilities in their learning which are different to those you yourself use. They may choose to use their own virtual spaces (such as WhatsApp for example) in which to engage in group work, for example, and indeed decisions may need to be made about the degree to which you follow them into these new spaces, or keep the formal learning space within the virtual learning environment (VLE).

Teaching Tip
Talk to students about the way that they use technology in their everyday lives, and consider whether this can be incorporated into the learning materials you develop.

Consider the Extent to which You are Being Directed and Supported in the Development and Delivery Process

It is highly likely that support will be available to you, whether it be from within your faculty at a university, or an external commercial company focused on learning design and development. Any specialised partner will bring advantages to the programme and module design process, typically including instructional design, an understanding of current technology and pedagogy and experience of adapting face-to-face modules to online delivery. Critically, when working on individual modules, they should have that understanding of the broader programme expectations and learner needs and the developmental and operational programme issues as the development processes takes place. This overview is essential in supporting a level of consistency to a programme.

There is the potential for huge variations in the nature of this support, so we strongly recommend that you take time to understand what is available to you and develop a working relationship that works for you in your local context. Understand what is being asked of you and engage in pilot work to test the relationship, and don't be afraid to push back if the output is not what you wanted. In the delivery phase, support is likely to shift towards existing programme teams. Again, be sure of who is doing what and when, and specifically what your responsibilities are – the critical importance of 'little details' such as setting up groups, discussion spaces or scheduling webinars will become very apparent.

Teaching Tip
Identify what technology you are going to be using, and be clear whether there are any specific features that you must include in your materials for consistency reasons.

DESIGN

We have found that the design process is vital for effective understanding of what is to be developed and to understand the time allocation needed to develop the various elements that need to be in place to teach online. At the end of the initial design phase you should have identified the learning objectives; the pedagogy; the technology to be used in delivering your module; and the route that the student will be taking through these. There are numerous instructional, eLearning and curriculum design models available. We have found that both the ADDIE and ABC models are useful tools for selecting the appropriate (or perhaps available) pedagogical approaches to meet the required learning outcomes. We advocate an approach where the module developer considers the learning outcomes and maps these to activities and resources, and then considers appropriate technologies to facilitate and engage.

> In the online learning environment, just as in the traditional courses, consideration of alignment of instructional content and assessment measures with learning outcomes is critical to successful learning outcomes and satisfaction. (Kauffman, 2015)

Identifying the Type of Content You will Need to Create or Source from Elsewhere

You will need to create content that transfers information. This is a combination of instruction and guidance on the learning journey, what to do, why, how and when, and probably lecture-type content where you introduce specific subject matter. Some of the teaching content might be sourced from elsewhere, but beware of reliability issues of other web resources (for example, YouTube content comes and goes and is barred in some regions) and geographical limitations of resources such as Box of Broadcasts. Be realistic in the sort of recorded media that can be created in-house, particularly the design and maintenance issues related with even the most basic multimedia content.

Teaching Tip
If you are developing materials for an international audience remember that some sources are not accessible in all countries.

Identifying the Type of Communications, Engagements or Individual and Group Activities that are Needed

This element will be greatly conditioned by both the type and expectations of the student cohort. If they have signed up for a specific model, you need to know and adhere to this – again this links back to the stage one analysis of what is expected/required for the programme.

Business school students, especially those with experience, are likely to expect to be able to network and share experiences. Undergraduate students may need a more traditional approach of delivery, followed by engagement. A key element here again is that students understand that there is a reason for engaging:

> Where possible, appropriate and well-designed communication tasks that align with the learning objectives of the course may be a way forward to enhance academic retention. (Rientics and Toetenel, 2016)

You might also want to consider the role of tutor-to-student communications during the module.

Teaching Tip
Additional emails or announcements that remind students of what is coming up next, preparation or group work before an event can be very successful in motivating and keeping students engaged in online modules.

Activity design will consider what engagements occur between the student(s) and resources or tools and other people (students, tutor) over a determined period of time with the aim of meeting defined learning outcomes. Will you evaluate this learning and if so how? Can this learning be collated and be reflected on by the learner(s) in online journals or ePortfolios?

Group work requires particular design consideration and there is perhaps a tendency to rely on group work online in the same way that we do in face-to-face teaching. However, for online learners there might be a considerable organisational challenge in effectively engaging in group work, which can considerably reduce the flexibility of their studies.

Some key considerations include the following: do you want groups to work unsupervised, or do you need to be able to observe and guide? Will group tasks run over days or weeks or will they take place in webinars? Group size, if too large, will enable members to potentially 'hide' and not engage. However we need to consider perhaps that part-time students may need a bit of flexibility and realistically will not find it easy to engage in everything. Design again will be driven by an understanding of learner needs (plus a dose of reality regarding what and how you can afford to facilitate and support).

Structuring the Resources in the VLE

In initial development you might be given considerable individual freedom in how learning is presented in the VLE. However, as you progress you will gain greater awareness of what structures appear to work well and there is often an increasing drive from some programmes to have a level of consistency between modules to enhance the learners' experience. A key question to be answered and understood in your own context is how will you structure your content in the VLE, for example, by week, by theme, by resource type?

For a face-to-face or blended learning programme, it will be very tempting to build your content around a weekly or fortnightly model, especially if there are weekly face-to-face elements, and regular if less frequent seminars. For online you can be more creative and perhaps build your content around themes or topics, which may span several weeks. Design becomes an important issue in the eLearning environment as both the tools available and the layout choices in the VLE can represent a very blank canvas into which a horrendously complex menu can be inserted! Hopefully, templating, guidance and support has been considered at the programme level. If you're working on your own, go back to the student journey and consider what information and tools they need to engage with at particular times. This will often help you to produce a logical and simple structure.

BOX 20.1   PRACTITIONER INSIGHTS 1: DESIGNING THE MODULE

STRUCTURING CONTENT ON THE VLE

My experience of running online modules has transformed my use of the university's Virtual Learning Environment (VLE). I had previously regarded the VLE as merely a repository for learning materials and paid little attention to how learning materials should be organised and labelled.

But with my first exposure to online delivery, it soon became apparent that having a clear structure for the content, and using labels which made the navigation as intuitive as possible, are critical to a positive online student experience.

Online students will soon become frustrated and discouraged if it is not obvious to them how they find what they need, or if it takes several clicks through a seemingly never-ending hierarchy of content folders to get there. But as well as being less frustrating for students, a clear and easy-to-navigate structure and more descriptive labels for content can also help students with their learning too, as it helps them to understand the overall structure of the module and make connections between the different areas of content.

My advice is to first organise content around topics rather than by type. So, for example, whereas I might previously have created different sections for each of the following: learning content, exercises and formative tests, I now organise this content so that it is embedded within the content sections for each topic.

Second, use labels which describe content in a way which helps the student. So, for example, whereas I might previously have described content sections using vague labels such as 'Week 1' or 'Unit 1', I now use more informative labels such as 'Unit 1: Introduction to Financial Accounting'.

Having a clear structure for content on the VLE is helpful for all students of course, so I now apply these same principles to the design of face-to-face modules too.

DEVELOPMENT

The design for a module should ideally be shared and evaluated before development takes place: is it feasible, does it fit with the programme director's vision and programme specification? It is really essential to engage in some form of prototyping that involves all the key resource types and engagement activities for one topic to evaluate the design in the chosen environment. Here, again, the relationship with the developer or wider team is critical. If you have any particular needs such as the ability of students to share their own content in virtual classroom sessions, this is the point to meet with the technical experts to be sure that it is feasible in your available learning environment. If it is, the wider team will be able to consider additional induction requirements. If it isn't, you've still got time to look at alternative approaches.

Allen (2006) argues that the scope of development has gone beyond the individual, and now involves a team; this is again particularly pertinent to online learning, which involves increasingly specialised elements rarely found in one individual. Any team approach will require timescale considerations: allow a six-month period if you are working on a single module; allow for lead-in times for software or hardware to be ordered; if working with a developer you may need to compromise according to mutual availability; there will be a review phase and potentially edits to be made, and so on.

Creating Content – Identifying the Tools

If there is a need to create recorded content ensure it is reusable as it can be a considerable investment in time. Experience has shown us the benefits of using tools which are locally supported by a team who are able to assure that output meets accessibility requirements.

Teaching Tip
Avoid dates, mention of module numbers, and the sort of things that change regularly and might require you to re-record regularly!

Presenting the Learning Materials to Students

Clearly state the aims and learning outcomes of each section. Provide an introduction to each section, including the sort of engagements and type of resources they will be working with – and if it's not already obvious, over what time frame.

A sample structure for presenting content is illustrated in Figure 20.1.

IMPLEMENTATION

The implementation of an online module requires careful consideration, especially in relation to student numbers and the implications for tutor support (how many students can a tutor effectively support?), setting up groups, discussion boards, scheduling virtual classroom sessions, setting up assessment hand-in tools etc. Depending on local circumstances this might be you or other support staff setting these up, but as your name is on the module it is worth being sure! When modules grow beyond pilot phases, there may be training or induction needs as new tutors are drawn in to support facilitation.

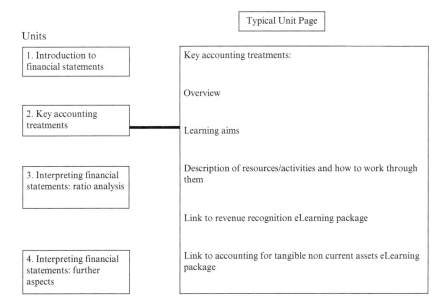

Figure 20.1   Presentation of content

Teaching Tip
Student induction is of critical importance because it can help:

● *Set and explore expectations*
● *Provide an opportunity to try out communication tools*
● *Iron out technical issues before formal teaching starts.*

EVALUATION

An easily neglected element of the above process is acting on any evaluation that is made both during and after the module has run. Mayfield (2011) suggests in the context of the ADDIE model that we consider:

> 1. How well were learning goals met? 2. How efficient were the training methods? 3. Were there any technical problems? 4. Are there any new training opportunities? (Mayfield, 2011)

All of these can be recorded and reviewed if a mechanism is put in place (for example via a programme-wide review) and a timely approach is taken to refine subsequent module runs. Student input on their experiences is key to ensuring that expectations are met and addressed and to update

BOX 20.2   PRACTITIONER INSIGHTS 2: DEVELOPING THE MODULE

CONTENT CREATION

When preparing for my first online module, I remember my main concern was the creation of a series of eLearning packages which were an attempt to provide students with relevant subject matter content. Initially, these packages mirrored the content of the equivalent face-to-face modules and therefore these packages would cover several different areas of content and might take students 45 minutes or more to complete.

I soon realised, however, that smaller, 'bite-sized' content packages focusing on a single topic would not only be more effective for students but would also be more flexible, as these 'chunks' of content could be reused more easily in other modules which might involve a different combination of topics.

Several years and several online modules later, my approach has evolved further. I now focus much less on creating additional subject matter content – not least because there are so many sources of good quality content available already – but instead on designing content and activities which promote and support student engagement and learning.

So nowadays, 'content creation' for me involves the following:

1. Creating an overall learning pathway for the module which is derived from the desired learning outcomes and involves creating a variety of activities and formative assessments to achieve the following:
    a. to help students to engage with and build confidence with the content;
    b. to accommodate a range of different learning styles; and
    c. to provide a means through which I am able to monitor the students' engagement and performance in the module and intervene as appropriate.

Examples of these activities include:

    a. Weekly discussion board activities requiring students to research and then share how that week's accounting concept is applied within an organisation of their choice, which I then review and provide feedback;
    b. Group wiki pages which encourage students to work collaboratively to solve accounting challenges;
    c. Weekly formative multiple-choice tests which provide an opportunity for students to practice the application of concepts learned and receive automatic feedback on their progress.

2. Creating short text or video content which provide:
    a. context, to help students understand why a topic is important and in what situations a tool or concept can be applied;

b. topic summaries, to help students appreciate both the key content and learning objectives for a topic, to help students make connections between content areas in the module and, if appropriate, with the module assessment, and, finally, to help students gain an overview of the work required.

BOX 20.3 PRACTITIONER INSIGHTS 3: DELIVERING THE MODULE

It might be tempting to think that there is little or no work required of a tutor in the 'delivery' of an online module. On the contrary, I would suggest the delivery of an online module can be just as, if not more, time-consuming than a face-to-face module. For me, the key to the successful delivery of an online module is frequent, clear, consistent and encouraging communications with students.
I adopt the following routine:

- On Monday morning I post an announcement which is emailed to students welcoming them to that week's topic, briefly explaining its importance, providing an overview of what they will be doing that week and reminding them of any upcoming events (such as virtual classroom sessions) or deadlines, and that explains what if any preparation is required, what resources they should bring with them, and provides direct links to the relevant areas of the VLE where these are located;
- On the day of a virtual classroom event I post a further announcement which serves as a reminder of the time of the upcoming event and of the preparation and resources required;
- On Friday afternoon I post another announcement which reminds students of what they should have been working on and reminds them of that week's discussion board activity, recommending they post their response by a specified deadline.

Online students can become confused by even small differences in the wording used so it is best to use consistent language in your communications. Do not expect students to necessarily recognise that when you refer to 'Worksheet 1' and 'Task sheet 1' you are describing the same document!

I save these announcements in a Word document which makes it easier for me to reuse in the future.

I also think it is important to adopt a friendly and encouraging tone in communications with students, particularly when responding to individual discussion board posts. Try to find some merit even if a post has very little, and even if a student's post seems negative try to respond positively. For modules with large cohorts rather than responding to each individual post it can be more appropriate to provide an overall summary, in which case again accentuate the positives and try to adopt a sympathetic and encouraging tone when addressing misconceptions, and in which case rather than 'naming and shaming' ensure your response maintains the anonymity of the original authors.

ourselves on how online learners study. Much of this information can be gathered from conversations in the virtual classroom, before or after the formal teaching time.

Teaching Tip
Module leader gatherings, to share how other modules are being taught and sharing experiences of how effective different approaches or technologies have been used, are of great value in enhancing the quality of modules over time.

CONCLUSION

The development and delivery of online modules requires time and planning and a different skill set compared to on-campus teaching. More development takes place beforehand, instructional design skills are needed and have to be developed, often involving partnerships with a wider group of stakeholders, and a greater attention to detail and clarity of instruction is essential. Facilitation is different, but can be incredibly rewarding as access is opened up to diverse learners who are increasingly savvy about what it means to be an online learner, and actively begin to take 'ownership' of their own learning. We have also seen that the increased time taken in development is offset over time as reusability factors become apparent and content and learning design is shared between programmes.

SUGGESTED FURTHER READING

ABC Curriculum Design Model. https://blogs.ucl.ac.uk/abc-ld/ (accessed 4 May 2019).
Allen, W.C. (2006). 'Overview and evolution of the ADDIE training system', *Advances in Developing Human Resources*, 8 (4), 430–41.
Debattista, M. (2018). 'A comprehensive rubric for instructional design in e-learning', *International Journal of Information and Learning Technology*, 35 (2), 93–104, https:// doi.org/10.1108/IJILT-09-2017-0092.
Jaggars, S.S. and D. Xu (2016). 'How do online course design features influence student performance?', *Computers and Education*, 95, 270–84.
Kauffman, H. (2015). 'A review of predictive factors of student success in and satisfaction with online learning', *Research in Learning Technology*, 23.
Mayfield, M. (2011). 'Creating training and development programs: Using the ADDIE method', *Development and Learning in Organizations: An International Journal*, 25 (3), 19–22.
Newman, T. and H. Beetham (2017). 'Student digital experience tracker 2017: The

voice of 22,000 UK learners', London: JISC. Available at: https://digitalstudent. jiscinvolve.org/wp/2017/06/26/student-digital-experience-tracker-2017-the-voice-of-22000-uk-learners/ (accessed 4 May 2019).

Rienties, B. and L. Toetenel (2016). 'The impact of learning design on student behaviour, satisfaction and performance: A cross-institutional comparison across 151 modules', *Computers in Human Behavior*, 60, 333–41.

Thought 12

Soumyadeb Chowdhury, Oscar Rodríguez-Espindola, Ahmad Beltagui and Pavel Albores-Barajas

In a modelling and simulation lecture, students represent physical models in a virtual form, experiment in different conditions using a suitable technology, and finally propose a solution. Students are often intimidated by the technicalities of building and testing the virtual form of a model in the computer, and their desire 'to be the best' implies aversion to risk and failure, which limits their learning experience.

To overcome the 'fear of failure' and 'getting it right straight away', models and simulations are linked to more familiar contexts during class activities. For example, the students work in groups to describe their experience in a coffee shop by answering probing questions: where people enter and exit, the tasks involved such as ordering and payment, how long these take, people behaviour and what might make these things vary. Groups create sketches to represent these details and then share these with a neighbouring group to comment.

Next, the groups address the comments by discussing and refining their sketches. There are several benefits from this process of requiring students to create and debate representations: it encourages discussion between the students in an interactive learning session; it shows the significance of iterative learning; it helps to move away from the perception to get it right straight away and avert failure; it helps to develop an appreciation of the importance of experimenting; and finally, it aids in linking theory with practice to support decision making.

21. Successful teaching in virtual classrooms

Richard Terry, Jon Taylor and Matt Davies

INTRODUCTION

The ability to plan and deliver a successful 'virtual classroom' (or 'webinar') is an increasingly important skill for university teachers. The rise of the virtual classroom has accompanied the recent global growth in online and blended programmes for which they provide an important opportunity for synchronous tutor-to-student and student-to-student interactions. Yet we are also seeing an increase in the use of virtual classrooms to support traditional face-to-face programmes, driven in part by a growing appreciation of the advantages afforded by the medium.

Whilst we predict the delivery of virtual classrooms will become an increasing proportion of a teacher's 'load', we recognise that some colleagues will have reservations about this vision of the future. Some will have concerns about the extent to which the medium can facilitate effective (and enjoyable) interactions between teacher and students and between students, and others may be daunted by the apparent technological challenges involved.

We have been using virtual classrooms since 2010 and in this chapter we draw on those experiences to explain the opportunities and advantages provided by the virtual classroom medium, and provide advice on how best to exploit these whilst mitigating the potential risks.

The chapter is organised as follows: first, we explain what we mean by a virtual classroom and why we prefer this description to a 'webinar', despite the latter being much more commonly used in practice; second, we discuss key considerations for planning for the use of virtual classrooms within a programme or module; third, we discuss issues relating to the design of effective virtual classroom interventions; fourth, we discuss how to select appropriate activities for virtual classroom sessions; and, finally, we provide some practical guidance for delivering virtual classrooms.

WHAT IS A VIRTUAL CLASSROOM?

We use the term 'virtual classroom' to describe an online synchronous session to support student learning delivered via a Web-conferencing technology (in our case, Blackboard Collaborate) which potentially incorporates voice, text, images and video. There are many benefits of using 'virtual classrooms'. They represent a cost-effective medium which allows the tutor to quickly switch between tutor-led and team-based activities, and potentially provide an opportunity for tutors to provide support and feedback to many more students than is possible in a traditional classroom context.

We prefer to use the label 'virtual classroom' to 'webinar' as the latter has become synonymous with a 'one-way' communication from presenter to audience, which is common with promotional webinars delivered in the corporate world. The phrase 'virtual classroom' implies students will be actively participating in the session, not merely listening.

PLANNING THE USE OF VIRTUAL CLASSROOMS

Why bother with virtual classrooms in the first place? What value do they add to the teaching and learning on a programme? In these sessions we aim to provide a quintessential classroom environment, a space devoted to the practice of real-time teaching and learning (Martin and Parker, 2014). Because of this emphasis, virtual classrooms, as with their physical counterparts, offer the possibility for teachers and learners to purposefully engage in both the knowledge transmission and the co-creation of knowledge that help underpin transformational teaching (Kelly, 2009).

When planning virtual classrooms, it is crucial to bear in mind the value the session adds. This is especially important in the current context of online learning, when access to content and means of interaction with it are widely available through a variety of digital platforms. The unique value of the virtual classroom session always needs to be borne in mind, centred on the roles of teacher and learner. Even peer-to-peer sessions, though making full use of the interface features on offer, may only make sense in terms of the programme or module objectives when undertaken in the context of a specific teaching intervention. Examples of such interventions in a virtual classroom context might include using virtual break-out sessions prior to an online plenary feedback session, or an online group discussion of new conceptual understanding.

This holistic perspective means that planning virtual classroom sessions needs to take account of the pedagogic preferences of the individual teacher, to ensure that the use of learning technology is driven by the teaching design rather than the other way around. This standpoint presupposes that individual teachers have a clear idea about their own pedagogic preferences in relation to design decisions taken at both module and programme levels, but, importantly, also understand the opportunities and limitations of the virtual classroom technology. This also depends on the overall programme philosophy and the preferences of the other academic teaching staff on that programme. This approach to embedding the technology into the overall design helps guard against the risks of a formulaic use of the teaching and learning opportunities offered by the virtual classroom space. The teaching potential of specific features, for example whiteboard use or break-out rooms, should always be evaluated in terms of the module's objectives and learning outcomes.

Depending on the teaching context, a variety of ethical issues also need to be borne in mind. For example, using virtual classrooms as part of the process of creating evidence for the impact of learning may raise ethical considerations such as confidentiality and awareness of the risks involved in suggesting alterations in the workplace. This is especially important given virtual classrooms' potential as environments for the co-creation of knowledge, in which empirical evidence is forthcoming that may be valuable to the research interests of academic staff. In a blended learning context, virtual classrooms are integrated into programmes and modules that are taught primarily face-to-face. To maximise the effectiveness of this integration we need to assess the implications for curriculum and programme design, and ask what this blended approach will mean in the context of both the programme and module.

Teaching Tip
Ensure all blended learning innovations align with the overall expectations of the programme. The use of virtual classrooms should support the teaching and learning objectives, not detract from them.

As blended-learning researchers have recently suggested, this integrative approach to matching appropriate delivery methods to programme and module objectives has major implications in terms of the general requirements for staff development (Alammary et al., 2014). These authors identify three levels of blended approach, each defined by an ascending intensity of training and development need:

1. Low-impact blend: where additional online activities are added to an existing programme.
2. Medium-impact blend: where online activities replace other activities in an existing programme.

3.   High-impact blend: where the blended programme is constructed from scratch.

Other research usefully identifies several key strategies to increase adoption of synchronous virtual-classroom sessions into blended learning programmes (Martin and Parker, 2014). These lead to the following teaching tips:

Teaching Tip
1.   *Provide support for teachers and students, and easy access to virtual classrooms.*
2.   *Conduct workshops demonstrating how to set up and use virtual classrooms.*
3.   *Organise experts on synchronous virtual classrooms to lead workshops on their use in blended programmes.*
4.   *Communicate to teaching staff how synchronous virtual classrooms can contribute to beneficial personal factors, such as reducing travel time and cost, improving teaching, and enhancing student learning.*
5.   *Make peer-support user groups available for teaching staff.*

DESIGNING AN EFFECTIVE VIRTUAL-CLASSROOM SESSION

When integrating virtual classrooms into programme and module design, the aims and learning outcomes are the key drivers, but pedagogic style across disciplinary boundaries and the preferences of each individual teacher also need to be recognised. Pedagogic approach in the programme and module design will influence the decisions about the format, timing and structure of virtual-classroom sessions.

Recognition that virtual classrooms are pedagogic events means that planning and design follow established pedagogic principles that are then adapted to the affordances of the technology. The pedagogic aims of the session and activity should drive the design, not the feature set of the software tool, for example making the opportunities available for independent study and self-facilitated learning.

Engagement in the session by both teacher and learner is a strategic-level issue and will shape the experience of the classroom session. This in turn raises issues of engagement expectations, in which the nature of engagement may determine a maximum class size and require additional teaching or moderation support within the session.

Teaching Tip
Consider using an additional person present in the session in a teaching or moderating role if using parallel breakout sessions or to manage the chat channel.

The marketing of programmes and subsequent student expectations will also impact on programmes in terms of student requirements for engagement. This issue should be addressed in the design stage when differentiating between postgraduate and undergraduate cohorts, especially where, for example, higher-degree learners may be expected to demonstrate a deeper critical awareness of issues through discussion. How this issue is dealt with in the design is dependent on the overall programme philosophy and the expectations driven by this. If an undergraduate programme is sophisticated in its approach to engagement in all contexts, for example requiring seminar presentations, then this will also reflect the student expectations in terms of their virtual classroom engagement. Similarly, cultural variation within the student cohort should be borne in mind, with its implications for expectations relating to critical reflection and critically evaluating concepts, theories and models, both of which are potentially enriching in the context of virtual-classroom experience. Effects of cultural variation may also be evidenced in differing levels of engagement in classroom and virtual-classroom activities by the same students. This is another potential advantage of the virtual environment.

SELECTING YOUR VIRTUAL-CLASSROOM ACTIVITIES

The versatility of the virtual classroom medium combines the strengths of the lecture and the syndicate group. The space can be instantaneously transformed to suit a different engagement format, for example moving swiftly from lecture to group work or whole group discussion. This demonstrates one clear advantage of the virtual space over certain physical environments, such as the lecture theatre. In planning and designing the activities for virtual classroom sessions, the onus is on programme-level designers to ensure that students are made aware of these advantages and that the virtual classroom environment is available for group work, virtual meetings etc.

Again, this stresses the importance of a high-level pedagogic design that is flexible in approach. Students should be free to use the virtual classroom space on their own initiative, for example using a customised group space to encourage self-directed engagement and peer-to-peer, networked learning (Cochrane and Narayan, 2016).

BOX 21.1 PRACTITIONER INSIGHTS 1: DESIGNING A VIRTUAL CLASSROOM SESSION

As with any teaching intervention, the design should be driven by a combination of factors, the most important of all being the learning objectives for the session. Other factors are:

- The functionality provided by the specific virtual classroom technology you are using
- Your own level of confidence with the technology
- Students' familiarity with the technology
- The nature of the subject matter being covered.

I have developed an approach to Virtual Classrooms that works well for me and my subject area of accounting and finance. This involves designing PowerPoint slides that provide a clear structure for the session and incorporate the following content:

- An introductory warm up quiz to check understanding and act as an 'ice-breaker' to the session
- A brief summary of key learning content
- Activities and multiple-choice questions to provide an opportunity for students to practise application of concepts and techniques on short, clearly structured activities. This reduces the risk that students could become lost and frustrated, which is perhaps possible with longer and less well-structured activities.

I have found this to be a very effective approach to engage students and to allow me to quickly identify misconceptions and tailor my support accordingly.
Virtual classroom features I particularly like:

- 'Chat': I encourage students to use this in response to directed questions and also to simply share questions and comments as the session progresses
- 'Raise hand': this allows students to indicate they have a question requiring a response. I encourage students to use microphones to communicate but for various reasons they are often more comfortable to use Chat
- 'Polling': this allows students to respond to a question which may be a simple 'yes' / 'no' or a multiple-choice poll with responses from 'a' to 'd'
- 'Timer' feature: this can help students manage their time on set tasks.

Once I was reasonably confident with the above features I attempted to use the more advanced features: break-out rooms, application sharing etc., but only sparingly, and often only if I have the support of another moderator!
    Another important aspect of the design of a virtual classroom session is 'flexibility'. You may well hope that users have completed the preparatory work, brought with them a scientific calculator, have with them a functioning microphone and headset, turned up to the right session for their group, but it is a good idea to ensure that you have built in sufficient flexibility so that the session will still work even if these hopes are not realised!

BOX 21.2   PRACTITIONER INSIGHTS 2: PREPARING FOR YOUR FIRST VIRTUAL CLASSROOM

We strongly recommend that you practise running a virtual classroom with a colleague before you run one 'for real'. This helps build confidence with the technology, knowing how to find and operate the various affordances you need. Just as important is building confidence with the medium: talking into a computer without being able to see your students' reaction can be more than a little unnerving, but this reduces with practice.

It is also a good idea to experience the virtual classroom 'as a participant' too, to gain an appreciation of how it all works from a participant's perspective and avoid the confusion arising through highlighting something to participants which only you as the moderator can see on your screen.

It is also a good idea to sit in the same room as a more experienced colleague, so you can see how they do it and discuss issues arising after (or even during) the virtual classroom.

DELIVERING A VIRTUAL-CLASSROOM SESSION

Building an understanding of the etiquette and the pedagogy of the event is crucial to successful teaching and learning in the virtual classroom. While planning and session design are critical, running sessions can be even more taxing than face-to-face teaching, because of the potential uncertainty of using a new environment and the lack of visual cues online. A clear plan of how the session time is to be used will keep things on track and inform and reinforce the expectations of the session to participants. Bearing in mind that engagement levels may be higher than expected, care should be taken not to overestimate the volume of content that can be covered in the session. The responsibilities as a session facilitator also include technical aspects that will require thought being given to a backup plan, testing and familiarity with the interface, provision of technical support and planning for software functionality changes between versions.

The tone used in the session and the additional detail required for a global audience will need to be considered, especially where the native language of participants is not the same as that of the teacher. Sessions work more effectively when they support various forms of engagement and discussion that rely on the participants' understanding of the etiquette and the pedagogy of the event. Approaches might include:

- Blended group presentations based on pre-organised knowledge construction.

BOX 21.3   PRACTITIONER INSIGHTS 3: DELIVERING AN EFFECTIVE VIRTUAL CLASSROOM SESSION

WHAT TO DO BEFORE

Before the virtual classroom is delivered, some planning and communication is obviously required. Students need to know what preparation is required and what materials or equipment they may need during the session.

It is also a good idea to review the list of student names and check the pronunciation if necessary. Unlike a face-to-face session where eye contact and a simple nod of the head from the tutor can be a sufficient cue for a student with their hand raised to respond, the tutor running a virtual classroom must address a student by name.

We also advise that you arrive early yourself (at least half an hour before the webinar is due to start) to allow plenty of time for setting up the session, checking audio and video features, and for uploading relevant documents and checking they appear as expected. An early start also allows you to welcome students as they arrive, helping break the ice and build rapport. I find these informal conversations before the session starts are usually the best way for me to find out how students are really getting on, and what the issues and queries are that I need to respond to.

Students should be encouraged to arrive at least 10 minutes before start time so they can set up in plenty of time, but don't be too surprised that many will arrive at the moment you start (or later!). If you do have to step away before start time, change your 'status' so that participants know you are not present. Leave a 'welcome' message informing everyone you will be back soon, and a reminder of what they will need for the session.

WHAT TO DO DURING

During the webinar itself we recommend the following:

- Use your video feature for just a few seconds at the start to say hello, but then turn your video off;
- Establish the 'etiquette' that only the person speaking has their microphone turned on, and that if a participant wants to speak they should 'raise their hand' and wait for you to pass control of the microphone to them;
- 'Time lags' can be a problem: when conversing with a participant, use a phrase like 'over to you' to indicate you have finished speaking and are waiting for a response;
- Don't be afraid of the inevitable 'silences' that occur during a virtual classroom. If there are no immediate responses to a question, it might be tempting to jump in and assume students are stuck and need your help. In my experience, it is best to sit tight and the responses will come;
- Allow yourself time to read chat messages and decide how best to respond. My approach is to respond directly by name to those messages which have merit, but to respond on an anonymous basis to messages which reveal misconceptions to avoid the perception of 'naming and shaming'.

- Blended prepared presentations followed by synchronous task-based work in-session.
- Directed learning with question-and-answer sessions.

More detailed instructions for tasks may need to be provided, especially for initial sessions. It's also useful if using break-out rooms to pre-populate them with task details if possible. When designing any session, it is vital to be sure that students can complete the task, both from the perspective of understanding it, and ensuring that the environment permits them to produce the desired output. For example, if the product of a discussion in a break-out room is a list of a few key points or decisions, there may be a need for a whiteboard facility that allows this to be shared with the whole group, or another tool may have to be used to capture the group's output in a form that can be shared with the whole group.

CONCLUSION

In our experience, we have found that the inclusion of virtual classrooms offers significant benefits to both teacher and learner. For purely online and also for blended courses, these sessions add the essential value of real-time interaction and feedback between teacher and student, and between students themselves. As in the case of real-world classroom activities, the virtual sessions require careful planning, design and execution to maximise their potential benefits. The versatility and flexibility that the virtual environment offers help make a compelling case for their integration into courses, but specialist advice does need to be sought in advance, and the need for professional development of faculty should always be borne in mind. Successful teaching in the virtual world is as dependent on these considerations as any other form of intervention. This in turn requires the wider commitment of the institution as a whole, in order to ensure the necessary arrangements for both pedagogic and administrative support are in place. With these support networks secured, the benefits of successful teaching in virtual classrooms, for both students and faculty, are far more likely to be achieved.

SUGGESTED FURTHER READING

Alammary, A., J. Sheard and A. Carbone (2014). 'Blended learning in higher education: Three different design approaches', *Australasian Journal of Educational Technology*, 30 (4), Australasian Society for Computers in Learning in Tertiary Education, https://www.learntechlib.org/p/148495/ (accessed 3 July 2018).

Biggs, J. (2014). 'Constructive alignment in university teaching', *HERDSA Review of Higher Education*, 1 (1), 5–22.

Cochrane, T. and V. Narayan (2016). 'Nurturing collaborative networks of practice', *Mobile Learning Futures – Sustaining Quality Research and Practice in Mobile Learning*, p. 57.

Higher Education Academy (2018). UK Professional Standards Framework (UKPSF). https://www.heacademy.ac.uk/ukpsf (accessed 4 May 2019).

Kelly, A.V. (2009). *The Curriculum: Theory and Practice*, London: Sage.

Martin, F. and M.A. Parker (2014). 'Use of synchronous virtual classrooms: Why, who, and how', *MERLOT Journal of Online Learning and Teaching*, 10 (2), 192–210.

Thought 13

Soumyadeb Chowdhury, Oscar Rodríguez-Espindola, Ahmad Beltagui and Pavel Albores-Barajas

Students learning to code for the first time tend to focus on the end result, without understanding the process, which is usually viewed as a black-box.

For example, they look for a sample program to execute, without understanding what it means and why it is there. To overcome this challenge, a pair programming approach is used to encourage collaborative learning and help students understand what they are doing – not just get the right result.

The session starts by dividing the class into pairs, with each given a distinct program containing multiple errors. Students work like a detective in a crime novel, using critical thinking to uncover the errors (in this context, the culprit). The task encourages them to examine each line of code and, with reference to taught elements, question what it should do. And narrowing down the source of the error leads them to iteratively correct the code – so it becomes natural to try small modifications and test the effect they have.

The activity enables students to 'get their hands dirty' with the code, in a collaborative environment and with support from the tutor. There are several benefits stemming from this approach of requiring students to rectify errors in a program by working in pairs: it shows the significance of collaborative learning; it aids the students to harness technical skills by developing a better understanding of the program and its corresponding logic; finally, it helps to develop an appreciation of the significance of iterative learning.

22. Managing online learning

Nicholas Theodorakopoulos

INTRODUCTION

This chapter focuses on some of the key issues in the design and delivery of online modules. Any intervention in general, and pedagogic ones in particular, must be theory-informed/evidence-based and practice relevant. There are many ways to think about the role of theory in the design, development and delivery of online Higher Education courses and one has to consider the relationship between pedagogy and technology. Ideally, pedagogy should lead technology. However, technology sets the parameters, enabling and constraining in computer-mediated learning (both human and technology aspects). I use the transformation model, which is often applied to operations and performance management, as an organising framework for discussing the implications of this to design, delivery and evaluation of an online module. While this chapter has been authored, having in mind the modules that I teach, which are centred around the topics of entrepreneurship, strategy and change management, the issues discussed here are generic to online modules/programmes.

ONLINE LEARNING AS A TRANSFORMATION SYSTEM

The principles of constructivist learning environments hold that module/progamme design and delivery should support active learning systematically and draw on cognitive and social learning theory. Considering online learning from a constructivist perspective has implications for the design, development and delivery of online education.

PROCESS

In line with the tenets of knowledge constructivism, my learning activities are aimed at stimulating and enhancing conceptual interrelatedness, interdisciplinary learning, and multiple perspectives, granting learners control of their learning to an appropriate level. To this effect, real-world examples/live cases and exploration, scaffolding, experiential learning/self-reflection are used in individual work modes as well as group-based work that promotes cooperation and social negotiation, aiming predominantly at higher-order learning.

A case in point is the online postgraduate module 'Strategy, Change and Leadership'. The module involves a mixture of learning methods, with a view to engage learners synchronously and asynchronously. These include instruction, demonstration, case studies, individual/group work and a range of practical skills and activities. An element of self-directed study underpins such activities, which link to the assessment and attainment of the specified intended learning outcomes. Different types of media are used to help create new ways to exchange diverse experiences and perspectives for collaborative learning. Indicatively, the following means are used: podcasts, giving the highlights of a lecture, video interviews of practitioners demonstrating problems and solutions, and storyboard templates, which show how a concept/framework of change can be applied to practice. Webinars and online synchronous discussions often entail learning activities involving problem-based work individually and collaboratively. Discussion boards, group email and wikis enable asynchronous interaction and are often used to enrich the learning experience. Moreover, the use of reflective learning and personal development planning are central to the achievement of the learning outcomes and the effective development of learners.

Moreover, courseware usability is a crucial element in the process of online learning. The design of the course/module interface is critically important because it has a positive or negative impact on user performance. Concerning the latter point, one has to take into account that learners are sensitive to the readability of onscreen text.

Teaching Tip
Use screen-friendly fonts and web-safe colours in order to create a standard consistent look.

Studying long texts from the screen is not easy and people do not like to go more than three clicks far from the main page. I usually suggest a navigation frame to online learners and employ strategies for cognitive error recognition, diagnosis and recovery (e.g. providing feedback and direction through appropriate communication).

OPPORTUNITIES AND CHALLENGES IN ONLINE LEARNING

With web 2.0 technologies and the growth of different types of offshore courses, opportunities for new types of learning are provided, dismantling traditional boundaries. These technologies allow individuals to connect in real time to others anywhere in the world, as higher education institutions use multiple technologies to facilitate, complement and support international experience and intercultural connections. As Higher Education is increasingly able to supersede geographic boundaries, colleagues and classmates may very well be on the other side of the world. Importantly, technology has made international experience much more accessible to students unable to study abroad because of limited financial resources or time. As a result of the expansion of online learning courses there is now a wealth of information available about online learning and virtual learning environments (VLE) and elements of effective practice.

The online education process should engage participants, create for them a sense of common space and identity and stimulate their active learning. To achieve this, my online modules are designed and delivered with a view to enable learners to:

- Participate in interactive modes of instruction, synchronously and asynchronously
- Engage with authentic/near-authentic activities and multidisciplinary tasks
- Work collaboratively in a heterogeneous group
- Progress through exploration and reflection to achieve higher-order learning
- Maximise the benefits of facilitation provided by the lecturer and the tutors.

In essence, I sense that the lecturer/tutors should be acknowledging and supporting participation, assessing student learning, providing feedback and guiding students. However, while online education can be empowering, where courses are taught wholly online there can be additional challenges for building teaching relationships and motivating students. These challenges stem from the diversity of the student body and the disparities in terms of *geography, national culture, age, skills, experience,*

Table 22.1   Amplifications and reductions in online learning

Themes	Example of amplification	Example of reduction
Flexibility, convenience	Removal of temporal, geographical and situational barriers. Students stay in their own homes and communities. Their private lives remain unchanged and a first priority.	When students' private lives remain a priority, learning becomes a second priority. Coursework is subordinated to immediate responsibilities and both students and instructors may experience a loss of sense of belongingness.
Course design	Online learning technology can increase the quality of course design and cost effectiveness.	A text-based asynchronous learning environment can result in loss of teachable moment, campus culture and teaching as a scholarly activity.
Equity, equality	As physical and cultural characteristics are not visible, there is a more equal and equitable platform for communicating.	Because physical and cultural characteristics are not visible, students are not forced to confront their biases and prejudices.
Thinking, learning sills	Technology is a catalyst for more interactive and meaningful activities that facilitate higher-order learning.	Text-based discussions do not develop verbal skills.

Source: Adapted from Kanuka and Rourke (2008).

situational factors (e.g. work/family commitments) and motivations with taking up and exploring online technologies. Kanuka and Rourke (2008), in exploring amplifications and reductions associated with online learning, point out the main advantages and disadvantages that should be taken into account when designing and delivering online courses. These are summarised above in Table 22.1.

Problems related to online intercultural learning in HE focus primarily on two interrelated issues: (a) online learning, which frequently requires new ways of interacting and collaborating with others; and (b) intercultural learning, which may include learners and instructors with differing worldviews, communication practices and technological issues. Studies commonly refer to mismatches between learning and teaching cultures, language, assessment difficulties, disciplinary differences and social presence. Hence, while collaborative learning is a very significant pedagogical approach, lending itself to shared experiences and novel ideas for lecturers/

tutors and students alike, it presents additional challenges in an online context.

In line with relevant literature, local English-speaking students tend to report greater satisfaction with online learning than international students. There is little doubt that the international dimension of online learning and the cultural diversity involved in communications relating to online courses posit severe challenges. Students can find it difficult to make positive connections with students from other cultural backgrounds online. Although this echoes much of the literature pointing to difficulties in communication in face-to-face courses, while cultural differences are not unique to online courses (which tend to have a very diverse/international student body), they generally tend to be much more pronounced and more difficult to address without face-to-face interaction. On this note, cultural and institutional differences are difficult to accommodate in the design and delivery. For instance, enterprising and strategising approaches may differ in different countries and people have different ideas about what a good leader – one who brings about successful change initiatives – looks and acts like.

Using multimedia and asynchronous communication can help create new ways for students to exchange their diverse experiences and perspectives for mutual learning. Also, some international students report that online environments can give them the time and the 'safe space' they need to formulate their responses and the more 'anonymous' context can be less intimidating. However, others say that they can feel intimidated by the longer and more articulate posts of local students. Moreover, although synchronous learning can be enabled by various means, such as webinars, online forums, discussion boards, chat and tutoring, different time zones can pose a challenge.

Teaching Tip
To accommodate those with less certainty about their posts in an online discussion forum consider setting a word limit for posts.

EXPLOITING OPPORTUNITIES AND ADDRESSING CHALLENGES

Which Way is Up?

Considering relevant literature there are, in my experience, certain elements of good practice that could help address these challenges effectively and in some cases turn them into opportunities for inclusive, active online learning. These are outlined below:

- Monitoring the levels of student participation and providing encouragement or prompts when necessary. Careful moderation of online posts and discussions can encourage 'risk taking' by students who may feel less confident about their language skills through positive responses to their contributions and the inclusion of their contributions in the main discussions.
- Although all communication about the module must be posted online, students should have the option of contacting the tutor by email for more individual issues or matters of a personal nature.
- Providing information about support available for developing writing and online participation skills.
- Expectations around requirements and online behaviour should be outlined in a welcome email or post from the tutor and through careful and sensitive intervention by the tutor when necessary. Modelling respectful forms of dialogue and participation and making explicit rules of online group work is important. For instance, the use of greetings, the formality/informality of postings, the levels of personal disclosure, rules about avoiding slang and idioms, expectations about the speed of responses, expectations about whether, and how often, the lecturer or tutor will post comments. Addressing any inappropriate or discriminatory language or responses immediately is of paramount importance.
- Internationalising the curriculum can help create a more inclusive online group working. This involves providing students with global perspectives of their discipline, enabling them to develop a set of values and skills to operate in diverse cultural environments (often labelled 'intercultural competencies') and considering how professional practice differs in different cultures/countries.
- Providing opportunities for students to identify and post relevant sources of information or examples from their own cultural settings. Posts can include a variety of resources including pictures, videos, media stories, articles, as well as links to other websites. This will allow them to make connections between what they know and what they are learning.
- Posting weekly messages summarising the content for the course to date or for that week pointing to what students will have been expected to learn. This can help students understand the bigger picture and the development of their learning which can also help to maintain their motivation and feelings of inclusion.
- Requesting students to provide their own short summaries of readings, of their thinking or their own findings, and 'eureka' moments to increase motivation and collaborative learning.

ENHANCING ENGAGEMENT

As mentioned above, an online module should engage students in real time and asynchronously such that they address the right level of knowledge, usability and aesthetics. Indicatively, the following means could be used:

- Podcasts – giving the highlights of a lecture
- Video interviews of practitioners demonstrating problems and solutions/tips
- Learning tools using a Storyboard template – showing how a theory can be applied to practice – linking with video interviews.

Using synchronous and asynchronous collaboration tools is vital for effective online learning. Such tools are central to ensuring collaboration within online problem-based learning teams and include chat, discussion boards, video conferencing, group browsing and discussion group email. The use of bulletin boards, where Q&A/Solutions are posted, and wikis for asynchronous group interaction can enrich the students' learning experience. Other methods, individual or group-based, include webinars where learners can ask questions and receive answers and online consultancy sessions over a specified time. As mentioned, the tutor's presence is crucial for creating a sense of an inclusive, active learning space. To stimulate participation, the tutor must not take for granted that social interaction will automatically take place just because the environment makes it technologically possible. In that respect, it is important not to restrict social interaction to task-specific activities aiming at cognitive processes. Interventions aimed at socio-emotional and affective processes must not be ignored, neglected or forgotten, as these seem to make a crucial difference.

CONCLUSION

Finally, I endeavour to not lose sight of the aim of learner-centred design: know how learners prefer to learn, understand their motivation or incentive to engage in online learning, what their needs are and how they feel comfortable when using online applications. Needless to say it is important to know what the users' experiences with online learning are. Therefore, the need for evaluating regularly the online learning system and identifying pedagogical and technological areas for improvement is imperative.

SUGGESTED FURTHER READING

Kanuka, H. and L. Rourke (2008). 'Exploring amplifications and reductions associated with e-Learning: Conversations with leaders of e-Learning programs', *Technology Pedagogy and Education*, 17 (1), 5–15.

Koohang, A. (2012). 'Active learning in E-learning: Advancing a systemic model', *Issues in Information Systems*, 13 (1), 68–76.

Lea, J. (2015). *Enhancing Learning and Teaching in Higher Education: Engaging with the Dimensions of Practice*, Maidenhead: Open University Press.

McLoughlin, C. (2001). 'Inclusivity and alignment: Principles of pedagogy, task and assessment design for effective cross-cultural online learning', *Distance Education*, 22 (1), 7–29.

Neary, M. and H. Beetham (2015). 'The nature of academic space'. In Lea, J. (ed), *Enhancing Learning and Teaching in Higher Education: Engaging with the Dimensions of Practice*, pp.103–12, Maidenhead: Open University Press.

Pachler, N. and C. Daly (2011). *Key Issues in e-Learning: Research and Practice*, Continuous International Publishing Group.

Rees, T. (2010). 'International students' experience of online learning activities: An annotated bibliography', Higher Education Academy Evidence Net. http://www.heacademy.ac.uk/assets/EvidenceNet/International_students_experience.pdf

Rogers, P., C. Graham and C. Mayes (2007). 'Cultural competence and instructional design: Exploration research into the delivery of online instruction cross-culturally', *Educational Technology Research and Development*, 55 (2), 197–217.

Stefani, L. (2009). 'Planning teaching and learning: Curriculum design and development'. In H. Fry, S. Ketteridge and S. Marshall (eds), *A Handbook for Teaching and Learning in Higher Education*, pp.40–57, London: Routledge.

West, C. (2010). 'Borderless via technology', *International Educator*, 19 (2), 24–33.

PART V

Teaching Content

23. The use of short in-class games

Jon Guest, Maria Kozlovskaya and Matthew Olczak

INTRODUCTION

The process and implications of decision making by firms/consumers/governments is an important topic in many subjects taught in business schools. We often construct simplified models to examine their behaviour.

One common example is the famous prisoner's dilemma (the name for the game comes from its original setting in which two suspected criminals are captured by the police, locked up in separate cells and given the choice of whether to confess to (compete) or deny (cooperate) a crime they are accused of committing). Both players are jointly better off by cooperating with one another, but each has an individual incentive to compete. As we discuss further below, this model has a wide range of applications across a diverse range of disciplines.

One approach to teaching models of decision making is to, first, outline the logic behind the choices people might make when faced with this kind of situation, then explain the implications of the predicted behaviour.

However, in our experience, there is a better way to teach it. Rather than students simply sitting in a classroom listening to an explanation by the tutor, why not get them to actually make decisions in an environment that recreates the incentive structure of the hypothetical model? The playing of simple, short in-class games in which students make decisions and find out the implications for their payoffs (winnings) can allow you to do this. These can be used to teach a diverse range of theories and applications. We believe that getting students to experience incentives in this way makes it easier to teach the underlying theory and bring out the implications of the resulting predictions.

Unlike most simulations (see Chapter 11), a short game only takes between 20 and 40 minutes of class time. They typically take place over a number of rounds with the participants responding to the outcomes from their own and their classmates' previous behaviour. Games can either be paper-based or played online. Below we consider the advantages of each approach and at the end of the chapter provide several examples of games that can be played using either method. Before that, we discuss in more detail the potential benefits of using games in your teaching and address a number of regular concerns that arise.

THE POTENTIAL BENEFITS

Using games has a number of advantages that help to explain why they have become more widespread in business education over the last ten years. In particular:

1. Breaking up the monotony of instructor-led teaching sessions
    They enable the instructor to break up lectures into smaller and more manageable chunks by running games between standard presentations. This helps the students to process the material.
2. Increasing student engagement
    Compared to the traditional 'chalk-and-talk' approach they encourage students to engage with the content, weigh up the evidence provided in the scenario of the game and arrive at their own solutions. In many games, they get to 'feel' the impact of incentives at first hand rather than simply listening to an explanation of how people will respond.
3. Dealing with heterogeneity in the classroom
    They are an effective way of teaching students with different prior knowledge of the subject. For those who have studied the subject before, a game is a different way of experiencing the material. For those with no prior knowledge the game can be an effective way to introduce new material.
4. Helping the tutor to cater to different learning styles
    Games can be a particularly effective way of teaching students with a more active style of learning. These students might perform poorly if they only experience traditional styles of passive teaching.
5. Helping students develop a range of transferable skills that will assist them in their future careers. These include:

    ●   Learning by doing: participating in a game motivates students to identify questions and create new knowledge.
    ●   Students can learn to increase their overall payoffs by learning to cooperate with the other players.
    ●   Peer learning: the interactive nature of many games means students need to listen to the arguments of their peers and understand their motivation in order to maximise their own payoffs.

SOME CONCERNS

Despite the potential benefits of using short games, a number of factors might still deter you. Four concerns regularly expressed by colleagues are:

1. I will not be able to cover enough material
   Using contact time to play games inevitably means less material can be covered and explained in class. However, one criticism of more traditional approaches to teaching is that they try to cover far too much. Constraints on concentration and processing capabilities means that only limited amounts of new material can be absorbed in intensive sessions. This approach may also signal that only surface learning is required. Students may achieve a deeper understanding of the material if tutors spend less time talking and make greater use of more active methods of learning such as games.
2. The students will not take the game seriously and I will lose control of the class
   Our experience suggests this is very unlikely to occur. Even with hypothetical payoffs, the desire to outperform peers, the fun of taking part and the belief it supports learning keeps the whole group engaged.

   Teaching Tip
   Try to make the hypothetical payoffs similar in size to those that students commonly experience in everyday transactions, i.e. £5, £10 and £20. People tend to learn more effectively when they can relate new knowledge to experiences from the real world.
   Sweets/chocolates or even cash prizes for the best performing or randomly selected participants can also help to keep the class engaged.

3. The game will not produce the expected results
   Most short games produce consistent and broadly predictable results. However, unanticipated outcomes can provide an opportunity to help develop critical thinking skills. For example, you can use follow-up work to ask students to consider (a) any limitations with the design and implementation of the game as a way of testing a particular theory; (b) different ways of improving the design of the game; and (c) potential limitations with the theory itself.
4. Introducing games will be very costly in terms of time and effort
   An unavoidable implication of introducing games is the incremental cost of changing the way you teach. These additional costs fall into three broad categories: (a) pre-class (b) in-class and (c) post-class. The pre-class costs include finding, adapting and introducing appropriate

games into the module. The in-class costs include collecting, calculating, recording and disseminating the results of the game. The post-class costs include the posting and integration of the results into teaching materials. From our experience, these costs are not as great as many colleagues expect. Both pre-class and in-class costs are now much lower than they once were because of the wide range of freely available resources on the Internet. These enable the tutor to choose between paper-based or online versions of the games. The next section will discuss the strengths and weakness of using each approach.

COMPARING PAPER-BASED AND ONLINE GAMES

A number of websites include numerous examples of paper-based games and provide copies of instructions and record sheets that can be easily downloaded, edited and copied. Many examples use ordinary playing cards to facilitate decision making and communicate decisions. This helps to keep set-up costs to a minimum. One advantage of using paper-based games is the face-to-face social interaction they generate between the students. Some actually involve physical activity, i.e. running around the room. Another advantage is the ability of the tutor to change the payoffs on the spot rather than having to adjust them in the software. An example of a paper-based game using playing cards is discussed in more detail later in the chapter.

Teaching Tip
With paper-based games, the in-class costs of collecting decisions, calculating payoffs and communicating results can sometimes impose considerable demands on the tutor. To reduce these costs ask the class for volunteers to help with the running of the game. Students who played the games in previous years are also usually willing to come and assist.

It is now much easier to play online versions of the games given that the vast majority of students have a mobile phone/tablet/laptop and classrooms are equipped with good wifi. Tutors no longer have to book computer rooms and it is possible to use games in very large lecture theatres. A range of websites (for example Veconlab, MobLab, economics-games.com) provide a diverse range of online games, often for free (including all the examples discussed below).

Teaching Tip
A good way to learn how an online game works is to set yourself up as the instructor on a laptop/desktop and as separate players on your phone and a

tablet. After playing a few rounds, it will become much clearer how the game works from both the perspective of the tutor and the students. This typically takes less than 10 minutes.

Online games can reduce in-class costs as the software collects, calculates and disseminates the results. These can then be easily presented to the class for feedback while the game is ongoing and for further discussion once it is completed. It is also easy to save the results for discussion later in the programme. One disadvantage over using paper-based versions is the extra setup cost of ensuring that all participants are logged in to the software. However, a major advantage is the ability to have all the students involved in making decisions, even in very large classes. This is important as research finds that those games where the class simply observes the actions of a few volunteers are the least effective. We have experience of using the economics-games.com website with around 100 pairs of students in a lecture theatre simultaneously playing the prisoner's dilemma game against one another.

Teaching Tip
Raffle tickets are a useful way of providing participants with a unique login number required for some of the online games.
With both paper-based and online games, get the students to make decisions in pairs or small groups. This makes it easier to play with larger numbers and facilitates discussion and peer learning.

Another advantage with online versions is the possibility of using games that are more complex; for example, involving random matching between players or a wider range of decisions for the players to make. However, one potential drawback is that some of the interaction between the tutor and students is lost. This is especially the case if the tutor leaves the students to read the instructions and play all the rounds of the game on their own. Online games are more effective when the tutor carefully talks the students through the instructions before the game begins and provides feedback and encouragement in between rounds. In our experience, engagement is amplified as the students wait for the lecturer to reveal the results from the previous round.

Another potential drawback with online versions is the increased anonymity of the participants. This increases the chances that some students will hold up the progress of the game by either delaying or failing to make a decision. With this in mind, it is important to note that some games include an option for the tutor to set a time limit on the decision-making process. Once this limit is reached, the software imposes a particular decision on those players who have failed to respond. Anonymity is also useful in some games as it enables the random matching of players and can be used to examine situations where players cannot communicate.

Teaching Tip
Revealing the players' identities in some rounds, while keeping them secret in others, can demonstrate how peer pressure affects behaviour in the game.

Overall, there are pros and cons of using paper-based and online games. The best option will depend upon a range of factors including the type of game you want to run and the class size. We suggest you experiment to see which of the options works best in your specific setting. Some illustrative examples of games that can be played online or in a paper-based form are discussed in detail in the next section.

SOME EXAMPLES

A Negotiated Price Market Game Using Playing Cards

This game (see Holt (1996) for further details) is a very effective way of introducing students to how markets operate. It works well for class sizes of between eight and 40. The tutor splits the class, with half the students acting as the buyers and the other half the sellers. They make decisions on an individual basis and their task is to negotiate an agreed price to trade one unit of a hypothetical good. The participants play the game over a number of rounds. At the beginning of each round, the tutor deals a black card to each buyer and a red card to each seller. The number on the black card assigns the buyer with a maximum willingness to pay for one unit of the good while the number on the red card assigns the seller with a cost of supplying one unit.

The following numbers work well with a class size of 32, i.e. 16 buyers and sellers:

- Black (spades or clubs): 10, 10, 9, 9, 8, 8, 7, 7, 6, 6, 5, 5, 4, 4, 3, 3
- Red (hearts or diamonds): 2, 2, 3, 3, 4, 4, 5, 5, 6, 6, 7, 7, 8, 8, 9, 9.

Before inviting the students to the middle of the room to negotiate prices with one another, the tutor carefully explains the following important points:

- The period of trading only lasts for two minutes.
- Irrational and loss-making trades are prohibited, i.e. a buyer cannot agree to prices greater than the number on their card and a seller cannot agree to prices below the number on their card.

- Sellers only incur costs if a trade is actually completed.
- Information on the cards must be kept private as it is highly unlikely in a real-world market that either a buyer would announce their willingness to pay or a seller would announce their costs of production.

The tutor then allows trading to commence. Once a buyer and seller have struck a deal they come to the front desk where the tutor is standing, place their cards face down and announce the agreed price.

The tutor checks the cards to make sure the trade is permissible and, if so, records the price that is agreed. The students return to their chairs and record the details of the trade on their handouts. After two minutes, the tutor announces that trading is over and collects any unused cards. He/she then deals all the cards out again at the beginning of the next round.

Typically, the variation in agreed prices falls as the rounds progress and converges to the market clearing level. It is easy to introduce taxes, subsidies and price controls in later rounds of the game.

Prisoner's Dilemma

In the prisoner's dilemma described earlier, if participants make this decision just once and act in their own self-interest, it is rational for them both to decide to compete. This therefore results in a worse outcome than if they both cooperated. On the other hand, if the same participants play against each other repeatedly, the possibility of building up trust and the fear of future punishment may allow them to achieve some degree of cooperation over time. This important insight can be brought out extremely well by getting students to play the game against the same opponents for a number of rounds.

This game has a diverse range of applications in economics, psychology, political science and biology. For example, it can highlight the difficulty in getting cross-country coordination on measures to reduce global warming. Likewise, it can illustrate the possibility that when firms interact repeatedly in a market they may be able to tacitly cooperate to keep their prices high.

Public Goods

In the public goods game players independently decide how many tokens to contribute to a common pot. The tokens in the pot get multiplied up by a given factor and are then shared equally among the players. The multiplication reflects the fact that the social value of public goods such as roads and parks exceed their construction cost, because they can be used by many people at the same time. The even division gives rise to the free-rider problem: each player is better off contributing nothing and enjoying their share of whatever is in the common pot. However, if all players follow this rational argument, no contributions are made to the common pot and all players earn less.

For example, consider a game with four players initially endowed with 10 tokens each and a multiplication factor of two. If a player contributes a token, the number of tokens in the pot increases by two and when the pot is shared each player only gets half a token back. Players do not have an individual incentive to contribute and end up with their initial endowment of 10 tokens each. However, everyone would be better off if they contributed all of their tokens, thus creating a common pot of 80 (after multiplication) and enjoying the payoff of 20 tokens each.

The public goods game is a multi-player version of the prisoner's dilemma. In both games the individually rational action (competing in the prisoner's dilemma and contributing nothing in the public goods game) is different from the collectively optimal one (cooperating and contributing everything, respectively).

In another version of the public goods game, known as the tragedy of the commons, players decide how much to take out from a common resource pool. The game is played over several rounds. The money left in the pool at the end of each round determines its size in future periods. Theory predicts over-exploitation and depletion of the resource, which in the end hurts all players. The game models many real-life scenarios of socio-scientific interest, such as air pollution, overfishing and antibiotics resistance. This wide applicability means it is useful for teaching economics, business studies, sociology, politics and biology.

We have used the game in a module on Corporate Social Responsibility. The students played the role of fishermen making harvesting decisions while using a joint pool. If the total harvest exceeds the sustainable fishing limit, the remaining population of fish is not enough to reproduce and replenish the pool for the next round. The game helped students appreciate the long-term benefit of sustainable business.

IMPACT ON STUDENT LEARNING

There is evidence to suggest that introducing games can have a positive impact on learning. In a number of studies, some students participated in short games whilst a control group received traditional methods of instruction. The differences between pre-course and post-course scores on multiple-choice tests are then used as a measure of learning. After controlling for academic ability and other student characteristics, studies by Emerson and English (2016), Dickie (2006) and Emerson and Taylor (2004) found the scores of those who participated in games improved significantly more than those in the control group.

Another important issue is raised by Gibbs (1988) who argues that: 'It is not enough just to do, and neither is it enough to think. Nor is it enough simply to do and think. Learning from experience must involve linking the doing and the thinking.' This very much chimes with our experience. The learning benefits from introducing games are maximised when the results are effectively integrated with the teaching of the underlying theory. This raises an interesting question. What comes first? The tutor's explanation of the theory or the game? This will vary to some extent depending on the class and the nature of the game. However, the experience of the authors is that the learning benefits are maximised when discussion of theoretical ideas takes place after the students play the game.

Furthermore, Cartwright and Stepanova (2012) found evidence that students gained a better grasp of the underlying theory the game was designed to illustrate, if they were required to write a report reflecting on their participation in the game. The more general message would seem to be that in-class games are most effective when the tutor fully integrates them into the module assessment. Making the direct relevance of the game to the assessment as clear as possible will also motivate the strategic learners to participate fully in the playing of the game.

A further interesting question concerns the way in which games are described to the students. Experimental evidence suggests that the language used can have significant effects, for example there can be different results if the same game is referred to in terms of an exchange rather than a contest (see for example Camerer and Thaler, 1995). Whilst the implications of this for the learning outcomes from in-class games has not been explored, it is worth bearing in mind that the context used may affect how students perceive a particular game.

CONCLUSION

With the amount of support material now available, it has never been easier to use either paper-based or online classroom games. They are a fun and effective way of introducing active learning and the feedback from students is very positive. We encourage you to experiment by introducing short in-class games into your teaching.

SUGGESTED FURTHER READING

Camerer, C. and R.H. Thaler (1995). 'Anomalies: ultimatums, dictators and manners', *Journal of Economic Perspectives*, 9 (2), 209–19.

Cartwright, E. and A. Stepanova (2012). 'What do students learn from a classroom experiment? Not much, unless they write a report on it', *Journal of Economic Education*, 43 (1), 48–57.

Dickie, M. (2006). 'Do classroom experiments increase learning in introductory microeconomics?', *Journal of Economic Education*, 37, 267–88.

Emerson, T. and L. English (2016). 'Classroom experiments: Teaching specific topics or promoting the economic way of thinking', *Journal of Economic Education*, 47, 288–99.

Emerson, T. and B. Taylor (2004). 'Comparing student achievement across experimental and lecture-oriented sections of a principles of microeconomics programme', *Southern Economic Journal*, 70, 672–93.

Gibbs, G. (1988). *Learning by Doing: A Guide to Teaching and Learning Methods*, London: Further Education Unit.

Guest, J. (2015). 'Reflections on ten years of using economic games and experiments in teaching', *Cogent Economics and Finance*, 3 (1).

Holt, C. (1996). 'Classroom games: Trading in a pit market', *Journal of Economic Perspectives*, 10, 193–203.

WEB RESOURCES

Paper-Based Games

https://www.economicsnetwork.ac.uk/themes/games
http://w3.marietta.edu/~delemeeg/games/

Online Games

http://veconlab.econ.virginia.edu/
https://www.moblab.com/
https://economics-games.com/

24. Teaching maths to non-mathematical students

Geetha Ravishankar

INTRODUCTION

Increasingly, a good understanding of maths is essential for successful completion of economics and business programmes. However, it is exactly those modules on mathematics and/or quantitative methods that students are often most anxious about. I found that the best way to help students overcome this anxiety was through a combination of clear, structured classroom sessions and a friendly, supportive, enthusiastic and encouraging disposition in delivering the same. Beyond that, my teaching approach is best summarised by a quotation from the mathematician Paul Halmos: 'The best way to learn mathematics is to do mathematics.'

As such, in this chapter I present the approach I take when teaching quantitative modules. The examples presented are based on modules I delivered on quantitative methods on undergraduate and postgraduate programmes, primarily in economics and finance. However, the overall approach, or aspects of it, are useful for audiences on specialist economics programmes or from other programmes across the business school.

The traditional format to teaching mathematics/quantitative subjects remains through lectures that are complemented with seminars/tutorials. It is also what I found to be the most effective way of communicating concepts and applications and I thus begin with a discussion of my approach to lectures followed by the same for seminars.

LECTURES

Essentially, my lectures were split into three components. I would start by *setting the scene*, i.e. explain why and how the topic/concepts was/were relevant and useful. For example, at times, where the topic allowed, I would begin with a diagram. Indeed, I find it useful to use a diagrammatic analysis both as a prelude to or as further explanation of a problem before embarking on

BOX 24.1   MOTIVATING MATHS TOPICS

The following is an example I use to help motivate my class on (quantitative) research methods and introductory maths. It is also one that fits well with other theory-based principles modules in first year economics. The example is based on the Independent Commission on Banking's (2011) final recommendations to improve the stability and strength of the UK banking system in the wake of the financial crisis. I specifically reference the following aim of the report, 'means a banking system that is effective and *efficient at providing the basic banking services'* (italics added for emphasis). In lectures, I start by giving students a couple of minutes to think about how such efficiency can be identified. What do we mean by efficiency in the context of banks? How can we measure such efficiency? What sort of information would we need?

Students typically identify cost control as an important element of efficiency, offering a natural segue to discussing cost and production functions. This can be linked directly to theory covered in other modules (namely microeconomics), thereby helping to highlight the interconnectedness of the various modules they take. With advanced classes, we move on to cost functions directly, but for introductory classes we begin with the idea that costs are allied to production. So, I ask students to think about how we characterise production for a bank. For example, what are the inputs and outputs? Most readily identify loans as outputs and labour as an input. With a few prompts, we identify assets and deposits as further inputs. They have thus intuitively identified a rudimentary production function, albeit verbally. I then demonstrate how this verbal information can be summarised using the f(. . .) mathematical notation, as follows:

Loans = f (deposits, total assets, labour)

Again, depending on the level of the programme, we can then move on to formalising the function, for example using a Cobb–Douglas production function. I would follow this by showing students the data that is needed to operationalise the estimation of the function. The question then is one of determining the precise relationship between each input and output (for example, the magnitude of change in loans from a given change in deposits assuming the other inputs don't change), which modules taken further on in the programme will cover. I stress that understanding why and how functions work is the first step to being able to use them in answering such questions later. I then preview the results of empirical research into the banking efficiency of the UK, thus showing the policy relevance of the same.

Throughout this empirical demonstration I explicitly state that the aim is to understand the intuition and make the link with real data and issues. The challenge in this is in simplifying the presentation so that students are not overwhelmed with the data and maths involved. When this is achieved, the informal feedback I receive is that it helps makes the maths seem less abstract.

the mathematical presentation. It helped build intuition. In other instances, I have used history and empirical research as motivations for a topic. For example, in introducing the idea of a generic function, $f(\ )$, I reference empirical research on bank performance which uses data from final accounts to determine a production function. We go over some of the data collected and I present and explain the estimated function. Or, for example, when introducing differential calculus, the Newton vs Leibniz debate can be referenced.

For students, especially at first year level, the empirical research presented is, admittedly, at an advanced level and I acknowledge this in lectures. However, a bird's-eye view of the motivation for the work, the role that the quantitative techniques play in revealing patterns in the data, and the resulting implications brings the subject to life. The quants of the textbook seem a little less abstract and a little more relatable. And admittedly, in the latter case, I am referencing my personal interest in history, which is, very likely, not everyone's cup of tea. So, some treat it as a mini-break (which in and of itself is useful to help retain attention) and others are rather bemused. Either way, it helps in the establishment of a rapport with the students and sustains their engagement with the lesson and subject.

I then move on to the key concepts and theories before using the remainder of the lecture to demonstrate the application of the theory/concept to problems. Throughout, I also find it useful to explicitly reference topics in other modules where the concepts are used.

Teaching Tip
For example, when covering differential calculus, I would explicitly reference the concepts of marginal costs and marginal revenues which students would have covered in their microeconomics module. This does two things. First, it contextualises the math thereby making it less abstract. Second, it counters any compartmentalisation of learning. In other words, by explicitly linking and signposting the applications of the mathematical concepts and techniques to topics in other modules, it highlighted the interconnectedness of the modules students took over their programme.

For the remainder of the lecture, I would demonstrate the application of that theory to a problem and solve it in real time using the visualiser, beginning, wherever possible, with a diagrammatic analysis followed by an exposition of the solution approach we would take. When working out the solutions on the visualiser, I would, importantly, demonstrate *all* steps, explaining the same as I continued with the demonstration. This included seemingly obvious ones such as isolating variables to one side of an equal to sign as a prelude to simplifying the equation and then solving for the unknown variable (see Table 24.1).

Table 24.1   Worked solution

$2x - 3 = x + 5$	(1)	Collect x values on left hand side; real numbers on right; change signs as do so
$\Rightarrow 2x - x = 5 - 3$	(2)	Simplify
$\therefore x = 8$		

As can be seen from Table 24.1, the right-hand margins of the page would be my *working area* where I would write short notes, complete rough calculations and incorporate explanations of the steps. Informal feedback from students indicated that this was particularly useful for review and revision after the class (informal feedback also helped improve lecturer penmanship!).

In as much as the theory behind the math is difficult, the language of mathematics is itself often a further source of anxiety. The mathematical operators and symbols are perceived as an explicit barrier to understanding the mathematical methods. Demonstrating and explaining the solutions in the aforementioned manner meant that the students learnt this language as they solved the problems and were thus less likely to be intimidated by it.

Teaching Tip
As an additional resource, I provided a notations crib sheet for quick reference. Overall, this approach also meant that the students were engaged for the duration of the lecture and in writing down the solutions were internalising the techniques, at least somewhat.

A potential issue with this approach is that students passively note down the solutions as demonstrated. This is mitigated to a certain extent in instances when the lecturer makes an error when working through the problem. However, I soon realised that the students would often spot my error before I did. And there was a palpable sense of accomplishment on their part as they were able to follow it through and identify the error – all of which served to boost their confidence in the subject. Indeed, I found this to be the real power of this approach.

Further, in amongst the humour these moments generated, it demonstrated to students that (a) mistakes happen; (b) they happen to everyone (even lecturers!); and (c) that the lectures and allied seminars were safe spaces to make mistakes. Indeed, while I would explicitly say so on many occasions, demonstrating it by actually making an error had a far greater impact. A final point to note is that demonstrating the solutions in real time as detailed thus far also enables the lecturer to point out topics that students typically found difficult or tended to make errors.

To further mitigate against passive note taking, having demonstrated a problem I would then set one for the students to try out in the lecture. This gave me the opportunity to wander around the lecture theatre to check student progress and take any questions. At the end of the set time, I would demonstrate the full solution in the class. Admittedly, the degree to which this can be adopted is dependent on the time available and the topic under discussion. I thus found it helpful to pre-select questions that students typically found difficult to both demonstrate in class and set as the subsequent problem for the students to work on. This also helped students familiar with the topics to retain interest in the same.

Finally, I upload all relevant PowerPoint presentations with the questions and solutions, along with the theory covered in the classes. Nowadays, with the increasing use of lecture-capture systems, the videos of the lecture demonstrations remain available for students to review. The lecture approach outlined thus far is fairly traditional. Increasingly, however, there is scope to incorporate a greater diversity of teaching formats that depart from the traditional lecture for core content delivery with allied seminars for practice on related topics. Such alternatives take the form of problem-based learning and flipped classrooms.

SEMINARS

In seminars, we go over problem sets relating to topics covered in the lectures. The questions reflected varying levels of difficulty. There would always be more questions than we could cover in the seminar, so I would select a mix of the more difficult questions for the students to try in class. The focus was not, however, in getting all the questions finished. Rather, it was to ensure that students understood the technique and felt confident in completing the set, be it in class or later as homework. To that end, I would demonstrate the most difficult question on the whiteboard towards the end of the session in the same manner I would in lectures.

Whilst the students worked through the questions, usually in their own groups, I could wander around, check answers and help with areas of difficulty. The benefit of the group work was that the students get a different perspective and explanation of the problem from that of the lecturer. And as for the student engaged in the explaining, what better way to check your understanding than by explaining it to someone else?

Finally (and arguably, most importantly), being positive, open and supportive encourages students to ask questions and counters any disillusionment when students feel their progress is slow.

CONCLUSION

To conclude, this chapter offers a summary of the approaches I find useful when teaching mathematics to non-mathematical students. The approach is primarily based on the chalk-and-talk method, updated to incorporate visualiser demonstrations, PowerPoint resources and online assessments. There is ample scope, however, to update this further with recently developed alternative teaching formats such as flipped classes and problem-based learning.

SUGGESTED FURTHER READING

The Economics Network, accessed 30 August 2018 at https://www.economicsnet work.ac.uk/.

Economics and Social Research Council and The Higher Education Academy, Quantitative Methods Initiative, accessed 30 August 2018 at https://www.quanti tativemethods.ac.uk/.

Fry, H., S. Ketteridge and S. Marshall (2009). *Handbook for Teaching and Learning in Higher Education: Enhancing Academic Practice*, 3rd edn, London: Routledge.

Thought 14

Pieter Koornhof

I was recently given the opportunity to further my formal academic training in education theory. As one of our assessments, we were made to attend a lecture from a discipline outside our own and reflect on it. I chose to observe a practical session forming part of the first year Biomedical Engineering curriculum. The purpose was to show students how to engage in simple programming and troubleshooting of circuit boards to serve as a stepping stone for more advanced techniques to be used later.

The lecturer started by reminding students of the ground rules and expectations for the seminar, followed by a brief theoretical overview. It was subsequently explained what the various tasks were for the session, and a brief demonstration was done. The focus was then shifted from the lecturer to the students. Students were encouraged to proceed with the individual tasks set for the seminar at their own pace. Those working at a faster pace were encouraged to help others, fostering a collaborative environment and making the general class experience seem relaxed. The lecturer then identified students who were struggling and assisted them. Rather than simply doing the task for them, the lecturer proceeded to demonstrate how, what and why something went wrong with the attempt and then expected the students to reflect on this and fix the problem themselves.

As an outsider looking in, the experience was decidedly foreign to me. It felt strange to be in a classroom environment and be wholly unaware of what was required. Even if I was shown how to work with the circuit board, it still would not be of any use to me as I didn't understand it at all! This made me reflect on two aspects of teaching. First, it made me think how we can take for granted the specialist nature of our content, and how important it is to make it broadly accessible. Second, it reminded me of the symbiotic nature of knowledge and skills within a professional degree, something which is also an aspect of law (even if it manifests in a completely different manner).

Upon reflection, I found that there were some practices which the lecturer used that I could easily infuse into my tutorials in order to improve them. I started expressly stating the outcomes of each tutorial and showed how the exercises related to the programme and the greater skill set required within the practice of law. I have also subsequently developed tutorials with an overt focus on skills such as contract drafting, which have been positively received. Sometimes it helps to ask yourself how your subject would be viewed by an outsider in order to reflect on how to make it both more practical and accessible!

25. How to embed Corporate Social Responsibility (CSR) in teaching

Muhammad Al Mahameed and Umair Riaz

INTRODUCTION

We aim in this chapter to provide a roadmap of how to embed Corporate Social Responsibility (CSR) in teaching business and management modules at both under- and post-graduate levels. Before you start digging into this chapter, we need to spell out a number of assumptions that we carried throughout writing this chapter: we presumed that as a reader, you are an educator in a business school and planning to embed CSR materials in your teaching. Also, we presumed that you have two burning questions as you are reading this and you would like to find their answers in here. They are: (a) what CSR materials would you have in your module? And (b) how would you embed/deliver these materials? Finally, we presumed that by embedding CSR materials you aim to provide your students with a fundamental awareness and understanding of the available CSR approaches that are currently undertaken by different-sized companies around the world.

Although we are not intending to discuss the philosophy and nature of education itself in this chapter, we think it is important to place our philosophical stance here. We believe in the socialising effects of education itself, which further materialises in the CSR teaching that is embedded in the wider business education. CSR education for us goes beyond collating and presenting CSR knowledge to the business student but is rather a process that produces complex economic, political and cultural power relations.

Another point that needs clarifying here is what we mean by CSR. This is not a straightforward argument to be made clear in a few lines, since there are diverse perceptions that have been developed around this topic across the different groups and departments in business schools. However, the best way to clarify this is maybe by stating our differences here and finding an overarching definition to be used throughout this chapter. In Figure 25.1 we tried to comprise what we believe are the main four definitions of the CSR concept in business schools. The differences within those four definitions appear to be down to the nature of teaching or research

*Figure 25.1   Different perceptions of the CSR concept across business and
             management topics*

topic that deals with CSR, which can be: (a) an accounting and reporting process; (b) an assessment mechanism; (c) a group of policies and
standards; or (d) a model for self-regulation. These different definitions,
however, refer to one or more ways companies try to show their commitments in taking responsibility for the social and environmental impacts of
their operations.

   Agreeing on this overarching concept of CSR, we can now talk about
topics that can be taught in the area of CSR, as well as the ways and
methods in which those topics can be embedded in business and management modules. Finally, we will conclude with different assessment styles
that can be adopted to ensure (a) achieving the outcomes of the embedded CSR teaching materials and (b) how well those outcomes have been
achieved.

TEACHING CSR: WHAT AND HOW TO DO IT

Looking at what CSR topics are accessible across business schools, a lack
of harmony appears to be present within what should be taught in CSR
education, with topics that currently comprise CSR in business teaching

being: (1) environmental and social accountability; (2) external reporting; (3) theoretical frameworks for CSR; (4) sustainable development; (5) comparative and international CSR; (6) CSR history; and (7) social and ethical reporting, and business ethics. This fragmentation and lack of harmony in the embedded CSR topics can be avoided by having clear learning outcomes that are attached to well-designed indicative learning contents. Therefore, the starting point here is thinking about what you want the learners to gain as a result of the learning process, thinking about statements that can predict these gains. The measurability of these statements is key since the learners will not just perceive them as what they can be able to do at the end of the learning period but also as criteria that will be used to assess the learners.

Besides their ability to be measured, these learning objectives should represent a balance between professional, intellectual and transferable skills. For instance, the embedded CSR topics should aim to develop the learners' (a) ability to apply CSR concepts to aid decision making (*professional skills*), (b) ability to assess and engage with the limitations of the traditional business model (*intellectual skills*), and (c) ability to work in teams and weigh the pros and cons of the available options (*transferable skills*).

Further, learners would expect to be told the type and level of the acquired knowledge and understanding of the proposed CSR topics and areas that would be gained at the end of the learning process. Therefore, we suggest here that one or more of the learning objectives represents the possible acquisition of the CSR knowledge and understanding, such as developing the learners' ability to discuss alternative forms of business which address a range of CSR areas and performance.

Thinking of your teaching targets makes the design of the learning pathway more efficient with regard to identifying the skills and knowledge that learners require in order to achieve the set targets. However, one challenge remains present in embedding the CSR topics in our teaching, which is how we can get the learners to engage with the designed teaching pathway. One approach that we think might overcome this challenge is aligning clearly the learning objectives of the embedded CSR topics with the indicative contents by identifying the appropriate delivery style. In Table 25.1, we are proposing five CSR topics that could be embedded in business modules, also we align these topics with what we believe to be appropriate learning objectives, indicative contents and delivery styles.

The success of this alignment could be reflected within the adopted teaching method, and how well this method can reduce barriers to learning and enhancing learners' skills. Therefore, adopting an appropri-

Table 25.1   CSR topics aligned to learning objectives

Topic	Learning objectives	Indicative content	Delivery style
Understanding CSR	Reflecting on key perspectives in CSR	Consideration of alternative CSR forms for the widely available business models and its historical development	Thinking
CSR Theories	Appreciating the rationale and dynamics of CSR application	Consideration of CSR theories	Thinking
CSR Frameworks	Ability to reflect on standards that frame CSR practices	Consideration of legal and quasi-legal frameworks for CSR	Thinking/ Doing
CSR Internal Process	Understanding alternative performance measurements	Critical examination of traditional models	Thinking/ Doing
Developments in CSR	Understanding the recent trend in the CSR practice	Contemporary developments in the area of CSR	Thinking
CSR and Business ethics	Understanding the link between Business ethics and CSR	Examination of ethical theories	Thinking

ate teaching method becomes rather significant when CSR teaching materials are embedded into business and management teaching as more links need to be established organically between these CSR materials and the predominant business and management teaching subjects. However, establishing these links appears to be the least popular task amongst business and management educators as more and more CSR materials emerge to stand alone rather than being integrated into the curriculum and pedagogy. We believe that these stand-alone CSR teaching materials could be an outcome of a particular teaching method that perceives the learner as a client rather than a partner in the learning process and believing that the teaching materials must respond to the market demand and directions.

Teaching Tip
We perceive the business and management educators as a bunch of experts in their subjects, whilst the nature of CSR education requires more of a facilitating role.

The link that closes the CSR teaching cycle and ensures a coherent knowledge transfer and efficient skills enhancement within the abovementioned teaching alignment is the assessment link. This assessment for learning and teaching CSR can be designed to carry additional learning and complement the rest of the teaching materials, finally followed by a diagnostic feedback for improvement. In order to capitalise on these characteristics, the planned CSR assessment should be aligned with the learning objectives via identifying the required indicative content. This achieves the assessment for further and additional learning rather than assessment of learning in which the learners would be quizzed with the offered teaching materials, whilst it offers little opportunity for additional learning. Consequently, planning the assessment and the assessment criteria for the embedded CSR teaching materials should follow and build on the identified learning outcomes. This paves the way to the educators to find out the required CSR curriculum and pedagogy. Due to the nature of the CSR materials and the different angles that learners and educators can adopt in CSR education, the diagnostic feedback becomes rather important to draw the attention of the learners for possible ways for improvements, which we can call 'feed-forward' instead of feedback. Further, the given marks and comments become equally important in this assessment philosophy, where learners are expected to better engage with formative feedback and show improvement in the future learning. For the rest of this section we cover two examples from the five CSR topics that we listed in the table above, which can be embedded in teaching business and management modules with regard to learning objectives, teaching methods and assessment.

Example 1: Understanding CSR

It appears to be rational to start embedding CSR in teaching by introducing the key perspectives of CSR, then facilitating the understanding of alternative CSR forms. However, what seems to be less rational at this stage is offering the learners a range of concepts/definitions around CSR topics and expect the learners to comprehend such a complex area. Therefore, introducing CSR to learners is all about giving the first impression, where learners would construct their opinion about these teaching topics as being 'cool' and necessary or 'boring' and excessive. Bearing this in mind, we can construct the desirable image of the CSR among our students by starting with clear and logical learning objectives that are aligned to study paths of essential and supplementary activities. We would suggest the following sub-learning objectives that could achieve the holistic objective of this topic, where the learners should be able to:

- Reflect on key perspectives in CSR
- Understand the historical development of CSR
- Understand current concerns for CSR
- Reflect on the limitations of the current business practices
- Reflect on the dynamics of CSR practices
- Reflect on CSR philosophy from ethics.

These suggested learning objectives for this topic are aimed to achieve a balance between professional, intellectual and transferable skills, as well as representing knowledge and understanding acquisition. To better achieve these objectives, we have designed an engagement assessment for the learners, where they are required to identify a CSR report and provide a 10-minute presentation covering the following questions:

- What are the key elements of the report?
- What is the focus of the CSR report?
- How relevant is the information provided in the CSR report to different groups of stakeholders?
- Should CSR be regulated as the financial reporting?
- Who should set standards?
- Does CSR give any stakeholder any enforceable rights?
- Do good CSR practices equate with ethics?

Based on this engagement assessment and learning objective for this CSR teaching topic, we identify the indicative content that will shape the required skills of learners to achieve the holistic objective of this area. We divide the content into three topics of learning: (a) introduction to CSR, (b) concerns for CSR and (c) investigating the dynamics of CSR as well as business ethics. Then, we attach learning activities to these topics. For the first topic, we direct the learners to reflect on different perspectives on corporate social responsibility by considering the characteristics that a truly sustainable company exhibits. We facilitate the learners' contributions through online tools such as 'Discussion Boards' and 'Wiki'. These tools would foster additional learning throughout the teaching period. The second topic of learning comprises an activity that encourages the learners to consider what aspects of the company's business are not reported in CSR and how the unsaid may have an impact on various stakeholders as well as on the future direction of the company. Further, the activity of the final topic of learning engages with the learners to consider the following questions: (1) Why are there often huge gaps between what is said in a company's reports and a company's actions? (2) What barriers may there be to preventing companies becoming more socially responsible? (3) How can the logic of a corporation be changed?

One more teaching component to take into consideration is supplying the learners with a navigation exercise that draws a map for the learners to enhance their learning experience. For instance, in the navigation exercise for this topic, the learners are advised to begin by completing the essential reading for the topic, where key items from the essential reading are explained in greater detail in the lessons. In addition, a range of activities including blog posts, journal items, wikis and surveys have also been provided to help learners reinforce and consolidate their learning. However, learners will regularly need to be referred back to the 'Study Path: Essential Activities' list to plot their route through the topic. For learners who wish to explore additional items, they should be directed to do so. The navigation should point out that the supplementary activities are not a mandatory part of the learning, they have just been provided for learners who wish to delve deeper.

Example 2: CSR Frameworks

The primary aim of the topic of learning is to introduce the learners to key CSR frameworks with an emphasis on focal practical challenges, which are relevant to different stakeholder groups. Within this topic we have a secondary aim to explore some key CSR practices through which the learners can develop their ability to comprehend the reporting materials. Further, during this learning space, we direct the learners to examine a selection of issues with the current practices of CSR which affect different stakeholder groups. Therefore, we suggest the following learning objectives, where the learners should be able to:

- Discuss the need for 'generally accepted principles' for CSR
- Discuss the nature of these principles and which phase of the process of CSR it covers
- Evaluate the usefulness of a range of frameworks in a given industrial context
- Discuss the challenges that companies and/or stakeholders might face in implementing these principles.

Unlike the first example, in this advanced topic we focus on enhancing the learners' professional and practical skills, while trying to capitalise on the developed intellectual and transferable skills, as well as further develop the acquired knowledge and understanding from previous topics of learning. We aligned these objectives with engagement assessment that ensures additional learning through independent study time. In this engagement assessment we argue that they should appreciate the significant role of

CSR frameworks and how the number of the global firms that have adapted one or more of these frameworks is increasing. The learners are given a particular company that has adapted specific framework/s, and they are asked to look at their CSR reports and activities and review the following questions:

- What is the scope of this report? Who is the audience?
- What standards had been used in this report?
- Is the report externally verified?
- Comment on the assurance process, if any.
- What are the distinctive features of its reporting process?
- What are your evaluative comments on the quality of the report in terms of accountability and transparency?
- What governance structure is in place?

Before attempting this engagement assessment, the learners will have engaged with the planned indicative content of the topic of learning, which we divide into three sub-topics. As it is shown in Figure 25.2, this content is integrated in a study path that represents seven learning tasks that lead to the achievement of the learning objectives.

This study path comprises essential activities that are designed to facilitate the introduction and comprehension of the planned core indicative learning content. First, introduction to CSR frameworks, the learners will be introduced to the widely used CSR frameworks through learning activities that are largely based on online activities that carry the teaching materials such as a video mini-lecture, designated reading and discussion points. The second sub-topic explores and reviews a number of CSR frameworks through face-to-face lectures. Finally, the third sub-topic reviews the limitations and how the CSR frameworks operate and who influences them via an online mini-lecture and planned engagement activities.

CONCLUSION

In this chapter we have discussed the ways teachers could think about what material to teach and how to teach for CSR modules. More specifically we have proposed the way CSR as well as ethic topics could be embedded in business modules to align them with the appropriate learning objectives and indicative contents. Furthermore, we have divided the content into learning spaces and have suggested supplying a navigation exercise to learners. The aim that we are trying to achieve is to introduce the learners to key CSR frameworks and key CSR practices that could develop

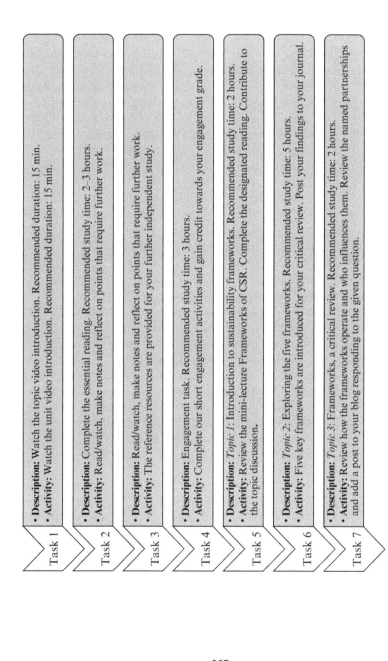

Task 1
- **Description:** Watch the topic video introduction. Recommended duration: 15 min.
- **Activity:** Watch the unit video introduction. Recommended duration: 15 min.

Task 2
- **Description:** Complete the essential reading. Recommended study time: 2–3 hours.
- **Activity:** Read/watch, make notes and reflect on points that require further work.

Task 3
- **Description:** Read/watch, make notes and reflect on points that require further work.
- **Activity:** The reference resources are provided for your further independent study.

Task 4
- **Description:** Engagement task. Recommended study time: 3 hours.
- **Activity:** Complete our short engagement activities and gain credit towards your engagement grade.

Task 5
- **Description:** *Topic 1*: Introduction to sustainability frameworks. Recommended study time: 2 hours.
- **Activity:** Review the mini-lecture Frameworks of CSR. Complete the designated reading. Contribute to the topic discussion.

Task 6
- **Description:** *Topic 2*: Exploring the five frameworks. Recommended study time: 5 hours.
- **Activity:** Five key frameworks are introduced for your critical review. Post your findings to your journal.

Task 7
- **Description:** *Topic 3*: Frameworks, a critical review. Recommended study time: 2 hours.
- **Activity:** Review how the frameworks operate and who influences them. Review the named partnerships and add a post to your blog responding to the given question.

Figure 25.2   Study path with essential activities

a critical understanding of CSR and ethics concepts, which has become more than ever a vital phenomenon to both industry and business schools.

We believe that integrating CSR and ethics into a well-designed curriculum would help teachers develop the capabilities of business students to work for an inclusive and sustainable economy by making CSR a natural and essential part of their thought process. Having mentioned the ways of aligning learning outcomes to the indicative content, it is important to incorporate CSR into curricula to better prepare students for entrepreneurship and employment opportunities. Furthermore, initiatives to promote CSR should be taken to accelerate the academic and industry dialogue and collaboration. This for instance could be done by organising highly interactive discussions and workshops with teachers, media, NGOs and business to promote the CSR education and bring harmony in topics.

Although business, management and organisation are the disciplines that mostly integrate CSR in their curriculum, a number of disciplines including accounting, marketing and human resources could embed CSR issues and values as an integral part of a well-defined curricula. As Melé (2008) suggested, the crisis in business ethics not only signifies a change for companies and business, but also an opportunity for education and research to expand and improve in the field of CSR. In order to make university education more sustainable to human society and wellbeing, the curriculum at universities will have to be rethought so that it equips professionals with the appropriate CSR skills and concepts. Finally, the debate over whether CSR should be incorporated as a stand-alone CSR subject or whether it should be integrated into a variety of subjects as a cross-sectional topic is still an ongoing discussion (Setó-Pamies et al., 2011). However, we believe that each university will have to espouse their own integration strategy that is most suited to its teaching environment, availability of specialised staff members and the accreditation process.

SUGGESTED FURTHER READING

Apple, M.W. (2012). *Education and Power*, Revised Routledge Classic Edition, New York: Routledge.
Dyment, J.E. and A. Hill (2015). 'You mean I have to teach sustainability too? Initial teacher education students' perspectives on the sustainability cross-curriculum priority', *Australian Journal of Teacher Education*, 40 (3), 2.
Elobeid, D.E., U. Lele and B.A. Kaifi (2016). 'Corporate Social Responsibility in Higher Education institutions: The experience of the College of Business and Economics at Qassim University', *International Leadership Journal*, 8 (1).

Green, M. and M. Somerville (2015). 'Sustainability education: Researching practice in primary schools', *Environmental Education Research*, 21 (6), 832–45.

Håkansson, M., L. Östman and K. Van Poeck (2018). 'The political tendency in environmental and sustainability education', *European Educational Research Journal*, 17 (1), 91–111.

Melé, D. (2008). 'Integrating ethics into management', *Journal of Business Ethics*, 78 (3), 291–7.

Memon, Z.A., Y.M. Wei, M.G. Robson and M.A.O. Khattak (2014). 'Keeping track of "Corporate Social Responsibility" as a business and management discipline: Case of Pakistan', *Journal of Cleaner Production*, 74, 27–34.

Rezaee, Z., N. Rezaee and S. Homayoun (2016). 'Integration of business sustainability education into the business curriculum', *International Journal of Finance and Managerial Accounting*, 1 (2), 1–8.

Setó-Pamies, D., M. Domingo-Vernis and N. Rabassa-Figueras (2011). 'Corporate Social Responsibility in management education: Current status in Spanish universities', *Journal of Management and Organization*, 17 (5), 604–20.

Stevenson, L., J. Ferguson and D. Collison (2014). 'Sustainability accounting and education'. In *Sustainability Accounting and Accountability*, pp. 48–66. London: Routledge.

Tormo-Carbó, G., V. Oltra, E. Seguí-Mas and K. Klimkiewicz (2016). 'How effective are business ethics/CSR courses in higher education?', *Procedia-Social and Behavioural Sciences*, 228, 567–74.

Warr Pedersen, K., E. Pharo, C. Peterson and G.A. Clark (2017). 'Wheels of change in Higher Education: A collaborative, multi-stakeholder project as a vehicle for sustainability education', *International Journal of Sustainability in Higher Education*, 18 (2), 171–84.

26. Teaching law to business students

Adam Shaw-Mellors and Pieter Koornhof

INTRODUCTION

It is not uncommon for new law lecturers to cut their metaphorical teeth by lecturing in introductory or cursory law courses aimed at business students. Such courses are often perceived as a 'safer' or 'easier' environment for law lecturers to develop their own ability to both present and critically analyse the law, as the target cohort is traditionally seen as less knowledgeable in, and therefore generally less critical of, the subject matter being taught. We contend that this is not necessarily a sound approach as the skill required to effectively convey relevant legal principles in a practical and accessible manner to business students can at times differ from how similar concepts would be presented to law students.

In this chapter, we reflect on some of the best practices we have developed in order to most effectively teach law to business students. These practices stem not only from our own experiences, but also from advice we have received over the years. In the first two sections we focus on how best to identify and develop the content that should be taught in law for business modules, whereas in the latter two we consider various methods and teaching approaches that may assist both new and established lecturers in this regard.

TEACH LEGAL RULES, NOT 'LAW'

A key aspect of our approach to teaching law to business students has been to focus carefully, during curriculum design and through the delivery of materials, on the specific needs and objectives of these students in relation to their study of the law. Students studying law as part of a business-related programme are not studying a law degree and the general purpose of their exposure to the law is, therefore, necessarily different to that of law students. With business students we take the view that their principal objectives are to understand core legal principles that will be relevant to working in a business environment and to appreciate how these principles practically apply. Teaching from this starting point has enabled us to think about what business students need to know and what they should be taught.

Teaching to law students typically involves exposing students to a range of different sources (such as case law and statutory provisions), often requiring students to research and understand the law's historical development to enable them to articulate views and recommendations. There are good reasons for doing this: a thorough understanding of the law requires an appreciation of its development, as well as changes in attitudes and policy behind it. This is, however, much less relevant to business students and the objectives we earlier identified for such students.

With business students, we focus on teaching what we term 'legal rules', rather than teaching law in the way we traditionally would do to law students. By legal rules, we mean core legal principles, taught in a systematic way that allows business students to learn these rules and identify and apply them in different contexts. Moreover, when we identify the legal rules we believe business students should be taught, we are careful to ensure we focus on rules relevant to businesses and on issues typically faced by those working in businesses. As such, in contrast to our approach to teaching law students (where students are encouraged to think critically about the law and its development), our concern with business students is teaching the relevant law in its current form, meaning we refer to the law's general development only where to do so helps to explain the relevant rules.

Linked to this are the expectations we have in relation to business students' independent study. Whereas law students are typically required to spend time researching legal principles and thinking critically about the law, we prefer to focus business students' independent research on thinking about identifying legal issues and how they apply in practical situations.

Teaching Tip
A typical exercise for business students might be to direct them to a business-related event or news item and require that they identify pertinent legal issues and think about the advice they would give to resolve such issues. They then come back to the lecture the following week ready to discuss their thoughts.

Our preference for focusing on rules does not, however, mean students should not be exposed to broader concepts where they are relevant to enhancing their understanding of the application of legal rules. One example we have found to be particularly relevant is teaching the law's approach to the interpretation of commercial contracts. By exposing students to the law's development in that particular area, we have been able to teach students much about the courts' general attitude to commercial contracting, and the relevant policy behind it, in a way that informs students' understanding of legal rules and how the courts regulate activities and transactions between businesses.

RECOGNISE TRANSFERABLE SKILLS AND TECHNIQUES

Once we have identified the relevant rules we think business students should be taught, we have two principal aims in the way we assess and interact with students. The first aim is to ensure we take the most appropriate approach to getting students to demonstrate and articulate their understanding of the principles we think they need to know. The second aim is to help students to develop a broader set of skills that will enhance their overall employability and workplace performance. In doing this, we take the view that there is more that business students can gain from studying law than legal knowledge alone and believe legal study can be an important source of skills relevant to business students' appreciation of key business concepts. We have found three particular skills to be capable of development through studying legal principles.

The first is the skill of procedure and rule application. A standard feature of law courses is to assess students by requiring that they apply legal principles to fictional practical scenarios, in order to reach conclusions and advise as to legal positions. We have, in the previous section, cautioned against assessing business students by requiring that they unnecessarily learn and apply detailed legal principles. When the relevant legal principles have been identified, however, we consider it important to expose students to practical scenarios of the kind they are likely to encounter in the workplace and we then require that students identify how the legal principles apply in those scenarios.

Teaching Tip
Use examples that business students might have encountered, maybe in part-time jobs. Ask them what was the law that applied to their situation? Were they treated fairly, and in accordance with the law?

In our experience, business students often find the task of identifying and applying legal rules to be difficult. A successful method we employ to assist students with this is the use of a 'roadmap'. This provides a basic step-by-step framework of factors students should consider in their application of legal principles. First, we encourage students to identify the relevant legal issues that have arisen in the scenario given to them and recommend that students summarise these issues in their own words. Second, we suggest students identify the relevant legal rules to be applied (and at this point, where possible, we provide guidance as to different areas of law to consider). Third, we recommend students analyse the relevant law and its application to the facts. Finally, students are encouraged to state their conclusions and advise as to the legal position and any practical steps they think should be taken.

We have found two benefits to this approach. First, it means students are exposed to the practical circumstances in which legal issues arise, enabling them to learn how they apply in circumstances similar to those they will encounter the workplace. Second, it enables students to enhance their appreciation of the application of rules and procedure in a more general way. This means students can develop a set of relevant skills that are important when performing activities in the workplace, such as acting on clients' instructions or applying company or industry rules, policies or procedural requirements.

The second skill we contend is developed through legal study relates to students' ability to analyse complex concepts and principles. A key aspect of legal study is the need to assimilate and marshal technical, complex and sometimes seemingly contradictory rules. In the workplace, students are likely to be faced with unfamiliar concepts and be required to understand what these concepts mean and how they fit together. This will require more than simple application: students will have to reconcile apparent inconsistencies and understand difficult concepts by understanding the context and rationale behind the principles they apply. Exposing business students to complex legal rules and requiring that they not only apply these rules but understand more fundamentally why they exist and how apparent inconsistencies within the law can be resolved can help students develop skills that will help them tackle such issues in the workplace.

Thus, returning to the example of the law of contractual interpretation, students might be required to interpret and follow contractual principles in the workplace, and so understanding how the courts interpret contracts will be important. Yet, this area of law, as is true of many others, is also important because it reveals different – and arguably inconsistent – approaches the courts take to establishing the relevant legal principles. This means it requires a reconciliation of contradictory and complex principles and propositions. The level of analysis required when tackling such principles will help students develop analytical and practical reasoning skills, thereby enhancing their overall employability and skills they will need in the workplace.

Teaching Tip
Tell students about a case that is relevant to the topic being studied. Ask them to discuss it in pairs and decide the outcome. Then, ask everyone to vote on what they think the outcome was. When the vote has happened, ask students to argue their case before you tell them what the courts ruled.

A third skill is the presentation of analyses and recommendations. We earlier referred to our preference for exposing students to practical scenarios and requiring that they identify legal rules relevant to these scenarios. One method we have used to achieve this is through requiring students to produce a report to an organisation's board of directors in which they identify key legal issues relevant to a scenario provided to them and make recommendations as to the course of action to be taken by the organisation in response. This method not only allows students to demonstrate their understanding of relevant legal rules but also encourages students to think carefully about the advice they provide, the implications of their recommendations, and the potential practical consequences of particular courses of action. These are important skills relevant to the workplace, where students will often be required to undertake analyses of complex documentation and other materials for the purpose of reaching conclusions and recommendations.

Teaching Tip
An assessment for a law course for business students is best if it includes practical situations where the student has to give advice. This allows them to practise the skills that they will need when they enter the world of work.

USE THE LANGUAGE AND CONTEXT OF BUSINESS

Fundamentally, a key skill for lawyers is the ability to present specialised knowledge in a relatable and accessible manner. A very sensible piece of advice that was once given by a senior colleague was that when one speaks to business people – especially when trying to explain a particular point of law in order to persuade them – you should speak the language of business rather than law. We would contend that this is not only an effective way of conveying concepts and principles to individuals in business, but also to business students.

An easy example of how one can use the language of business to make one's content more relatable is to switch from the phrase 'case law' to that of 'case study'. Whereas law students are used to the former, business students are not. However, they would have been exposed to a variety of factual scenarios presented in a manner to illustrate a particular principle and to be used for subsequent discussion and analysis. We would also contend that there is very little reason for business students to be taught the names of cases or in which court a judgment was made. Instead, the relevant facts and principles can be abstracted and presented through a basic summary. Simply framing your content in a different manner requires relatively little effort but goes a long way towards making it appear less foreign to the student.

Effectively teaching law to business students not only relates to the actual language being used, but also the context being provided to students. When teaching law to law students, most of their other subjects will be reinforcing a particular language, style and skill set being used and conveyed. For business students being taught a legal subject, this will not be the case. As such, it is up to the law teacher to adapt to the context of the business student. Often the type of law modules taught to business students tend to have a commercial focus, and therefore phrasing examples and questions in a way that relates to such an environment is beneficial and sensible. This is again not necessarily an arduous task. For instance, when teaching intellectual property to business students one could easily relate the importance of the content by placing them in the metaphorical shoes of a rights holder that may be dealing with a potentially litigious matter. Another example would be to place the student in the shoes of an employer dealing with an employment matter, or a director of a company that needs to ensure that its board meetings are in line with regulations so that decisions taken are not subject to review. In doing so, the law teacher moves away from simply referring to dry provisions in a statute or explaining a legal concept in the abstract. Instead, one is able to breathe life into content by making it a business problem involving the law.

We believe that developing this facet of one's teaching not only improves how you are able to relate to business students, but also helps you to develop a skill which you can use when teaching in other contexts. First, the ability to abstract and simplify concepts and principles from statutes and case law is useful when introducing law students to new areas of the law that they may not have been exposed to before. Second, it helps you to relate the law to the real world, showing how (especially commercial legal) aspects would operate in a business environment.

As we stated before, an important skill for a lawyer is the ability to communicate their knowledge to a client, not only to provide advice, but in order to obtain proper instructions on how to deal with a matter going forward. We submit that law teachers should not only develop the above skill for their own benefit, but also assist in developing this skill in their law students. Whereas the ability to explain complex concepts in a relatable and accessible manner is a key requirement for a successful law graduate, it is not one always directly taught or assessed within a law school. Through using the experiences gained in teaching law to business students, this can be done. For instance, there is no reason why roleplaying as an employer, a director or a rights holder cannot be used to provide the same context and understanding to a law classroom, or in assessing them on their ability to convey information to a client. Again, oral assessments at law schools are not uncommon, and so it is again a case of changing the focus rather than reinventing the wheel. This could further be assessed through the use of videos or presentations where the ability to convey information is expressly measured.

MANAGE STUDENT EXPECTATIONS (ALONG WITH YOUR OWN)

We contend that it is important to be realistic in your expectations of what you want a course to achieve. It is important to be mindful that, when teaching business students, a discrete aspect of the law is being conveyed. Whereas in a previous section we reflected on how there should be a focus on teaching relevant transferable skills to students, it is important to note that a teacher is not able to teach all necessary aspects of the law within the confines of a single course. To assume that a law student will be an expert in employment law after a single term would be misguided to say the least. Given the context of a business student – something we reflected on above – this assumption would be even less appropriate.

When developing a programme for business students, it has been our experience that some law teachers will unfortunately simply take their existing programme and simplify it. This is the wrong approach. In doing so, you do not necessarily reflect on what the outcomes of the course are and how these may differ for business students. Whereas you would expect a law student to be able to identify and solve a particular legal problem, this is not necessarily what you can or always should expect from a business student. It is therefore important to determine what is most appropriate in terms of the knowledge or skills you as lecturer would like to convey.

The question of what is or would be the most appropriate content may in part be determined by the nature of the module. A programme broadly catering to a variety of students should look different to one being taught to a specific cohort. For instance, a company law programme for finance students would likely look different to one for entrepreneurial students. Equally, an employment law course for human resource managers could also be slightly more tailored to the context of employee relations from the side of the employer. Reflecting on the outcomes and content will help you define the parameters of your course. Naturally there will always be aspects within certain subjects that are seen as non-negotiable, but we contend that you should provide as flexible a framework as possible for you to adapt your content and style for particular groups.

Providing a framework that is flexible but with defined outcomes for students creates a solid point of departure for managing the expectations of both students and the lecturer. This way the lecturer has a clear idea of what they ultimately wish to teach, and this should then be broadly set out for students. Within these stated parameters a lecturer can then determine which teaching activities and assessments would be most appropriate for a module. It is even possible, within reason, to involve the students in this process. Adopting a flexible framework allows you to ask students if there are any particular topics or aspects they would like to cover. On the presumption that a suggestion is sensible and fit for purpose, it may then easily be included. It is even possible to pre-empt an answer to the dreaded question of 'Will this be in the exam?' in doing so.

For instance, a lecturer could still allow for student involvement by proposing a range of optional topics to be covered and offering students a choice. If you know what's coming, it's possible to craft interchangeable questions and include them in an exam. Alternatively, students could prepare and present on these additional topics and that could form part of the module's assessment. In larger classes where in-class presentations may not be feasible, a similar result could be achieved through having students prepare video presentations to be played in class, for instance. There are various creative ways to ensure that it is clear to students what the expected outcomes are of a module, and – perhaps more importantly – that these outcomes sensibly speak to the broader context of their particular discipline. This will go some way to avoiding frustrations and missed opportunities on the part of both student and lecturer.

CONCLUSION

Some of the most rewarding lectures we have presented have been to non-legal cohorts, and the feedback we have received from it has assisted us in improving our teaching in general. It is therefore not entirely inaccurate to assert that teaching law to business students can make you a better lecturer. What we would still however contend is that this is not the case because it is necessarily easier. Instead, it allows for experimentation and challenges you in different ways than a cohort of law students would. We believe that this encourages law lecturers to think more carefully about their teaching practices and why they are teaching what they are teaching (in terms of both content and method) in a way that traditional law teaching does not necessarily do.

The aspects that we have reflected on above are only some of the ways that a lecturer can adapt to tailor their content and style to be more effective when teaching to business students. We do not proclaim that the advice given here is even the most effective way of doing so, but hope that it may contribute to the marketplace of ideas by assisting (both present and future) colleagues in reflecting on and developing their own best practices.

SUGGESTED FURTHER READING

Allen, V. (2005). 'A reflection on teaching law to business students', Paper presented at the Society for Research into Higher Education Conference, University of Edinburgh, 13–15 December 2005, available at http://www.leeds.ac.uk/educol/documents/151912.htm (accessed 3 September 2018).
Butler, N. and O. Madhloom (2016). 'Teaching company law to business students: An effective framework', *Law Teacher*, 50 (2), 160–71.
Dove, L. and N. Bryant (2016). 'Law in translation: Challenges and opportunities in teaching international students in business law and legal environment courses', *Journal of Legal Studies Education*, 33 (2), 263–91.
Endeshaw, A. (2002). 'Teaching law to business students: An inquiry into curriculum and methodology', *Law Teacher*, 36 (1), 24–43.

Thought 15

Adam Shaw-Mellors

When it comes to assessments, traditional methods on law programmes require students to write essays about legal principles and provide advice concerning issues contained in fictional problem-based scenarios. Teaching law to business students meant I had the occasion to consider whether this style of assessment was the appropriate one for business students studying law, given the different purposes and objectives behind these students' study of the law. In particular, I have concerned myself with how to ensure business students learn about the types of legal issues and practical problems they are likely to encounter when working in businesses and organisations, as well as what skills they will need to resolve them.

Reflecting on these issues led me to think more generally about the nature of the way I teach and assess law students. In particular, I thought about the extent to which students appreciate the skills they obtain through assessments and whether they realise the relevance these skills have in relation to their overall development and employability. This in turn led me to think about whether I could do more to help students identify and apply these skills.

It is a common assumption amongst law students that they are assessed through the traditional methods I have described because these methods best enable students to demonstrate the knowledge of the law they are deemed to need if they are to become successful lawyers. What became apparent to me, however, was that students do not always appreciate the broader set of skills they develop and demonstrate in these assessments, nor how they relate to different career types. For example, when teaching law, we tell students we expect them to demonstrate critical analysis when writing an essay, but perhaps take for granted their ability to make the connection between the skills they develop when analysing complex legal principles and the analytical skills they will be required to demonstrate when pursuing their desired career. As such, it has become a part of my teaching practice to dedicate time to explaining to students why I have decided to assess them in the way I have and to highlight the skills to be developed through the assessment and their relevance to the workplace.

I have found two particular benefits to getting students to approach assessments with a more fundamental understanding of the skills the assessment will enable them to develop. First, it means students think more pragmatically about their assessment, thereby improving their engagement with it. In other words, students can see the assessment as more than work they must complete: it becomes an opportunity to reflect on and develop important skills of wider relevance. Second, it helps students to recognise the skills they are developing and to appreciate the relevance of these skills to their overall employability. I have found this not only improves the quality of students' work, but also helps them to focus on the skills needed to help with their careers.

27. Practitioner module partnership and sponsorship

Keith Glanfield

INTRODUCTION

Teachers in higher education (HE) are under ever-increasing pressure to make their modules and degree programmes relevant to professional practice. This is especially the case in business schools. The expectation is for HE teachers to directly apply theory and research to a relevant profession (accountancy, law, marketing, supply chain, and so on), to demonstrate how the profession works in practice. However, we all approach our teaching and research from slightly differing perspectives. For example, some, like myself, might have entered HE teaching from a practice background. In contrast other colleagues might have entered the profession by the conventional doctoral route. Irrespective of our differing backgrounds, the challenge remains the same for us all – to apply what we teach in order to improve the student experience, student employability and student satisfaction.

There are many different methods available to us to integrate professional practice into our teaching. They range from teaching to pre-prepared academic case studies, taking relevant vignettes off YouTube, having practitioners with us in the room when we teach and setting practical-based forms of assessment. No matter how we go about this, there are challenges for us as HE teachers. Arranging this activity is very time-consuming and requires detailed planning. Many different parties are involved. It potentially relies on the teacher having an active and reasonably extensive network of contacts. Given the extensive effort needed, HE teachers must want and be committed to including a practice dimension into their teaching.

This chapter explores a method of integrating practice into business school HE teaching that aims to minimise the above challenges. The method is labelled 'module sponsorship'. It simply involves a module leader forming a partnership with a business; a collaboration where the business informs the teaching of theory and research and the theory and research informs the practice of the business. Having used this method many times in my own HE teaching, I use one particular example of module sponsorship to practically demonstrate the method's components and features (Advanced Marketing Communications), including an honest appraisal of the benefits and reduced challenges of using this method for both students and HE teachers.

THE BACKGROUND OF THE MODULE AND THE PRACTICAL CHALLENGES I FACED

Advanced Marketing Communications is an undergraduate marketing module I teach in the BSc Marketing programme's final year. The module integrates several foundations of the marketing discipline, i.e. consumer behaviour, marketing communications and marketing strategy. It presents students with an opportunity to understand how the marketing problems faced by organisations can be addressed through the effective use of advanced marketing communications techniques. In other words, I aim to teach how the effective development of marketing communications campaigns can address practical marketing issues. These may include repositioning poorly positioned brands to improve an organisation's market share, extending brands into new market segments and launching new products to combat competitive threats.

I deliver the module in the final term of the degree's final year, the very time when students wishing to enter a marketing career are facing rounds of job applications, interviews, and assessment centres for marketing graduate schemes, internships and full-time marketing positions with advertising agencies and client-side blue-chip organisations. At a minimum employers are looking for candidates who can, on paper, effectively frame, analyse and understand marketing problems that lead to the development of feasible and practical solutions. Employers are in addition looking for 'exceptional' candidates who can evidence a practical understanding and experience of:

- Persuasively pitching and presenting solutions to marketing problems to senior stakeholders and key decision makers
- Taking a solution from paper and delivering a cost-effective and innovative campaign
- Campaign development from both a client and agency perspective
- Evaluating new and emerging marketing communications tools
- How client organisations and advertising agencies manage what can be a very tricky relationship.

As the module leader, my challenge was to develop the module to address these pressing and practical requirements, to operationalise theory and research to demonstrate its relevance and applicability to developing solutions to practical marketing problems.

THE SOLUTION – MODULE SPONSORSHIP BY A MAJOR LONDON ADVERTISING AGENCY

A major London advertising agency, with important clients such as LloydsTSB, Nestlé and GlaxoSmithKline, agreed to sponsor the module. They agreed to provide the following to develop students' practical skills and experience:

- *Joint review and amendment of module content from a practitioner perspective.* The Agency and I reviewed and amended the module, from a practitioner perspective, integrating and incorporating the activity set out below.
- *Practical assessment – provide a 'live' and current client problem, being worked on by the agency, for students to develop a commercially compelling marketing communications campaign.* The Agency and their blue chip company provided a 'live' marketing problem which the agency were working on at the time. Working in groups the students were to develop a campaign solution for the 12-week module period. The challenge was to reposition a well-known fast-moving consumer goods drinks brand, from a night-time drink taken prior to sleep to a relaxing and early evening drink.
- *Briefing of students by the agency/client and ongoing contact through the campaign development process.* The students were briefed directly by the Agency and their client on the marketing problem. This was followed by a discussion on the importance of client briefing, how to manage this vital activity, accompanied by follow-up sessions to take questions on the brief and for the brief to be challenges. This included providing students with packs of the product to taste and give them a practical feel to the product's packaging and merchandising.
- *Provide guest lectures on related practical skills, 'the art of pitching', etc.* The Agency provided practitioner guest speakers to deliver sessions on the practical challenges of pitching, campaign development and creativity in advertising. These were delivered as component parts of lectures, in support of relevant theory and research.
- *Provide the main participants of a pitching panel, where each group pitched their solution to the agency/client and a number of industry*

experts. Each of the 28 groups, over a 2-day period, pitched their campaign solution to key members of the agency, their client, the Regional Director of the Chartered Institute of Marketing and an external pitching consultant. This was not a false, staged environment. Rather it was a realistic opportunity to sell a campaign solution to industry experts, including the opportunity for students to gain a paid summer internship at the agency and also for groups to receive a best pitch first, second or third award. The contents of the pitches were considered for incorporation into the agency's ongoing development of solutions for their client.

- *Award a number of paid internships for students based upon their performance in the campaign pitches.* Based upon students' performance in the pitching assessment, a number of students were invited for interview by the Agency, with several paid summer internships awarded to students. As a result a number of offers of full-time employment were made.
- *Award prizes of 1st, 2nd, 3rd for pitch performance.* Based upon students' performance in the pitching assessment, the top three pitches were awarded prizes by the Agency which were formally recognised and certified by the University.

ADDITIONAL SUPPORT TO COMPLEMENT THE SPONSORSHIP ACTIVITY

With 28 groups developing campaigns over the course of the 12-week module, I thought it essential each group had the opportunity to discuss their campaign with me a number of times throughout its development. Each week I scheduled three one-hour tutorials. Each group met me biweekly, totalling six meetings over the course of the module.

In addition to the guest lectures provided by the Agency, I also included a small number of guest lectures delivered by practitioner subject matter experts, i.e. brand equity measurement, campaign evaluation and media planning.

The Chartered Institute of Marketing, given its role to develop future marketers in the West Midlands, aided the development of the module in assisting in the development of the assessment criteria and in the form of their Regional Director, marking and providing feedback on the student pitches.

LEARNING AND TEACHING BENEFITS

The learning and teaching benefits of the newly formatted module, when compared to the previous year, were markedly improved. These included improved student evaluations, coursework and exam performance, along with directly attributable benefits for student employability.

- *Improved student evaluation.* The overall student satisfaction of the module, against the previous year, improved from 3.0 to 4.0 (out of 5).
- *Improved coursework and exam performance.* In overall terms the mean mark moved up to 60.53 per cent (sd 8.96) from 51.12 per cent (sd 8.84) the previous year. Exam performance increased by 12 per cent and coursework assessment moved from a mean of 56.74 per cent to 61.75 per cent. Other factors may have influenced this improvement, however strong narrative student feedback emphasises the value of the practical nature of the module in applying theory and research to practice.
- *Central theme to integrate research and theory with practice.* The 'live' marketing problem provided a central theme for lectures. Each week I could apply and discuss the lecture's research in this context. One central theme provided continuity and the opportunity to practically integrate frameworks and models.
- *Likely increased ability for students to integrate and apply research and theory in an exam setting.* Compared to the previous year students demonstrated a greater ability to apply research and theory in an examination setting. The year-on-year increase in exam performance of 12 per cent can be directly attributed to students arriving at definite and relevant conclusions based upon using their experience of the 'live' case assessment, to consider the relevance of theory and research.
- *Opportunity for the teacher to integrate and build relationships with a large student group.* Sometimes it can be difficult for HE teachers to build relationships with a large student group, in this case 190 students. Meeting each assessment group six times during the module meant I had a common point of reference for class discussion, and a means of building a stronger two-way relationship between myself and the module's students.

EMPLOYABILITY BENEFITS FOR STUDENTS

The intention of changing the delivery model of the module was to practically support students in their search for their first role in marketing, providing an opportunity for students to develop specific work-based marketing technical skills (pitching and pitch development) along with experiencing specific client and advertising agency processes first-hand:

- *Internships, employment and incentives.* As a result of the Agency seeing and jointly assessing the 28 student pitches, 15 students were invited for interview. A number were offered and accepted paid summer internships, resulting in some full-time job offers. The potential of these internships, the pitching prizes plus the added incentive of working on a 'live' practical problem, acted as an incentive for students to commit to the module and its assessment.
- *Developed practical work-based skills.* Students in a 'live' setting were equipped with first-hand experience of the client/agency briefing process, translating a brief into a marketing problem that required a solution, end-to-end campaign development (including creative development) and crafting and delivering a pitch to experienced industry and agency practitioners.
- *Experience for use at interviews and selection.* Students successfully used their pitch development experience and their exposure to campaign development, to enhance their CV during recruitment and selection. This experience was very valuable during competence-based interviews that required students to demonstrate how they had addressed practical work-based challenges.
- *Network growth.* Many students took the opportunity to extend their professional and social networks using electronic media to connect with practitioner guest speakers and their organisations.

LEARNING AND TEACHING CHALLENGES

Although this model of delivery achieved several important and relevant teaching and learning benefits, a number of challenges accompanied it. I experienced an increase in the preparation time and resources needed over and above taking a more conventional model of delivery. However, this was likely far less than if I were to have addressed the module's challenges by not using module sponsorship:

- *Change module sequence and content to cope with new lecture format.* In order to integrate guest lectures into lecture time, I changed the emphasis of the module in response to practitioner feedback. This included the incorporation of a 'live' marketing problem and changing the content, structure and sequencing of the lectures.

- *Greater tutorial time and out-of-lecture support.* I had to build in greater face-to-face time in tutorials for students to gain the maximum benefit of working on the 'live' marketing problem and to prepare each group for their practical 'pitch' assessment.
- *More administration.* I did slightly more administration in the form of the ongoing management of the partnership and making arrangements for additional guest lectures etc. requires greater administration from the lecturer.
- *Greater lecture preparation.* Linking and integrating guest lecture content into lectures increased lecture preparation time.

DISADVANTAGES

The numerous opportunities the module presented for students to improve their prospects brought with them a number of challenges:

- *Increased workload and effort required to optimise the opportunities in their final term.* During their final term, where final year students are most under pressure, students had to commit to achieving tight and demanding deadlines in order to deliver an innovative and practical piece of coursework. This mirrors the challenges faced by many in practitioner marketing roles, requiring students to work in a professional and organised manner, and substantially commit to dedicating the requisite time and effort to deliver high-quality output.
- *More group work.* Although more group work was required for final year undergraduates in the final term, the practical work-related nature of the task positively contributed to the favourable teaching evaluations.

THE FOUNDATIONS OF AN EFFECTIVE 'MODULE SPONSORSHIP'

I have applied the model of practitioner module partnership and sponsorship to other modules, with similar results. The model has the potential to be applied outside of the marketing discipline to other business school disciplines. In reflecting upon my experience, the transferability of the 'module sponsorship' model is dependent upon a number of factors:

- *Partnering with an organisation that is willing to share commercial information and open up their organisation to the University.* Gaining in return access to a pool of employable undergraduates and receiving a diverse set of solutions to a business problem that is central to the organisation's future success.

- *Sourcing a business problem or organisational issue where a suitable solution can be developed at a distance*, i.e. without students having to work in the organisation for a significant period of time or become directly immersed in its day-to-day operation.
- *The business problem lends itself to a practical form of assessment that mirrors a real-life professional experience*, i.e. the presentation of an advertising solution to an advertising agency client in the form of an 'agency pitch'.
- *The teacher is willing to recognise and work within the practical commercial and operational constraints of the partner organisation.* Making the necessary trade-offs to accommodate the need for students to develop a practical solution to the business problem and make themselves available for press and PR activity.
- *The partner and sponsoring organisation is willing to invest time and resources* in briefing the business problem, delivering guest lectures, supporting the students in development of their solutions and participating in marking and evaluating the module assessment.

CONCLUSION

This chapter is not designed to present a precise, empirical and generalisable statistical study into the effects of practitioner module sponsorship on enhancing the student experience and its positive influence on student employability and satisfaction. Instead in this chapter I recount my own personal experience of using this method of introducing practice into my teaching and setting out the benefits I derived from its introduction. This approach may suit certain colleagues and the modules they teach but may not suit others. It is not presented as a 'one-size-fits-all' solution, merely an alternative to be considered. As an advocate of the practitioner module sponsorship model, it is not for me to decide upon its merits; that is a matter for you the reader.

PART VI

Assessment

28. Demystifying the assessment criteria

Gayatri Patel

INTRODUCTION

Few would contend the claim, possibly reluctantly, that assessments form the central focus of students' learning and teaching at Higher Education (HE) (Ramsden, 1992). This may be because the final transcript is possibly the most significant physical representation of their academic performance over the years spent on the degree programme, and will usually have lasting influence in defining a student's overall experience at university. For this reason, the students' performance in assessments, particularly at modular level in the initial years of any programme, can have a dominant influence over their passion, work ethic, self-confidence and motivation towards the subject, but also define the nature of the relationship between the students and the lecturer. At programme level, the pattern of assessments over the programme can contribute to defining the quality of guidance and support that they actually or perceive to be receiving from their institution.

The significance attached to assessments is reflected in the design and management of them, which forms an integral part of any programme design, and often has a dedicated team to manage and administer assessments at either school or university level. The implications of the actual or perceived lack of support received in relation to assessments can be significant to both internal and external operations in a university. Externally, implications in relation to assessments are reflected in the prominence given to them in the National Student Survey, whereby over a fifth of the questions are currently directly related to assessments, feedback and the support received in relation to it. Internally, ambiguity and inconsistency can lead to actual or perceived lack of support in relation to assessments, and can perpetuate feelings of discontent and failure in meeting expectations amongst the student cohort.

This is significant, as unlike secondary or further education, the design, delivery, assessment and marking is largely undertaken by the same module team members. The responsibility of lecturers in relation to assessments can create a complex and conflicting role with their identity as a teacher in

HE. In this context, it can be relatively easy, consciously or unconsciously, to be overtly defensive in relation to assessments during interactions with students to maintain impartiality and objectivity.

Whilst, naturally, a strong commitment to maintaining academic integrity of the programme and the institution should be upheld, any degree of a cold and defensive attitude towards assessment by academics contributes to the often held perception of the mystification of assessments and the assessment criteria. In an attempt to demystify the criteria, and how the work is going to be marked, students often resort to believing hearsay narratives of certain lecturers being more lenient than others; implement strategies to dedicate time to certain subjects on the module and avoid the study of others; and spend time repeatedly writing to academics with a number of queries, rather than dedicating this valuable time to assessment itself. At worst, the chasm between the assessment expectations and criteria and the student's meaningful understanding of it can lead to a breakdown in the trust and learning and teaching partnership between students and lecturers, and breed cynicism and antagonism.

The aim of my practice was to begin to dilute the myth that the judgement of assessments was undertaken by the 'elite' academics, who exercise their 'academic judgement', which itself was mysterious in nature and beyond the grasp of students. It is not enough to simply expect students to refer to the assessment criteria, or naively rely on mere verbal communication of the criteria and presume students have acquired the knowledge in relation to the assessment. Instead, a more structured intervention was required, which resulted in students having a meaningful understanding of the assessment criteria so that it can be used as an active tool in the learning process.

THE PROBLEM

Pedagogic research has provided support to the commonly held belief in academia that the interpretations of assessments criteria can, to some extent, vary between individuals even within the same faculty (Webster et al., 2000). This may explain why some students might feel compelled to attempt to construct a cohesive interpretation of components of the assessment criteria through a process of trial and error and elimination, by submitting assessment pieces over a period of time. Not only does this exercise take a lengthy period of time, often not available in a modular environment, but this misdirected dedication of time and effort does not facilitate best student achievement. Evidence of this problem materialised in my module, taught to second year students on the programme. The

Business School's assessment criteria has been tailormade for the discipline, spanning the areas of:

- Research
- Subject knowledge
- Use of authority and analysis
- Identification and application of relevant legal principles
- Communication and presentation and referencing.

Each area consists of a descriptor with detailed expected performances, which is aligned to the appropriate grade ranging from fail, to a higher first class. The assessment criteria are exceptionally comprehensive and clearly written. At the beginning of my first lecture of the year, I decided to undertake an, admittedly non-scientific, experiment. I distributed a copy of the assessment criteria, and made clear to the students that this was a personal experiment and the students were strongly encouraged to be entirely honest. They were asked whether they referred to the assessment criteria, before, during or upon reading their feedback. Only 10 per cent of the students stated that they even referred to it, with some students admitting that they were not aware where it was located to access it.

From this brief survey in my module, it can be observed that despite the best intentions and efforts of the faculty, the clear and explicit assessment criteria did not provide any meaningful understanding of the standards and criteria against which the students' work was going to be assessed. From the informal written and oral feedback I received from my survey, I observed three main points.

- First, students failed to understand a number of the key terminologies and phrases used in the assessment criteria.
- Second, students struggled to articulate what the criteria and descriptors may look like in practice, and how they would meet the requirements in their work.
- Third, students did not have any meaningful understanding of the differences between the grade descriptors, and again how such differences materialised in practice.

One student's observation about the assessment criteria was very revealing as he stated that 'submitting an assessment is like a stab in the dark, you just hope you get the grade that you want'. This demonstrated the distance that the students experienced in relation to the assessment criteria, which was not, according to them, incorporated as part of the learning process. The assessment criteria were perceived as something that is largely used and applied by the academics, and not an active tool that can be useful to the student learning process in achieving the learning outcomes of the module.

THE SOLUTION

At the core of my teaching practice is the belief that assessments should be designed *for* learning, rather than *of* the learning. This is particularly pertinent for my module, as at the core of the module is the intention to develop the student's ability to be critically evaluative, and to present and defend a position in a clear, coherent and justifiable manner. Thereby, an assessment *of* the learning would be aligned with the learning and teaching outcomes of the module. In order to incorporate the assessment as part of the process, I decided to design and implement a new assessment support and guidance initiative to be part of the teaching schedule.

I replaced a tutorial on the teaching schedule with an 'Assessment Workshop' which lasted for a duration of 90 minutes. It was made clear to the students that the focus of the workshop was not to examine the content of the module, but to examine the criteria and the expectations of the assessment. In preparation for the workshop, the students were asked to read through the assessment criteria, highlight the terminologies and reflect on their understanding of them. The workshop itself was divided into two parts.

For the first part of the workshop, I put together a selection of slides that consisted of highlighted key terms in the assessment criteria. As a group, I led the discussions on the interpretations of these key concepts, and I provided an input to define, clarify, or expand on the interpretations provided. These discussions were pivotal as they not only helped the students to evaluate their own understanding with components of the criteria, but also how it specifically applied to the module and more broadly in the second year of the programme.

This is significant as terms such as 'highly evaluative' and 'critical analysis' are inherently, and unavoidably, ambiguous; the precise meanings of which are based on a number of factors including the assessors, the nature of assessment and the academic level at which the assessment is set. Alongside each terminology, I provided an explanation as to the meaning of the term in relation to the module, and provided extracts from students' essays from the previous year, who demonstrated meeting the assessment components from varying different grade bands. These discussions were quite lengthy, as we compared and contrasted the example extracts from the different bands, and how they met the criteria. Not only did this provide a clarification of the students' own understanding of the assessment components, but also across the different grade descriptors, thereby completing a horizontal and vertical examination of the assessment criteria.

Teaching Tip
Spend time working carefully through the meaning of circulated assessment criteria with students to ensure their understanding of the assessment criteria.

The second part of the workshop was more practical in nature. Here, using the assessment criteria, and their improved understanding of it, students were required to mark a selection of anonymised essays from the previous year, each from a different grade band. The students were required to work in small groups to review and grade each assessment in light of the discussions and explanations provided in the first half of the workshop. As the workshop was taking place in the second teaching period, the students had sufficient knowledge of the content of the subject to undertake a comprehensive review of the essays provided.

Once all the essays had been reviewed and graded, I led the group discussion for each essay, whilst discussing why the students have awarded the marks, and the justifications for them in light of the assessment criteria and grade descriptors. I provided the actual mark for each essay, together with my annotated feedback of the assessment on a power point slide. The students engaged in further discussions, drawing comparisons with their own assessments and mine. The students were remarkably surprised with the accuracy of the marking.

Teaching Tip
Students enjoy marking anonymised examples of former students' work, using the assessment criteria to guide them.

Towards the end of the workshop, the students asked if they could have an electronic version of the essays from the previous year. I refused and explained that the rationale of the workshop was to focus on the criteria, and not the content of the answers. This also avoided the risk of students focusing entirely on the content of the answers, and replicating it for the submissions, which is often associated with distributing sample answers. Instead the use of hard copies ensured that the task was entirely focused on understanding the assessment components and reviewing how it materialised in practice.

THE IMPLICATIONS

The Assessment Workshop not only forced the students to engage actively with the assessment criteria, but also to facilitate a meaningful and practical understanding of the criteria and grade descriptors. Just from the observations and informal feedback at the end of the Assessment Workshop, it was conclusive that it was very well received, and this was again reflected in the formal feedback for the module.

The Assessment Workshop addressed the three problems that were identified earlier on in this chapter.

- First, it provided a comprehensive and reflective explanation of the key components of the assessment criteria.
- Second, the marking task of the workshop exposed the students to the practical examples of how students in the previous year had demonstrated meeting the criteria.
- Third, the culmination of both aspects of the workshop facilitated an understanding of how the criteria was applied to this specific module across the different grade brackets, together with practical examples.

In comparison to previous years, the results of the assessments showed a significant improvement in the quality of the answers submitted for the assessment, with a significant increase in the number of students achieving an upper second class, and higher, with a large fall in the number of students that received a lower second class grade.

This practice of intervention has been beneficial for the student beyond the modular level. At programme level, the approach actively to engage students with the criteria also encouraged them to assess how the faculty criteria specifically applied to the other modules on the programme. On a more broader and abstract level, the assessment workshop was a significant step forward in making the students more inclusive to the assessment process. The facilitation of providing a meaningful interpretation of the assessment criteria, and how it is applicable to the module content across the different grade descriptors, is a significant step forward in breaking down the perceived or actual barriers between lecturers and students in relation to the assessment and the marking. Inviting students into the assessment process ensures that the assessment itself is a learning tool itself, and thereby facilitates an assessment for learning, rather than assessment of learning.

CONCLUSION

The introduction of the Assessment Workshop is a significant step forward in demystifying the assessment criteria, and shattering the perception that the assessment criteria is beyond the grasp of students, and to be used largely by academics undertaking the marking. The workshop helped the students to gain a meaningful understanding of the criteria to the extent that it can now be utilised as an active tool in the student learning process in achieving the learning outcomes of the module. In this way, the students develop an evaluative ability in themselves, an ability which is a precursor for being able to be in the advantageous position of being able to monitor one's own learning, which is the central tenet of being a student in HE, and preparing them for life beyond university.

SUGGESTED FURTHER READING

O'Donovan, B., M. Price and C. Rust (2004). 'Know what I mean? Enhancing student understanding of assessment standards and criteria', *Teaching in Higher Education*, 9 (3), 325.

Ramsden, P. (1992). *Learning to Teach in Higher Education*, London: Routledge.

Rust, C. (2003). 'Improving students' learning by developing their understanding of assessment criteria and processes', *Assessment and Evaluation in Higher Education*, 28 (2), 147.

Webster, F., D. Pepper and A. Jenkins (2000). 'Assessing the undergraduate dissertation', *Assessment and Evaluation in Higher Education*, 25 (1), 72.

Thought 16

Bimal Arora

I was invited to deliver a three-hour session to a class of 40 students on an International Business postgraduate course in a business school, on voluntary sustainability standards (VSS), a specialised topic. The topic of VSS does not find coverage in the standard courses and curricula in business and management, including in corporate social responsibility and sustainability courses/modules. VSS have been argued to be a form of private regulation. My research and work suggest that consumer-facing and branded VSS such as Fairtrade, Forest Stewardship Council (FSC) and Rainforest Alliance, have grown in prominence over the years and touch the lives of individuals everywhere, particularly in Europe. With this in mind and an aim to make accessible the complexities involved and issues relatable to students, I decided to deliver a workshop-style session instead of a lecture.

No additional resources were provided, so I had to manage only with standard audio-visual teaching aids available in a classroom. I bought products such as a banana, a coffee mug, a chocolate bar with Fairtrade and FSC logos. I used these products, which students use in their daily lives, to set the context. I then divided the class into groups and asked them to work with different VSS – I developed questions which directed the students' search for answers using the Internet. The questions were targeted at understanding different aspects of VSS and I guided the search in my interactions. The groups of five had to answer five questions each on the allocated VSS in 60 minutes and had to prepare a presentation for the class.

Given that VSS was a completely new topic, it was challenging for the students. Students were suggested to divide one question per student and search for information using their laptops/smartphones to answer the questions for the group. I closely observed each group and responded to queries and confusions as requested and needed.

The exercise became an opportunity for harnessing students'

creativity. These 60 minutes offered a challenge and space, time and opportunity to interact and collaborate, search for, gather, unpack and make sense of complex information on an unknown topic, interpret, synthesise, work in a group, be playful, and present. There was indeed time pressure for preparation and delivery, but each student in every group presented concise information in answering the allocated group questions. They used different ways – from using paper, to a PowerPoint, to interactive style. By the end of the session the class knew about different VSS discussed and could appreciate the closure talk I delivered which highlighted the several challenges associated with VSS.

Overall, the workshop feedback was positive and many students enjoyed the exercise. Some students walked up to me after the class and expressed interest in choosing VSS and related areas as topics for their dissertation.

29. Using posters in academic assessments

Kris Lines

If you can't explain it simply you don't understand it well enough.

INTRODUCTION

The quotation above (variously attributed to Einstein and/or Feynman) very much sums up the essence of academic posters. A good poster should be concise, visually effective and easy to understand. Somewhat ironically though, these strengths also represent its greatest disadvantages. Students (and indeed some academics) can often conflate clarity of expression with a lack of academic rigour; while a focus on creativity can particularly challenge those students drilled in the traditional orthodoxy of timed exams and expansive essay writing.

What follows below are my best-practice recommendations for integrating posters as a form of assessment (whether summative or formatively). For ease of reading, I have grouped the reflections into five themes.

ACADEMIC CREDIBILITY

While academic posters have become commonplace within the sciences, their integration in a business or law school curricula is often seen as more unusual. This can lead to perceptions that the posters are there for novelty value or as a 'soft option' at the expense of more traditional forms of assessment. Indeed, this can be particularly jarring where students expect to be performing the same work that they see in depictions of their profession on television. There may also be inaccurate views that posters belong firmly in junior schools and are not for 'serious' studies at university.

If these perceptions are the case, then students may not appreciate until much later in the programme (and by then it may be too late!) that a poster often necessitates using a different set of skills to produce the work. The earlier in a programme that these perceptions and expectations can be managed, the greater the likelihood will be that students will engage with the assessment.

A good example of how visual communication has become increasingly important to businesses can be seen in regulatory or consumer contractual notices. Indeed, the very essence of a Creative Commons licence is that 'normal' members of the public can read and understand the licence summary. Simultaneously, lawyers and editors can look beyond the summary at the dense legal code. The same is true of a poster. A good poster does not simply entail cutting, copying and pasting an essay in its entirety, but rather involves a more visual way of communicating concepts and arguments to an audience.

Teaching Tip
Producing a series of testimonials from practitioners, industry partners or conference organisers talking about the importance of posters and visual communication will help to demonstrate the relevance of posters within an academic and professional context. Similarly, if an instructor has access to past examples of previous exemplar posters on the course, this can be very useful in contextualising what exactly is required of an assessment.

ORIGINAL RESEARCH?

An integral part of every assessment is the alignment of the task to the specific learning outcomes of the module, and poster assessments are no exception to this rule. Before the students start to produce their work, it is therefore important to decide what the poster is actually being used for. The level and type of programme will make a significant difference here.

At a postgraduate level, for many early-career academics or research students, a poster presentation often represents their first foray into disseminating their research at conferences. Much like the Three-Minute Thesis (3MT®) competition aimed at doctoral candidates, the inherent space limitations of a poster forces researchers to distil their concepts into a much more condensed form than a traditional 2000-word essay might. This can make it easier to assess whether the poster presenter has understood the key ideas being conveyed. Similarly, MBA students may be more comfortable in producing posters as this may be akin to product pitches.

Using academic posters for undergraduate business or law students does however bring with it several additional challenges, particularly in relation to the format of the poster. As undergraduate students may not be presenting original research, or conducting experiments, it will be important to spend time initially in deciding what content or section headings need to be included in the work, and in what layout they should appear on the poster. This will help to standardise marking (particularly if students are communicating about different topics), but also give the students a means to scaffold their learning.

Teaching Tip
If posters are being used for undergraduate business or law students, consider providing set headings to help structure the work – for example through the identification of a business problem, or the analysis of a specific case.

DESIGN AND LAYOUT ISSUES

One of the chief complaints I have encountered in using posters for summative assessment is that communicating visually is unfamiliar to many students, and this can engender an initial sense of fear, reluctance or inadequacy.

One way to overcome this is through the provision of a series of design constraints. While this might seem somewhat counterintuitive, especially given that fostering creativity may be explicitly linked to the learning outcomes, such an approach will reduce uncertainty and minimise some of the more avoidable formatting errors. Indeed, we can see this fear removed in the essay-writing process through familiarity with ubiquitous software (for example Microsoft Word) and common writing protocols such as Times New Roman size-12 font, with line and a half spacing and margins of at least an inch around the page. By contrast, the sudden freedom of a giant, blank piece of paper with no rules, word count or guidance can be very unsettling.

Consider implementing similar rules on margins, minimum font size (for readability at least one metre away), file format (PDF is easier to print), as well as providing advice on background colour schemes, negative space (avoiding clutter), and on shaping how the reader views the poster content (for example columns, linked text boxes, flow charts etc.).

Although graphical elements will help to illustrate the poster concepts in a more visual way, care should also be taken to ensure that students understand the rules surrounding the copyright and fair use of images. Indeed, it is important that students realise the distinction between sharing a meme across their social media channels, and the need to attribute and ensure the appropriate licence for an image in an academic or professional setting. Guidance on the use and sourcing of Creative Commons (CC) images may be particularly helpful for these groups.

Teaching Tip
Consider delivering instruction on how to communicate visually, with accompanying design constraints. If you are not yourself confident in visual or graphic design, it can be helpful to collaborate with interdisciplinary colleagues to share good practice ideas.

QR CODES

One of the key differences between academic posters and traditional coursework assignments is the presence, or indeed absence, of references and bibliographic material. While a traditional coursework assignment might have copious footnotes or endnotes, there is an inherent trade-off between citing extensive references on a poster or utilising the (already limited) space for substantive content.

The students in my classes have managed to square this circle by utilising QR Codes.

For those unfamiliar with this technology, a QR Code is a pixelated image, much like a barcode, that allows web-enabled devices to perform a particular action such as hyperlinking to a pre-set webpage or document. While the technology has been around for decades, it is only comparatively recently that smartphone cameras have had the integrated functionality to decipher these codes. Nowadays, most if not all smart devices should be able to do so.

The difference that a QR Code has made to my students' posters is considerable. Students can now produce a 'traditional' bibliography or set of endnotes, and link this to the poster through a QR Code image in the corner of the page. Not only does this allow them to demonstrate their academic credentials, the space that this barcode image takes up is minimal, notwithstanding an accompanying heading and instructions of how/why to scan the code.

For anybody wishing to replicate this, there are three useful technical points that may assist:

- Although it is not possible physically to link footnotes or endnotes between the poster and document, it is easy to fake this through superscript text. At the point on the poster content where you wish to have a citation, insert the appropriate number and click 'superscript'. This should then appear to be a traditional reference. This same number can then be manually inserted in the same manner in the corresponding bibliography.
- Uploading a document to a cloud-based repository or website, for example OneDrive, Dropbox, etc., may be the easiest way to

produce the necessary hyperlink for the QR Code. However, the corresponding file url is likely to be long and complex, which will result in a similarly complex QR Code. The more complex the image, the harder it will be for a camera to decipher it. Instead, once you have the hyperlink, use a url-shortener such as bit.ly to shorten this link. The corresponding QR Code will be much clearer and easy to incorporate into your document.

- Remember that free QR Code generators will often produce static and fixed links. Some may also be time-limited (for example only operational for 14 days). If you wish to reuse your poster in the future, it is important to check whether the hyperlinked document is still accessible.

Teaching Tip
A QR Code can be used to link bibliographic material to a poster. Alternatively, researchers may wish to consider using the poster as a visual way of communicating only the key findings from their research, however, perhaps with QR Code links to the full manuscript or research data?

SHOWCASE

Finally, it is worth considering what attracted me to posters in the first place. Too often a student may graduate from a degree programme with nothing tangible to show employers or family members what they are capable of producing beyond a series of (often very specific) essays or their performance in a variety of timed exam papers. Posters provide tangible artefacts, in an aesthetically pleasing format that can be shared much more widely. The visual nature of posters also lends itself to showcase events where invited guests, practitioners, faculty and the public can celebrate the research and achievements of a group of students.

CONCLUSION

They say that a picture is worth a thousand words. A well-thought-out poster assessment will bring with it many advantages such as fostering creativity and confidence, allowing ideas to be distilled into more digestible chunks or the construction of a tangible artefact. But just as with any other skill, visual communication and graphic design needs to be practised and honed. This chapter has tried to provide some best practice tips to help navigate the most common difficulties but really the most effective approach is to experiment with what works for your classes and context and adapt accordingly.

SUGGESTED FURTHER READING

D'Angelo, L. (2011). 'Academic posters across disciplines: A preliminary study', *University of Reading Language Studies Working Papers*, 3, 15–28.
Duarte, N. (2008). *Slide:ology: The Art and Science of Creating Great Presentations*, Beijing and Sebastopol, CA: O'Reilly Media.
Reynolds, G. (2013). *Presentation Zen Design*, Berkeley, CA: New Riders, 2nd edn.
Zielinska, E. (2011). 'Poster Perfect' *The Scientist*, available at: https://www.thesci entist.com/careers/posterperfect42000.

30. Writing effective multiple choice questions

Simon Finley

INTRODUCTION

The use of multiple choice questions (MCQs) as a tool for assessment has courted controversy and stirred academic passions for decades. I am sure everyone has heard the arguments and counter arguments until they are, quite frankly, bored of them. In 2014, however, the Central Queensland University (CQU) took a bold step that may have provided clear strategic leadership on the topic – they banned them.

This chapter looks at some of the criticisms of MCQs that contributed to CQU's response and then provides counter arguments by discussing where MCQs are used successfully and how we can overcome some of their perceived limitations. The chapter concludes with a brief summary of some effective MCQ writing tips that I have learned through painful experience over a number of years of both writing and using this excellent assessment resource.

CRITICISM OF MCQs

One of the key arguments for CQU was that MCQs provide a mathematical potential for achieving a pass mark through simple guesswork (Ibbett and Wheldon, 2016). If presented with a MCQ test made up of questions with four possible answers, or 'distractors', then anyone could have a go at the test with no prior knowledge and expect to earn around 25 per cent of the mark.

I can almost hear the defenders of MCQs screaming 'But that's not enough to pass!' This might be true, but the art of writing good-quality distractors is challenging and candidates can use a range of techniques to eliminate distractors, giving them a better chance of guessing correctly. In fact there are now online resources that coach candidates in the art of detecting such 'clues'. Consider the following examples:

Q1   Which of the following is a recognised stage of Maslow's Hierarchy
      of Needs:
      A.   Self-recognition
      B.   Desire
      C.   Esteem
      D.   Middle age

Middle age is clearly not a need, so, in this example, candidates only need
guess from three possible correct options, increasing the likelihood of a
successful guess to 33 per cent.

Q2   An expense that has not yet been paid for is recorded in the statement
      of financial position as an:
      A.   Prepayment
      B.   Accrual
      C.   Non-current liability
      D.   Investment

The only grammatically correct responses are B and D because the question ends with 'an' so must therefore be followed by a vowel. So here the
candidate has a 50 per cent chance of guessing the answer. As you can see,
the odds of successfully passing MCQ tests through guesswork are significantly improved through careless crafting of questions and distractors.

Teaching Tip
*Read through any MCQs that you have written very carefully, to see if there
are any obvious reasons to discount an answer – which someone without
knowledge could identify.*

Another significant argument is that MCQs cannot test higher-level
learning skills (Scouller, 1998) and that they can only be used to assess
memorisation/recall, which is generally seen as one of the lowest levels of
learning complexity in models such as Bloom's Taxonomy (Bloom et al.,
1956). This, therefore, makes them inappropriate for degree-level qualifica-
tions where we need to test higher-order thinking skills.

   Other concerns are that MCQs present problems in ways that are not
typical of real situations; that they create ethical questions due to distractors being written in an attempt to mislead candidates; and that questions
are often overly complicated and too long.

MCQs IN ACTION

We need only to look at medical and accountancy training to see that
MCQs are being used as a central component of professional competence

assessment. If these highly regulated industries, where professional training standards are tightly controlled, can use MCQs successfully, why not the higher education system?

The answer lies, in my opinion, with one of my favourite quotations from one of the leading authorities on assessment design in higher education, Professor David Boud (1995): 'Candidates can, with difficulty, escape from the effects of poor teaching, they cannot (by definition if they want to graduate) escape the effects of poor assessment.'

If you think about the criticisms discussed previously, they are not really criticisms of MCQs; they are criticisms of badly-written MCQs. No form of assessment is immune to this; the design of good-quality assessment is a challenging and, all too often, overlooked component of excellent teaching practice. Let's be honest with ourselves, how often have you either set or seen essay-based questions that students are able to pass by doing little more than memorising and regurgitating lecture slides and quotations? This tests nothing more than the ability to remember, a key criticism levelled at MCQs. The fault is in the assessment design, not the assessment type!

TESTING HIGHER-ORDER THINKING SKILLS

Yes, MCQs can be used to test recall but they can do so much more. If we use Bloom's Taxonomy (Figure 30.1) we are able to demonstrate the use of MCQs to test up to, at least, analysis.

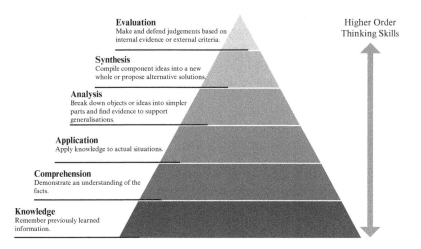

Figure 30.1   Bloom's Taxonomy

The following section provides illustrations of how MCQs can be used to test higher-order cognitive skills other than simple remembering/recall.

UNDERSTANDING

Q3 Which of the statements below most accurately describes the products in the following graph.

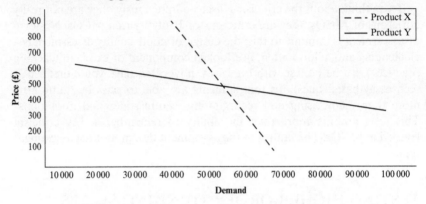

A.   Product Y is more price elastic than product X.
B.   Product Y is more price inelastic than product X.
C.   Product Y is perfectly elastic.
D.   Product X is perfectly elastic.

This question requires candidates to demonstrate an understanding of price elasticity in order to interpret the data presented in the graph.

APPLICATION

Q4   Using the graph presented in Q3, answer the following question:
Your manager has been told to increase the price of all company products in order to drive revenue growth but she is concerned that this will damage market share. She has asked for your advice. Which of the following solutions would you present as the most appropriate given the objectives presented?
A.   Increase the prices of both product X and Y by the same amount as this will have little impact on market share.
B.   Increase the price of product X proportionately more than product Y as this will have the least significant impact on market share.

C. Increase the price of product Y proportionately more than product X as this will have the least significant impact on market share.
D. Increase the price of neither product as this will reduce market share of both products.

In this example the test taker is required to take the model and apply it to a problem-solving task.

ANALYSIS

Q5 As part of their annual reporting a company publishes the following key performance indicators. Last year's results are also provided as a point of comparison.

	Year Ended	
	31 Dec 2018	31 Dec 2017
Return on capital employed	22.1%	26.7%
Operating profit margin	15.8%	15.7%
Sales revenue to capital employed	1.4	1.8

Which of the following observations about the company's performance is the most plausible?

A. The company's overall performance has improved in 2018. The most likely reason for this is an improvement in cost control and a consequent reduction in operating costs.
B. The company's overall performance has declined in 2018. The most likely reason for this is an investment in new capital in 2018, which has damaged the company's revenue-generating efficiency relative to its asset base.
C. The company's overall performance has improved in 2018. The most likely reason for this is an increase in overall sales volumes driven by investment in productivity expansion.
D. The company's overall performance has remained relatively stable. The most likely reason for this is a lack of new capital investment.

This question requires the candidate to interpret the data presented and use it to differentiate between the options presented to identify the most plausible explanation.

As you can see, MCQs offer a credible option for testing relatively higher-order thinking skills. In medicine MCQs are often used to present patient symptoms to candidates, who then have to diagnose the most likely medical cause, usually with conditions that can present with similar symptoms. This places candidates in real-world scenarios and appears to me to be an incredibly effective method of assessing these skills in this context. I do not see why we cannot do the same in business studies.

ENHANCING MCQs

Layering

As demonstrated previously, MCQs can be used to assess a range of thinking and learning skills. Good assessments use layering techniques in order to test this range and MCQs can also achieve this.

For example, consider a scenario on the topic of barriers to international trade. Questions could be created that require candidates to:

- Identify the correct definitions of key words (remembering).
- Classify examples of trade barriers under key headings such as tariffs, quotas and embargos (understanding).
- Identify suitable trade barrier options in response to specific requirements (application).
- Select the most significant ethical threats relating to proposed trade barriers (analysis).

If you wished to extend this even further you could insert a question where candidates are required to explain why the ethical threat identified was the most significant in relation to the case presented (evaluation). With the options available through most virtual learning environments, these sorts of short written response questions can easily be inserted at specified points in MCQ assessments. While this needs to be marked by an academic, the whole test can be administered online and the marking of the MCQ questions and provision of feedback will still be entirely automated.

Teaching Tip
Identify what you want the MCQ to assess. Questions requiring analysis will be less easy to pass than ones that simply require remembering.

CONFIDENCE-BASED MARKING

This method requires candidates to select a response and then select a confidence rating, which affects the overall mark awarded. This method has been

Table 30.1   Illustrative scoring regime for a confidence-based MCQ exam

Degree of Certainty	Low	Medium	High	No response
Mark if correct	1	2	3	0
Penalty if wrong	0	−2	−6	0

used effectively in medical examinations, as illustrated by this example (Table 30.1) from Gardner-Medwin (2006) as reproduced by David Nicol (2007).

The purpose behind this approach is to reward candidates for high levels of preparation and confidence in their knowledge and to reduce the impact of guesswork. This raises a number of concerns about the use of negative marking, which we will not explore here, but the principle works just as well without the penalty marks and only the enhanced confidence-based scoring.

RESPONSIVE TEACHING

Of all the uses of MCQs this is my favourite. We spend so much time preparing our lessons and assessments that we sometimes fail to step back and ask whether what we are doing is working. Sure, we all do post-module reflections and make changes for the next year, but what about the candidates who are sat in our lectures now; how do we support them to perform to the best of their abilities? I believe that we must be responsive to the particular needs of each cohort. MCQs offer a simple and effective tool to help in this regard.

With the evolution of mobile-phone technology, the design and implementation of in-class tests is now quick, simple and accessible to just about everyone. I have successfully used a number of different packages, such as Kahoot, Mentimeter, Poll Everywhere and Socrative. Others are available and many are free to use.

During lectures I like to do short presentations (15 minutes maximum), followed by a short MCQ quiz that students access through their mobile devices. The cumulative responses can be projected onto the main screen in the classroom through a website which can inform some class discussion. More recently I have used this to determine what I do for the remainder of the session and in future lectures. In this way I am able to adapt my content and delivery to ensure that students are sufficiently ready to move on to new topics. By doing this in every lecture I am able to constantly adapt content and out-of-lecture support to target the specific needs of each group I teach.

Nicol (2007) introduces another fascinating use of this technology, whereby the lecturer projects the results of a question and then challenges students to convince the person next to them what the correct answer is. The lecturer then repeats the question to see if the responses change before revealing the correct answer. This is a great way to engage candidates, to get them to articulate their thoughts into words and to encourage peer-led learning.

TIPS FOR WRITING GOOD MCQs

This section provides a brief summary of the lessons I have learned about writing good MCQs:

- *Identify the objective*
  Match the skills being assessed to the assessment type. If testing recall, understanding, application and analysis then MCQs are an option. For higher-order skills you need to mix it up.
- *Clear and concise question stems*
  Ambiguity and uncertainty create candidate stress and undermine assessment credibility. Keep question wording simple and always get someone to review it.
  Exclude all irrelevant material and 'red herrings'; these are not conducive to effective assessment.
- *Four or five distractors*
  In reality there is no limit to the number of distractors but this can undermine effectiveness. Too few options increases the probability of guessing correctly and with too many it becomes difficult to write plausible distractors. Four or five tends to work well for me.
- *Beware of 'clues'*
  Don't write 'throwaway' or clumsy distractors that are obviously not correct. Also check the grammatical accuracy of the question by reading out the question stem multiple times, each time with a different distractor. This helps to ensure that each option is grammatically matched to the stem. Also try and make the distractors a similar length; odd ones out often provide clues as to the correct response.
- *Time allocation*
  Think realistically about how much time each question will take to read, consider and respond to. The time allocation should be fair but not overly generous. If you are unsure, recruit someone to answer a couple of test questions and time them.
- *Avoid numerical answers*
  I am not a fan of requiring candidates to do calculations for MCQs. It is difficult to write multiple, plausible numerical distractors and I

have often found that these sorts of questions are littered with 'red herring' responses, where answers from one step in the calculation are given as a distractor. If there is a single correct numerical answer then why not simply provide a space to write the answer? Modern virtual-learning environments facilitate this in online tests and are capable of automatically marking this.

- *Presentation*
  I am a stickler for presentation but I believe it is vital for engendering confidence. If the font type and size varies, the text is misaligned and question spacing varies, it instantly makes me think that work has been copied and pasted, and carelessly to boot. In my experience this sort of work includes the highest incidence of errors. I want my students to focus on answering the questions and not be distracted by these concerns. We must also remember that we are trying to develop professional business attitudes and habits in our candidates and to do that we must also 'walk the walk'.

SUGGESTED FURTHER READING

Bloom, B., M. Englehart, E. Furst, W. Hill and D. Krathwohl (1956). *Taxonomy of Educational Objectives: The Classification of Educational Goals. Handbook I: Cognitive Domain*, New York: David McKay.

Boud, D. (1995). 'Assessment and learning: Contradictory or complementary?' In P. Knight (ed.), *Assessment for Learning in Higher Education*, London: Kogan Page.

Gardner-Medwin, A.R. (2006). 'Confidence-based marking: Towards deeper learning and better exams.' In C. Bryan and K. Clegg (eds), *Innovative Assessment in Higher Education*, London: Taylor and Francis, as cited in D. Nicol (2007), 'E-assessment by design: Using multiple-choice tests to good effect', *Journal of Further and Higher Education*, 31 (1), 53–64.

Ibbett, N. and B. Wheldon (2016). 'The incidence of clueing in multiple choice testbank questions in accounting: Some evidence from Australia', *e-Journal of Business Education and Scholarship of Teaching*, 10 (1), 20–35.

Nicol, D. (2007). 'E-assessment by design: Using multiple-choice tests to good effect', *Journal of Further and Higher Education*, 31 (1), 53–64.

Scouller, K. (1998). 'The influence of assessment method on candidates' learning approaches: Multiple choice question examination versus assignment essay', *Higher Education*, 35 (4), 453–47.

Thought 17

Kathy Daniels

As with many institutions, our postgraduate intake consists of a lot of international students. It always seems that international students soon form groups with others of their own nationality, and the integration that would be so beneficial to everyone's learning experience does not happen. To address this I have tried combining team activities with the teaching of organisational behaviour.

Students are divided into groups by myself, making sure that there is a mix of students from different nationalities. They are given a pack of paper straws and are told they need to build the longest bridge that they can, using just these straws.

To do this task they need to talk to each other, and as a result they start to get to know each other. This breaks down some of the barriers between the different groups that would otherwise form.

When the task is completed, with (hopefully) lots of fun, students are required to apply theory relating to organisational behaviour.

As a team how did they operate? This can be related to theory of team development, and also team roles. Did a leader emerge? This allows us to think about different leadership styles. Did any conflict arise? We can link this back to theory relating to conflict.

By the end of the session the students will have had a chance to get to know each other better, they will have had some fun and they will have seen theory relating to organisational behaviour in practice.

31. Peer assessment

Elaine Clarke

INTRODUCTION

A few years ago I was discussing a business student's particularly problematic circumstances with a colleague, and the colleague mentioned how
much easier it was in medical-related subjects to deal with such matters,
because students had to demonstrate 'fitness to practise' alongside their
subject knowledge. It was the first time I had heard the term 'fitness to
practise', and suddenly I realised that here was a term to sum up what I
had long felt about our business students. They too needed to demonstrate
'fitness to practise', even though in business and management there is no
formal assessment of this that would qualify them before entering into the
world of work. In medical professions the term means that a person has the
knowledge, skills and character to practise their profession effectively and
safely. In business and management studies at any level (undergraduate,
pre-experience Masters or post-experience) there is also a behavioural element to the learning process – what one could call 'fitness to practise' – not
simply acquiring the subject knowledge. Both of these areas – knowledge
and behaviour – require students to apply critical faculties, that is, to dig
beneath the surface to enrich their learning.

In whatever sphere students will find themselves following their studies
– in the commercial world, in the professions, in social enterprises, in
the traditional not-for-profit or public sectors, or pursuing their own
businesses – the same is true: it is the behaviours they have developed
throughout their studies every bit as much as the subject knowledge
they have gained (if not more so), that will enhance their employability
and determine both the *speed* with which they begin to contribute to the
organisation and the *success* of their contributions. It behoves us then,
as facilitators of learning, to ensure that the experiences we create within
and around the classroom bring about the development of appropriate
behavioural and critical skills.

WHY SHOULD WE INVOLVE OUR STUDENTS IN PEER ASSESSMENT?

Peer assessment is an activity that can contribute to some considerable extent towards the development of desirable workplace behavioural and critical skills. When we talk about peer assessment in the context of studies, we mean any activity in which students, or groups of students, rate and provide feedback in some form on the work of their fellow students. It can also be termed as peer review or peer evaluation.

It is the process of involving our students in assessing others' work that is most fruitful in terms of the behavioural and critical skills developed, enhanced by the feedback that each student will receive from other students on their work. We are asking students to make critical judgements, giving them responsibility to be fair and balanced in applying their own knowledge and experience to the work of their peers. They will also need to communicate those judgements to those whose work they have reviewed, drawing upon their skills in communication to explain their reasoning in a constructive manner. They will possibly also have cooperated with others in arriving at and communicating their views. These are important skills that students should be able to demonstrate to employers. Practising these skills will also refine a student's critical approach to their own work, reflecting upon feedback they have been given (which will be a constant occurrence in the world of work), on their own strengths and weaknesses, seeing their work in the context of others, learning from others' approaches and reinforcing their own subject knowledge.

WHAT FORM MIGHT PEER ASSESSMENT TAKE?

Peer assessment can possibly take as many forms as there are forms of assessment itself.

It could be written work, for example completed or draft essays, reports or research projects; peers could assess presentations, debates or other forms of 'performed' assessment, either in completed form or as a work-in-progress. Peer assessment could apply to the subject knowledge and/or the process of working with that subject knowledge, for example in the way in which the work is structured, or a particular argument is advanced. In performed assessment, evidence of behavioural skills could be assessed, for example in the clarity or the persuasiveness of the communication.

Peer assessment as part of a process towards an informal and ungraded output (formative) or a formal assessment that the students have to complete in the near future (summative) is particularly helpful. Assessing work from former students that has been anonymised is also valuable in students exercising critical thinking and in justifying their reasoning. Students can undertake peer assessment group-to-group, group-to-individual (when the individual is part of that group and it is a process that all group members undertake), or individual-to-individual. Group feedback could be a first phase in building up confidence before moving on to students assessing each other individually. The assessment process could result in students providing only feedback to each other, a grade only (more likely in quantitative subjects), or a grade along with feedback. Later in this chapter I will touch upon the issues associated with students giving formal grades in the summative work of their fellow students.

EXAMPLES OF PEER ASSESSMENT

1. Students are divided into pairs and are asked to provide feedback on another student's essay plan. As this is an essay plan, i.e. a piece of work at its earliest stage, it is likely that only the inclusion of subject knowledge and a small bit of process (in the way in which the student has proposed to structure the work), will be evident to the reviewer. The students will have been provided with a template against which to provide their feedback.

   By a certain deadline each student will submit a plan for an essay which will be an eventual piece of summative assessment. The plans are redistributed by the tutor. Either before the class, or during time put aside in class, each student will review the plan they have been given and make notes on the template. They will then get together and talk through their review with the student who produced the plan. This is best done in the classroom so that the tutor can circulate and support, and so that there can be a plenary discussion about the essay plans themselves, and the value of the exercise. During the one-to-one discussion, the reviewer can add to their written notes, and the recipient of the feedback can make their own notes. It is important to focus on what are seen to be the strengths of the plan, and on providing suggestions for improvements so that there is a balance of positive and constructive feedback. The author of the plan should be given the reviewer's sheet of notes at the end of the discussion.

2. Students are asked to peer assess presentations from groups of their fellow students that count towards the final grade for that module. All of the class review each presentation in its turn. Each student is provided with a template against which to provide feedback and a

grade, and will hand these in to the tutor at the end of the session. (Email could be used, however there is a likelihood that the tutor will not receive every piece of feedback, possibly disadvantaging some groups.) Students could comment on the depth of knowledge shown, the process of how logically and convincingly the case is argued, speakers' ability to engage with the audience, as well as more technical aspects such as how visual aids have supported the presentation.

3.   Students are given three anonymised pieces of earlier students' work, ranging from weak to strong, similar to the type of assessment that will be expected of them. Students are asked in their groups to agree on feedback and a grade, and then to discuss their reasoning with the rest of the class. The tutor can then reveal the actual feedback and grade that had been given to the work, and this can stimulate further discussion.

Teaching Tip
Do not ask students to submit assessments of their peers' work via email. Some students could be disadvantaged by having less feedback if their peers do not email any peer assessment.

The notion of students contributing to actual grades of their fellow students can cause unease in both the tutor and the students. It is more likely to be the tutor who feels unease, fearing a loss of control and potential problems with consistency of standards and internal regulations. A way to mitigate this is to restrict peer assessment in summative work to a limited weighting of the overall module grade. The tutor should also make it clear that s/he retains the final say in the grade that is awarded, having given due consideration to students' proposed grades. There have been a number of studies across disciplines of the extent to which student-awarded grades match those of the tutor when graded separately from each other and then compared. Although there is some variation in conclusions, there is a large body of evidence to show that, on the whole, student-awarded grades do mirror tutor-awarded grades given appropriate preparation, and that they mirror each other more closely the more practice students are given at assessing their peers (Dochy et al., 1999). With the safeguards mentioned, tutors should feel comfortable in applying peer assessment to summative work as well as to formative.

Teaching Tip
Any peer assessment that contributes to students' final marks should have a limited weighting in the allocation of marks.

PEER ASSESSMENT FOR LEARNING

The cognitive and behavioural skills required in any of these exercises are significant, and reflect important skills our students will need in the workplace. In business and management studies, we should be focusing on problem-based learning where possible, so that we are replicating the kind of activities students will actually be faced with in the workplace. We should look to provide them with examples to show that real-life business does not fall neatly into silos, and that there are usually a number of stakeholders, perspectives and implications to any problem. Peer assessment is likely to be valuable in any form due to its active, participative nature. When linked, however, with problem-based learning, it becomes a key tool in assessing *for* learning, as opposed to a traditional view where assessment is *of* learning, this latter being a test of the end result of what a student has learned. An assignment that has been designed with peer assessment in mind already contains important characteristics of assessment *for* learning. In peer assessment the students question what they see, they feed back and give suggestions for improvement. They learn from engaging in this process – in taking on the role of the tutor – as well as from reflecting and acting upon feedback they have in turn been given. This can reinforce their learning about the subject knowledge. More importantly, however, it enriches their cognitive and behavioural skills and reinforces their ability to manage their own learning through identifying ways in which to improve.

Teaching Tip
The more students are given the opportunity to engage in peer assessment, the better they become at making judgements, communicating constructively and applying judgement to their own work.

PREPARING STUDENTS TO ENGAGE IN PEER ASSESSMENT

For peer assessment to work effectively as a developmental tool for students, we as tutors need to take the time to prepare the students. It is worth spending time at the beginning setting up the process so that students engage fully and gain maximum benefit, having understood what is expected of them and having the tools to carry it out. Investment in preparation will also result in a more fulfilling experience for the tutor.

I suggested in an earlier example using a template against which students review each other's work. Of course, the tutor could design this template, taking into account the learning outcomes and assessment criteria. What would be more fulfilling for the students, however, and a richer learning experience, would be to allow them, in groups, to design any templates or checklists themselves. Research has shown that active involvement at this stage is one of the critical factors in students' perception of the value of peer assessment. If students are to generate criteria or design templates, this can be done in various iterations where the students themselves filter and refine each other's ideas. The tutor could do the final filtering or merging of ideas, however if they do so, they should explain their reasoning to students. It might be that this is appropriate if the peer assessment is to have any part in the actual grades the students are awarded.

If students are not to be involved in designing the criteria against which they will review each other's work (however I would strongly recommend that they are), then it is important that the tutor goes through the criteria one by one with the class so that students understand how each criterion is relevant to the whole assessment, and how to make judgements against that criterion. If we ask students, for example, to give feedback on the way in which fellow students have structured an argument, ought we not first to show them examples of how they can identify the actual arguments among the whole text and what a logical flow to an argument might look like, to look out for evidence to support that argument and to question the credibility of the evidence? Or if we want them to judge whether visual aids have been used appropriately in a presentation, ought we not spend the time talking about the purpose of visual aids and what the good and bad characteristics are? It might seem as if the time involved in doing so is considerable, however it doesn't need to be if guidance is shared in advance of a classroom discussion, or if a discussion takes place over a period of a few days on a VLE and is summed up in class before the peer assessment begins.

Teaching Tip
Consider asking students to help develop the criteria against which assessments will be peer assessed.

We are asking students to exercise critical judgement of their fellow students' work and we should be prepared to spend time developing their competence and their confidence to do so. Research shows students are largely happy to be assessed by their peers, so dealing with resistance is not likely to be an issue from that perspective. Building up confidence needs to be done in stages. An exercise in reviewing the anonymised work of former students could, for example, be an early phase in building up their confidence, as they simply discuss the good and bad elements of the work they see. Or, they could begin by working in groups to give feedback, preparing the ground for their being able to give individual feedback at later stages. Research has also shown that peer assessment is a fruitful and fulfilling exercise regardless of the stage a student is at in their studies. With careful preparation, first year undergraduates will gain as much from the peer assessment process as post-experience Masters students.

Preparation for peer assessment should also take into account the context of the students' earlier experience, for example, in their education, or in their being from different countries and cultures. Undergraduate, and a great deal of postgraduate, business and management courses do not stipulate specific subjects that the students must have studied beforehand. A classroom of students might therefore come from disciplines as varied as textile design, economics, engineering, social policy, each with different learning and assessment approaches. Business and management studies is also the largest subject area to attract international students, so classes could well contain students from cultures very different from the dominant culture of the home institution, or contain a large number of students from another different culture. A discussion with students about the expectations of assessment can expressly bring out these diverse factors and proactively explore how they can fit with the expectations of the assessment. This discussion can be combined with involving the students in designing the criteria/templates/checklists, as it would naturally fit into this activity.

Feeling comfortable and confident to provide feedback on a fellow student's work is likely to be influenced to a large extent by background and culture, so we need to work at breaking down any reservations and building up enthusiasm and confidence to participate. Technology can play a role in this, for example, all students contributing something short and written to a discussion board before the class; using a positive-only approach to comments students may give in reply; using personal voting systems in the classroom to filter ideas; building up the size of the 'audience' to which a student must contribute, firstly discussing one-to-one, then in threes, fours and so on; working through with students ways in which they can ensure everybody has a chance to contribute in their smaller groups, in however small a way at the beginning, so that confidence is built gradually.

CONCLUSION

The time and effort spent engaging students in peer assessment is far outweighed by the benefits to the individual students and to the learning culture in the classroom. There is an acceptance that participative learning is far more effective than when students are passive recipients of the one-way lecturer-to-student outpouring of knowledge. Peer assessment has been shown to improve attendance, motivation, engagement, memory of concepts, appreciation of performance, students' thinking and interpersonal skills, depth of learning, quality of output, relationships in the classroom and students' satisfaction with their learning experience. Students find it challenging, yet are aware that it develops important skills.

Peer assessment is appropriate in both formative and summative activities, yet in the spirit of assessment *for* learning, *formative* peer assessment is a more powerful intervention, especially when linked with problem-based exercises. We need to build the competence and confidence of tutors, through staff development, to embark upon peer assessment if they have not already done so, or to revisit it if they have had an unsatisfactory experience first time around. Preparation of both tutors and students is essential. Once prepared, the transformation in student learning is tangible and enduring, and will go a long way towards that essential element in their employability, their 'fitness to practise'.

SUGGESTED FURTHER READING

Dochy, F., M. Segers and D. Sluijsmans (1999). 'The use of self-, peer and co-assessment in Higher Education: A review', *Studies in Higher Education*, 24 (3), 331–50.

Falchikov, F. (1995). 'Peer feedback marking: Developing peer assessment', *Innovations in Education and Training International*, 32 (2), 175–87.

Ngar-Fun, L. and D. Carless (2006). 'Peer feedback: The learning element of peer assessment', *Teaching in Higher Education*, 11 (3), 279–90.

Vickerman, P. (2009). 'Student perspectives on formative peer assessment: An attempt to deepen learning?', *Assessment and Evaluation in Higher Education*, 34 (2), 221–30.

32. Providing effective feedback

Jon Guest

INTRODUCTION

An important and time-consuming part of a lecturer's job is making judgements about the quality of students' work. This involves giving feedback that is typically in the form of written comments on either electronic or hard copies of the work. We spend a significant amount of time writing these comments. The problem is that personal experience, conversations with colleagues and evidence from the research literature suggest that many students do not read, engage with or act upon the feedback we provide. What is worse, responses from the National Student Survey suggest that students are less satisfied with the feedback they receive than any other aspect of their learning experience in higher education.

This is very worrying as effective feedback plays a key role in effective learning. Why are students so dissatisfied with what we do? How can we increase the likelihood of more students engaging with the feedback we provide? This chapter will focus on different ways of dealing with this issue.

SOME SIMPLE WAYS OF IMPROVING WRITTEN FEEDBACK

This section will discuss a number of relatively low-cost ways of improving the effectiveness of traditional feedback comments. These include (a) the language we use; (b) where we write the comments; (c) the balance between strengths and weaknesses; (d) the tone and phrasing; and (e) reference to learning outcomes. Examples of possible feedback comments are included to help illustrate the impact of these factors.

DIFFICULTIES UNDERSTANDING THE LANGUAGE

Students find it difficult to understand the comments because we write them in (a) the specific disciplinary language of the subject and (b) the terminology of Bloom's Taxonomy i.e. synthesis, analysis, evaluation. This is often an issue when writing feedback for first year undergraduate students. Wherever possible, it is advisable to avoid excessive and unexplained use of academic jargon. Always remember the comments are for the students to understand and act upon rather than the external examiner. The external examiner's job is to judge how useful the students will find the feedback you have provided.

Teaching Tip
Always remember you are writing feedback comments for the students to act upon rather than other academics such as the external examiner.

WHERE DO WE WRITE COMMENTS?

If all the feedback appears at the end of the assignment, it might be difficult for students to judge where a specific comment applies in their work. It is useful to annotate work in the exact location where the comment is most relevant, i.e. writing in the margin or drop/dragging text when marking electronically. Highlighting and/or underlining relevant sentences/paragraphs can also help. If writing detailed feedback on the text or in the margin is difficult, you could include a comment along the following lines: 'For a more detailed explanation of this point see the second feedback comment at the end of the assignment.'

When marking large amounts of coursework it is difficult not to fall into the habit of writing one word in text annotations such as 'good', 'vague', 'confusing' or even '????' on students' work. It is best to avoid doing this. Evidence from the research literature suggests that students find them impossible to interpret. For example, survey respondents in Ferguson (2011) described one- or two-word feedback comments as being 'completely useless'. Whenever possible, try to write in-text comments in more detail. For example, some potential alternatives to writing 'vague' include:

> 'I think it would really improve the quality of your argument if you could be more specific about the research findings you are referring to here – see the underlined section.'

> 'It would really help the reader if you could provide more specific details to clarify what you mean in the highlighted section of your answer.'

'I found it really difficult to understand the meaning of the underlined phrase. See if you can have a go at rewriting this sentence to make it easier for the reader to understand.'

An alternative to writing 'good' is:

'The highlighted section is a clear example of where arguments have been built up in a logical manner. Try to continue with this style of academic writing in future assignments.'

An alternative to scribbling '???' is:

'Unfortunately I could not follow the line of reasoning in the highlighted section. It would have significantly improved the quality of the work if you had explained how this point is related to your previous argument.'

Try to refer to in-text comments at the end of the work. For example:

'The yellow highlighted paragraphs are good examples of where you have applied relevant theory to the issues raised in the question.'

Writing comments in more detail comes at an obvious cost because of the extra time and effort involved. It may appear daunting when you have over 300 assignments to mark. Too much written feedback may also overwhelm students, making it more difficult for them to know what to focus on. It is often more effective to explain three or four points in detail as opposed to identifying numerous strengths and weaknesses very briefly.

Teaching Tip
With limited time to mark each coursework, it is more effective to explain three or four areas for improvement in detail as opposed to identifying numerous strengths and weaknesses very briefly.

THE BALANCE BETWEEN STRENGTHS AND WEAKNESSES

One purpose of feedback is to motivate students to take appropriate actions to deepen their learning. If the comments only discuss weaknesses, it can have the opposite result. When marking, it is easy to forget the emotional responses people feel when reading comments on work in which they have invested a large amount of their own time and effort. As well as having a negative impact on self-confidence and motivation, students are likely to ignore feedback if it is overly negative. Always try to find something positive to say; otherwise there is a danger the students will take no notice of any of the comments.

THE TONE AND PHRASING

Students are more likely to engage with feedback comments if they:

- Avoid using harsh/judgemental language
- Stress the normality of making mistakes in the learning process
- Place greater emphasis on the importance of effort over academic ability.

For example, they are more likely to act on the second of the following two comments.

'This is wrong/incorrect – you do not understand this concept.'

'This is a common error. Many students find this concept difficult the first time they study it, but the majority obtain an in-depth understanding after a prolonged period of study and go on to do well in future assessments.'

MAKING REFERENCE TO THE ASSESSMENT CRITERIA/LEARNING OUTCOMES

Research suggests that feedback is more effective when it refers to the learning outcomes and assessment criteria for that particular piece of work. There is also evidence that this practice is not widespread.

Teaching Tip
Make sure you carefully re-read the assessment criteria and intended learning outcomes before reading the assignments and providing feedback.

A USEFUL FRAMEWORK FOR THINKING ABOUT FEEDBACK

I have found Sadler (1989) a useful framework for thinking about assessment and feedback. He argues that to be effective the process must enable students to:

- Develop a shared understanding with the tutor of what a 'good' piece of work looks like
- Identify strengths and weaknesses in their own work, i.e. recognise any 'gaps' and appreciate how big they are
- Take appropriate actions to close any identified gaps.

What can we do to make sure the feedback process meets all three conditions for success?

DEVELOPING A SHARED UNDERSTANDING BEFORE THE FINAL SUBMISSION

Do students know what they have to do in order to produce a high-quality piece of work? Do tutors make it clear or does it remain a mystery? This is an issue picked up by the National Student Survey. Question eight asks students the extent to which they agree with the following statement – 'The criteria used in marking has been made clear in advance'. A typical response to this issue is to provide more and more written guidance. This may include assessment criteria with performance descriptors for each grade. Assessment criteria are useful but a shared understanding of their meaning and application is difficult.

For example, does the assessment criteria include everything a tutor will consider when marking an assessment or do some important factors remain hidden? Many individual descriptors are very broad (for example 'depth of analysis') and inevitably involve the application of sub-criteria. Are these sub-criteria included in the written document? What is the relative importance of the criteria and sub-criteria? Do the students and tutors have a shared understanding of how they are weighted? How strict is the weighting? Can it vary between pieces of work? If it is possible to produce a document that articulates all of this information, it is likely to be unwieldy and of little use.

For these reasons, assessment criteria in isolation may not be an effective way of communicating standards. They become more useful when students see examples of how they apply to actual assignments. One low-cost option for tutors is to provide anonymised samples of students' work from previous years complete with feedback comments and assessment criteria. It is advisable to provide examples of these pre-submission exemplars across the whole range of grades. A more costly, but much more productive, option is to carry out an in-class marking activity.

In groups, students mark anonymised and 'clean' (i.e. feedback comments and marks removed) samples of work with the assessment criteria.

Towards the end of the session, the tutor provides fully marked copies of the same work so the students can compare their own application of the assessment criteria with that of the lecturer. It is important to spend some time identifying and discussing any differences of interpretation. A slightly more ambitious version of this activity is to ask the students to judge the quality of the work without the assessment criteria. They have to create their own version of the assessment criteria as they carry out the exercise. The tutor provides the actual assessment criteria towards the end of the session and discusses any important differences.

Teaching Tip
One potential issue with using exemplars is the danger that students will treat them as model answers to mindlessly copy when submitting their own work. To reduce the chances of this happening, provide very different examples of good answers.
Alternatively, rather than providing the whole assignment, copy a single page or paragraph.

CLARIFYING THE SIZE OF ANY GAPS

Traditional written feedback can be effective at identifying gaps. For example, commonly used comments include:

> 'The assignment lacks clarity and logical coherence.'
> 'There is not enough critical analysis.'
> 'Some concepts are not explained in enough detail.'
> 'The answer did not focus on the question.'

It is far more difficult to explain the size of any gaps. For example, the second comment above identifies that there is not enough critical analysis but says nothing about the level required to achieve a particular grade. Sadler argues that:

> 'It is difficult for teachers to describe exactly what they are looking for, although they may have little difficulty in recognising a fine performance when it occurs. Teachers' conceptions of quality are typically held, largely in unarticulated form, inside their heads as tacit knowledge.' (Sadler, 1989, p. 54)

One effective way to address this issue is to show students concrete examples of work that demonstrate the standard or the skill at an appropriate level. These are post-submission as opposed to pre-submission exemplars. For example, when marking assessments copy samples of answers that illustrate good performance on some aspect or aspects of the assessment criteria. Distribute these answers in class or post on the virtual learning environment. Referring to these exemplars in the written feedback can also save time by reducing the quantity of comments.

The use of post-submission exemplars can also play a very useful role when staff face students who appear disinterested in constructive feedback and just want to know why they received a mark below the one they believe they deserve. Spending a few minutes getting these students to compare their own work with examples of high-quality exemplars is an effective and efficient way of dealing with these difficult situations.

Teaching Tip
Rather than providing complete versions of the post-submission exemplars, copy a particular page or highlight a paragraph that is a good example of some element of the assessment criteria. In the feedback, include a sentence along the following lines – 'For an example of a piece of work that demonstrates excellent critical analysis see the highlighted section on exemplar A.'

RELEVANCE OF COMMENTS FOR FUTURE WORK

In the research literature there is evidence that some students ignore feedback because they believe it is specific to that particular assignment and provides no guidance on how to improve their future work. Evidence suggests that many lecturers write feedback comments as if the students have submitted a draft copy of the work for a later resubmission. How can we avoid doing this? Some feedback comments relate to the academic content of the assignment such as the choice/explanation of theories and application to any issues raised in the question. For example:

> 'To achieve a higher mark/grade for this assignment you need to have demonstrated a more in-depth understanding of theory X.'

When writing these types of comments, try to highlight cases where a good understanding of this same academic content is required for students to perform well in subsequent assessments. If this is the case, it is important to highlight this point in the feedback. For example:

> 'Try and study theory x again in more detail. Many students find it difficult first time around but you will need to gain a deeper and more thorough understanding of the material if you wish to improve your performance in future assessments.'

Other feedback comments relate to more generic skills development such as the structure of the answer, the balance of material, the quality of written communication and the ability to develop arguments in a logical manner. It is easier for students to see the relevance of improving these skills for future assignments but always signpost and make it as clear as possible. For example:

'In future assessment make sure all diagrams are fully labelled and clearly explained in the main body of your answer.'

ADVICE ON HOW TO CLOSE ANY GAPS

This is the trickiest part of the feedback process. It is difficult to specify/outline exactly what the student needs to do or what future actions they can take to improve. Comments such as 'you need to work harder' are unlikely to have an impact. Some alternatives include:

'Read lots of different examples of other assignments that received a high mark. Compare them against your own and try to identify their particular strengths and areas you need to work on to obtain higher marks in future assessments.'

'In the future, try to read through your work more carefully and amend any errors before handing it in.'

'Book an appointment with the support centre x at the university to receive extra support.'

'Try to attempt more practice questions.'

'Go back and read chapter x again in the textbook and try to gain a better understanding of theory y.'

SOME ACTIVITIES TO IMPROVE THE IMPACT OF FEEDBACK

This section will discuss a number of different activities to improve feedback, including (a) how to provide feedback quickly; (b) releasing feedback before the grades; (c) demand-led feedback; (d) peer review; and (e) audio feedback.

PROVIDING FEEDBACK QUICKLY

Students are more likely to engage with feedback if they receive it while the process of researching and writing the assessment is still fresh in their minds. Unfortunately writing detailed comments on hundreds of assignments can take weeks. By the time the marking is complete and the feedback returned, many students have started studying for subsequent assignments. The comments may no longer seem relevant as they focus on their next assessment. There are two different ways of providing feedback quickly – even on very large modules.

1. Provide feedback after reading a sample of assignments.
    Instead of marking all the students' work before providing feedback, read a sample of the assignments in the first couple of days after the deadline. Identify any common weaknesses and either discuss these in the next class or post announcements/handouts on the virtual learning environment.
2. Provide feedback before reading any assignments!
    Tutors can often predict/anticipate common mistakes or weaknesses in students' work before they have marked a single assignment. Rather than keeping this information private, produce a handout and discuss these anticipated weaknesses with the students in the first class following the deadline date. It is also useful to spend some of this contact time describing some of the key features of a good answer.

Although imperfect and rather generic, feedback provided in the first few days following a deadline may have a stronger impact on some students than more personalised detailed feedback provided much later.

RELEASING FEEDBACK BEFORE THE MARKS

There is evidence that once many students see their mark they ignore other feedback. There are a number of possible explanations. For example, if the mark is better than anticipated, students may believe they have mastered the topic and so do not need any feedback. If the mark is a lot worse than expected the emotional distress means they never want to look at or engage with the assignment ever again.

One way to address this issue is to release feedback without any marks. The students then have to provide an estimate of the mark based on the comments. They are encouraged to compare the feedback with their

322 *Learning and teaching in higher education*

peers and a grade incentive for accuracy is a useful way to incentivise the students to take the activity seriously.

Teaching Tip
A useful incentive scheme operates in the following way. If the estimated mark from the feedback is within five percentage points either above or below the final mark awarded by the tutor, the student receives a bonus of five percentage points. To avoid any attempts to game the system, add the five percentage points to the mark awarded by the tutor – not the estimated mark provided by the students.

DEMAND-LED FEEDBACK

Rather than providing feedback you believe is the most appropriate, ask the students to identify particular aspects of their work for which they would most like to receive feedback. It is useful to add a sentence along the following lines to the cover sheet for an assignment:

'I would like feedback from the tutor on' or 'I would like more guidance on the following' (list some potential areas).

You could also ask the students what types of feedback or which feedback comments they have found the best and the least useful.

PEER REVIEW

The term 'peer review' is a label for a wide range of different educational activities. In this chapter, the term describes an arrangement where students make evaluative judgements about the quality of the work produced by their peers. Peer review is not the same as peer assessment as the tutor still marks the work and awards a final grade. Any grade awarded by peers is for guidance only and does not count towards the final mark.

A peer review exercise based on draft versions of coursework has a number of advantages. It not only increases the quantity of feedback, students are more likely to act upon the comments for the following reasons:

- They receive the comments in a timely manner while the assignment is still at the forefront of their mind.
- The relevance of the comments is more obvious, i.e. the tutor provides them on a piece of work that is not yet completed.

- Students are more likely to write the comments in a language and style that other students will understand.

Perhaps the biggest educational advantage of using peer review comes from students having to produce feedback. This has the following advantages:

- Students have to engage with the assessment criteria as they evaluate the quality of their classmates' work.
- Seeing different approaches to a question helps to develop a more sophisticated notion of knowledge and learning.
- It promotes critical analysis of the subject content.
- It improves the ability to self-evaluate their own work.

Students may express the following concerns about peer review:

- The feedback will be low quality and unreliable because their peers (a) will not take the activity seriously, and (b) do not have the relevant expertise to judge the quality of the work.
- They feel uncomfortable about (a) making critical comments on their classmates' work, and (b) other students seeing and making critical comments on their own work.
- Other students will copy their work.

It is possible to implement a peer review exercise in a number of different ways. The exact design chosen by the tutor can help to address some of these concerns. For example, it is advisable to make sure at least two students peer review each piece of work and discuss the feedback. This increases confidence in the usefulness of the comments. Grading the exercise in some way may also encourage students to take it seriously. When I first implemented peer review, the quality of the feedback was marked. However, this is challenging because it is difficult to write an assessment criteria against which to mark the quality of the feedback. In addition, the marking process slows down the return of the reviewer's comments back to the students. For these reasons, it is better to use it as a 'gatekeeper' activity, i.e. any student who fails to engage with the process receives a mark of zero for the assignment. It also helps to make the whole process anonymous. Many virtual learning environments have a peer review facility that make it relatively easy to implement anonymity while also reducing the administrative burden on the tutor. To avoid concerns with copying, the students could peer review a partial draft, i.e. 800 of a 1500 word assessment. Fears of plagiarism lessen if the review is of a research proposal or literature review for a dissertation, i.e. on a different topic than their own work. However, students are less confident about judging the quality of a piece of work on a different subject area than an assignment where they are all answering the same question.

AUDIO FEEDBACK

An alternative to written feedback is to record and post audio files of spoken comments. Online marking software such as Grade Mark in Turnitin usually have this facility. One potential advantage of using audio files is efficiency. Some estimates suggest that one minute of talking provides approximately the same quantity of feedback as six minutes of writing. Vocal explanations may also convey meaning more effectively than written explanations. Some research suggests students find the comments more detailed, supportive and personalised.

Teaching Tip
Try replacing written with audio feedback. This enables tutors to provide far more feedback when they may have only 10 minutes per essay on large modules.

CONCLUSION

Providing students with feedback takes up a large amount of our time and yet students seem very dissatisfied with the outcome. Some relatively minor changes to the way we write, frame and present feedback can have a significant impact on (a) how well the comments are received and (b) how likely they are to be acted upon. Sadler (1989) also provides a useful and practical framework for thinking about feedback processes and policies. A number of activities such as peer review and exemplar marking classes are useful ways to make feedback more effective. They also help to illustrate an important point. Feedback is not just a few comments added to a piece of work during marking. Instead, it needs to be conceptualised as an ongoing process that occurs before, during and after the completion of assessments.

SUGGESTED FURTHER READING

Ferguson, P. (2011). 'Student perceptions of quality feedback', *Assessment and Evaluation in Higher Education*, 36 (1), 51–62.
Sadler, D.R. (1989). 'Formative assessment and the design of instructional systems', *Instructional Sciences*, 18, 119–44.

Index

ABC model 200
active discussion, encouragement of
20–23, 23–4
active learning 177, 191, 222, 239
ADDIE model of instructional
design 197, 200, 205
additional teaching or moderator
support 214–15, 216
Adobe's State of Create 2016 study
59
affective learning 111, 115, 117
Allen, W.C. 204
appointments 17, 77, 79–80, 320
Apprentice Challenge 145
apprenticeships 3, 5, 9, 110
assertiveness techniques 173–4
assessment criteria 280–88
ambiguity and inconsistency 280
anonymised essays from previous
year reviewed and graded by
students 284, 285
Assessment Workshop 283–4, 285,
286
audio-visual teaching aids 287
creativity 288
cynicism and antagonism 281
discontent and failure, feelings of
280
expectations 281
explanation of key components
280, 282, 285
feedback 280, 282, 288
group work 287
impartiality and objectivity 281
implications 285
interactive style 288
key terms, highlighted and
interpretation of terms
283–4
meaningful understanding 281
presentation 287

problem 281–3
solution 283–4
support 280
assessments
experiential learning and business
simulations 116
law: teaching to business students
269–70
quality 40
storytelling as teaching technique
105
see also assessment criteria;
effective feedback of lecturer;
multiple choice questions
(MCQs); peer assessments;
formative assessments; posters
in academic assessments;
summative assessments
attendance and engagement 10,
36–44
assessment method 38–9
breadth of understanding 40
breaking down of active learning
community for module 39
formal and informal feedback 38,
40
group presentations 70
implications 40–41
innovative methods 37
large group teaching 95
lectures 36, 37, 38, 39, 41
loss of opportunity for incremental
development 38
online presence 41
problem 37–9
quality of assessments 40
solution 39–40
tutorial reports 40–41
tutorials 36, 37, 38, 39, 41, 42
attention-seeking technique 172–3
audio-visual teaching aids 287

National Student Survey 124, 280,
   313, 317
nativist approaches to learning 2–3
natural stimulus 4
newspaper articles or editorials 51
Nicol, D. 301–2
note-taking 15, 16, 18

OneDrive 292
online learning management 222–8
   active learning 222
   amplifications and reductions 225
   anonymity 226
   asynchronous learning 223
   bulletin boards 228
   case studies 223
   cognitive and social learning theory
      222
   collaborative learning 223, 225–6
   constructivist learning 222, 223
   consultancy sessions 228
   cooperation 223
   course design 225
   courseware usability 223
   cultural and institutional differences
      226
   demonstration 223
   discussion boards 223
   email contact 223, 227
   encouragement or prompts 227
   engagement enhancement 228
   equity and equality 225
   experiential learning 223
   feedback 224
   flexibility and convenience 225
   group-based work 223
   individual work modes 223
   instruction 223
   intercultural learning 225
   internationalisation of curriculum
      227
   navigation frame 223
   opportunities and challenges 224–7
   participation 224, 227
   personal development planning 223
   podcasts 223, 228
   problem-based work 223
   process 223–4
   real-world examples 223
   reflective learning 223

   requirements and online behaviour
      227
   scaffolding 223
   self-directed study 223
   self-reflection 223
   short summaries of readings 227
   storyboard templates 223, 228
   student learning assessment 224
   support availability 227
   synchronous learning 223, 228
   thinking and learning skills 225
   transformation system 222
   video interviews 223, 228
   webinars 223, 228
   weekly messages 227
   wikis 223, 228
   word limits 226
online module: designing and teaching
      197–208, 210
   ABC model 200
   ADDIE model of instructional
      design 197, 200, 205
   analysis 197–200
   blended learning 202
   communications, engagements or
      individual and group activities
      needed 201–2
   content creation 198, 201, 204,
      206–7
   curriculum design models 200
   definition 198–9
   delivery of module 200, 207
   design 200–201
   development 203–4, 206–7
   direction and support in
      development and delivery
      process 199–200
   discussion boards 198
   eLearning design models 200
   engagement levels 198
   evaluation 205–8
   face-to-face or blended learning
      programme 202
   flexibility and interactions 198
   geographical limitations of e.g. Box
      of Broadcasts 201
   group work 199, 202
   implementation 204–5
   instructional design models 200–201
   journals or ePortfolios 202